*T*his bible of all that is cool and Jewish is the exclusive property of

_____

gmar hatimah tova

(make a nice signature here, *bubbeleh*)

## *Maternal History*

_____ begat _____

who begat _____

who begat _____

who begat _____

## *Paternal History*

_____ begat _____

who begat _____

who begat _____

who begat _____

**who had to ask what begat meant!**

# Cool Jew

*The Ultimate Guide*
*for Every Member of the Tribe*

aka

# The Heebster Handbook

Other Books by the Author

*Kabbalah Magic: Ancient Secrets to Help You Succeed*
*While Sleeping Through All Eighteen Lessons*

*How to Control Public Opinion as a Heebster in Hollywood*

*The Jewish Guide to Running the World on Ten Dollars a Day*

# Cool Jew

## The Ultimate Guide for Every Member of the Tribe

Lisa Alcalay Klug

**Andrews McMeel
Publishing, LLC**

Kansas City

# Acknowledgments

Heartfelt thanks go to ~~the Pale of Settlement, La Brea Tar Pits, Hula Swamp,~~ Jerusalem, Los Angeles, New York, and tribal affiliates everywhere; my honorary Sheeb editor Christine Schillig, designer Holly Camerlinck and the entire Andrews McMeel team supreme; my fearless illustrator Amos Goldbaum; my *gantza mishpoche* and beloved parents, teachers, *chevre,* and *malachim,* including esteemed rabbis and rebbetzins: David Aaron, Yonah and Rachel Bookstein, Naftali Citron, Menachem Creditor, Eliezer Eidlitz, Chanan and Jody Feld, Jonathan and Shifra Feldman, Yehuda and Miriam Ferris, Stephen Friedman, David and Jody Glickman, the much loved Ben and Judy Hollander z'l, Simon Jacobson, Kenny Kaufman, Asher Krupnick, Yosef Langer, Yosef Liebowitz, Ian and Rachel Pear, Yitzchak Schwartz, Alexander Seinfeld, Rav Shmuel, Sam Shor, Arie Strikovsky, H.Y., Dovid Zaklikowski, and Dr. Avivah Gottlieb Zornberg. *Tsnius* high fives, hugs, knishes, and jewcy thank-you *brachot* to David Abitbol, Alisa Adler, Deanna and Allen Alevy, Caesar Alfano of the Lower East Side BID, Kim Amzallag, the Author's Guild, Kim and Chaim Azizy, D'Shane Barnett of the Mandan, Hidatsa, and Arikara Nation of North Dakota, Aaron Bisman, Jacob Harris and Elliot Fox of JDub Records, Esther Bittleman, Tamar and Noah Bittleman, Michael Bloch, Rachel Brodie, Prof. Alan D. Corré, Jeremy Cowan, Linda Cies, Michael Dorf, Michael Franklin, and Dave Bias of Downtown Arts Development, Helit Edelstein, Dovid, Daniel and Rochel Chaya Feld, Debbie Fellman, Batsheva and Yossie Frankel, David Friedman, Frances Geballe, Phyllis Cook and Laura Mason of the San Francisco Jewish Federation Endowment Fund, Sheryl Giffis, Alex Goldberg, Beth and Daniel Gordon, Julie Gordon Mitrani, Rabbi Ayla Grafstein, Eliyahu Eckelberg and the Ruach BaMidbar Writer's Grant, Chaya Gottesman, Itzhik Gottesman, Yonatan Gutstadt, the Harizys, Marci Heit, Robby and Joanne Helperin, Tor Hyams, Joel ben Izzy, Jewlicious Festival, Sari Katz, Stacey Katz, Michael Kaye, Aaron Kenin, Aron Korney, Gwen Korney, Esther Kustanowitz, Sophie Miriam Lagnier, Wayne Lampert, Sarah Lefton, Craig Leinoff, Hillel Lester, Avi Levine, Avraham Lowenthal, Lori and Alan Lurie, Lois and Gary Marcus, Judy Massarano, David McLees and Dean Schachtel of Jewish Music Group, Aron Menda, Jeff Miller, Rachel Miller, Marisa Mimoun, Jeff Morgan, Nissim ben Chaim, Naomi and Zwe Padeh, Zev Padway, Paul Panish, Stephanie Pell, Yoav and Shira Potash, Regina and Kevin Richter, Ramona Rubin, Yehoshua and Leah Safran, David Scharff, Michalya Schonwald, Lou Schubert, Sara Schwimmer, Eleanor Shapiro and the Bay Area–based Jewish Music Festival, Jen Shaw, Yehuda Shifman, Zelda Shluker, Glen Stevick, Rob Tannenbaum, David

Fagin and Sean Altman, Bernard Taper, Alan Tigay, Amy Tobin, Morgan Thompson, Rhoda Uziel and PLP, Virginia Creative Center for the Arts, Jennifer Mary Williams, Steven Zelin, Chien Yuh-Ching, and Yuan Fang Zhu. Abundant thanks and appreciation to the archivists, artists, entrepreneurs, and individuals who contributed images to these pages; their names appear, with gratitude, in the credits. To anyone I inadvertently forgot, this ONE's for you!

And, to the Eternal Author of All

כדי להודות ולהלל לשמך הגדול
עַל נֶסִיך וְעַל נִפְלַאוֹתֶיך וְעַל יְשׁוּעָתֶך.

*Shkoiyach!*

# CONTENTS

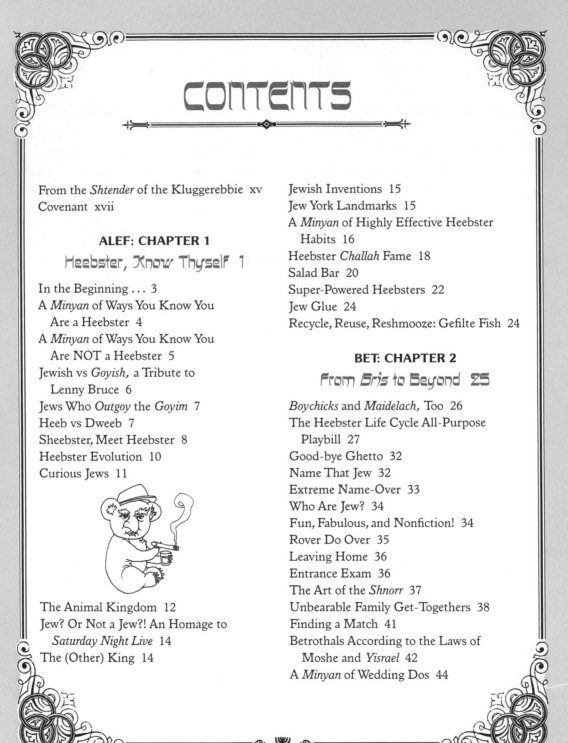

## VAV: CHAPTER 6

### Members of the Tribe  163

COOL JEW

# FROM THE *SHTENDER* OF THE KLUGGEREBBIE

As a bona fide member of the global Jewish conspiracy to make the world a better place, I hereby testify to the wisdom exhibited herewith by the author. With a deft pen and a happy heart, she has distilled the deepest soul, the **kishkes** of the Jewish people, into a remarkable work that would have made her **bubbie** so proud and full of **nachas** if it were not for those Nazi bastards who took her to the next world.

This is one helluva book. It's so **gevalt**! It's from the heart. Keep reading and rereading it until you've never been so proud and so utterly filled with joy to be a Jew.

I offer these words in the ancient rabbinic tradition of lending one's good name to the publication of an esteemed colleague. The author is, quite frankly, a **mensch**, and if she offends you or your Jewish sensibilities in any way, please don't let it get you all **farklempt**. And if you're not Jewish and you're still reading, please don't let any jokes worry you. In advance of anything that might rattle your feathers, the author and I ask that you please accept our humble request for forgiveness. We're all G-d's children. Some of us are just a little more, let's say, Heebish than others.

Oy, will you look at the time? Gotta get the flock outta here. **B'vracha shleima v'noymar** . . . With a complete blessing, let us say, **Oy men**!


With Eternal Tribal Affection,

לקברבי

The Forty-ninth Kluggerebbie

*The truth is not ashamed of appearing contrived.*
**ISAAC BASHEVIS SINGER**

✡

*When I pass from this world, and stand before the Heavenly Tribunal,
they will not ask me "Zusha, why you were not Moses or Abraham."
They will ask me, "Zusha, why were you not Zusha?"*
**REB ZUSHA OF HANIPOLI**

✡

*If I spend my life pretending to be someone else, who will be me?*
**THE KOTZKER REBBE AKA RABBI MENAHEM MENDEL MORGENSZTERN OF KOTZK**

# COVENANT

When I was a kid, my Panamanian/Israeli/Ladino-loving mother and my German/Polish/Yiddishe father had no clue how to teach me how to become an American. They had to figure that out for themselves. But they did teach me how to be a Jew—each one of them a somewhat different kind of Jew—but a Jew and a proud one at that. And maybe that's all I really needed to learn because when you think about it, being a proud Jew makes you a citizen of the world.

If you have no clue what this means, then this is the book for you. If you already know what this means, then this is the book for you, too. And if you're not even Jewish, wish you were, love someone who is, or are wondering what all the Jewish hoopla is really about, then this book is for you, too. In other words, it's the book for anyone who wants to understand, relish, or question something about being Jewish because as our ancient Sages taught, knowledge is power.

And if that's true, then being a

## Heebster

is really the carrot on your gefilte fish. That's because as G-DASH-D only knows, you can never be Heeb enough. And that's what being a Heebster is all about. But what, you ask, is this new word Heebster? You've heard of the word Heeb. Well, a Heebster is all that. And more. Much more.

A Heebster is someone who loves being Jewish, who is not afraid to be a total dork but who also has that certain Jewish *savoir faire* that makes him or her hipper than hip. What matters is how you feel about the Jewish world, the Jewniverse. As a Heebster you're proud, informed, and downtown, whether you live in Miami Beach or some landlocked farm in Middle America.

For anyone looking for a little inspiration, this book decodes contemporary Judaism and its hippest forms of cultural expression. At a time when it's never been more delicious to be Jewish, it is designed as a field manual for twenty-first-century Jews and the people who love them. The ultimate guide for this Age of Hilarious, this book is all about learning how to hip-hop your Hebraic with irreverence, good humor, and bona fide liberated Jewish self-expression. It doesn't matter if you love hip-hop, have never hip-hopped, or are bracing for a hip replacing. Whether you went to Hebrew school, volunteered on a kibbutz, or never stepped foot in *yeshiva,* the Heebster motto says it all: "I'm good enough, Jew enough, and *gevalt,* do I like me!"

The original Jewmor book, this collection provides all you need to know to Super Jew your own lovely Heeb self, celebrate the Mosaic lifestyle, and befriend the Jewish people whether your DNA be lily-white, black, or somewhere in between. It doesn't matter what kind of Jew you are: Ashkenazi, Sephardi, a little religious, a lot religious, not religious at all, not Jewish, Jew-friendly, old, or young. You're welcome whether you are a strongly identified Jew, more Jew-ISH, an Honorary Heeb, an ally, or a deprived Midwesterner who has never actually met a live one. Unbounded by age, geography, or even identification with Da Tribe, this book spells it all out, in Hebrew, Yiddish, Ladino, and then some.

Within these pages, you'll find everything from FYIs "For the Yiddish Impaired" to "Self-Help for the Christmas-Carol Intolerant." You can quickly pick up "Jewsticulations," compare the "Heeb vs Dweeb," and demystify the fine art of *frummin'* out. And for those *Yidden* who remain, nevertheless, as neurotic as ever, you can even score tips on "How to Behave in the South, Siberia, and Other Hostile Territories." This playful no-apologies approach to fully embracing being Hebraic helps put an end forever to Christmas tree envy.

So slap on your Groucho Marx glasses and come join the People'chood of the Thirteenth Tribe. Because who wouldn't want to discover new meaning in the old adage, "When you're in love, the whole world is Jewish!"

# IN THE BEGINNING . . .

the world was divided into two camps: Heebsters and non-Heebsters. Heebsters are Members and Friends of the Tribe who not only know what it is to be Jewish. They know it, flaunt it, dig it, and love it. And that is precisely what makes them Heebsters. If you're reading this, you might already be shining your Hebraic loud and proud. But what if you're not? Don't worry. No matter who you are or where you are, you can *always* become a Heebster. In fact, you're already on your way.

Deep, deep inside, every Jew is in some microscopic way already a Heebster. It's simply part of the Jewish spiritual inheritance. Even if you're *ohm*-ing in an ashram somewhere in Tibet, or raising buffalo in Dakota with nary a Jew in sight, there is something inside of you that has never stopped being part of the Tribe. It's a mystical birthright that traces its roots all the back to Mt. Sinai and has the power to light up countless generations ahead. All you need to do is fan the embers until that little Heebster spark catches flame.

And it will, my friend, because as a Heebster, you don't just survive, you thrive! Being Jewish is about much more than bagels and loxy. It's about moxie, about feeling *Yiddishe* foxy! Because when you're of *Da Tribe,* you've got *Da Vibe.* It's not about deprivation. It's about celebration, exclamation, and exaltation! When you embrace *Da Place,* you're blessed with grace. So let go of the pain. You're a link in the chain. Shun shame and embrace fame. Take charge and live large. Once the sweet Heebster harmony starts humming in your heart, you'll catch on fire with a burning love and pride for yourself, our people, and every fabulous facet of who we are! And to that, we say, "Ahhhhhmayn!"

Jew got questions? Jew got answers! When you don't care what it means to be Judaic, that's unHeebster. When you're down with all things Mosaic, that's oh so Heebster. How do you know who you are? For starters, it takes a *minyan.*

## FYI: FOR THE YIDDISH IMPAIRED

A *minyan* is a prayer quorum. "In Jewish," it takes ten to conduct a *Torah* service, to say *Kaddish,* the memorial prayer for the dead, and other assorted ritual festivities. Because of its mystical significance, a *minyan* may also be used to designate a certain spiritual quality that can be expressed only in the presence of ten. X-nay on "It takes two, baby." As every Heebster knows, it takes ten! It takes ten!

# A Minyan of Ways You Know You Are a Heebster

1. You still call the Jewish *Forward* newspaper by its original Yiddish name, the *Forvertz*.
2. On Saturdays, you skip a big breakfast, then hunker for pickled herring and Manischewitz 'bout noon—standard *noshing* hour at synagogues worldwide.
3. You know the true secret of floaters vs sinkers.
   (*For floaters, splash seltzer into matzah ball batter.*)
4. You're proud to know the first Israeli astronaut, Ilan Ramon z'l, ordered kosher meals on the space shuttle *Columbia*.
5. You send a *Rosh HaShanah* card to Rebbetzin Hadassah Gross, the ultraorthodox transvestite.
6. You spot your polyester booty getting down in the book, *Bar Mitzvah Disco*.
7. You wear panties that read "a great miracle happened here" across your tush.
8. You throw the word "f---in'" in the midst of Jewish phrases, as in *"Shomer F---in' Shabbos."*
9. You send all snail mail with U.S. postage stamp *dreidls* from your lifetime supply.

### And the Ultimate Minyan Maker that proclaims you are a Heebster:

10. You entered, judged, or won the annual Simply Manischewitz Cook Off!

# A Minyan of Ways You Know You Are NOT a Heebster

1. You have no interest in lox, gefilte, or *kasha varnishkes* and you have no clue what these words mean anyway.
2. You follow Martha Stewart's instructions for extending the life of your Christmas tree.
3. You circumcise the Jewish flourish—*mann, witz, berg,* or *stein*—from your surname so it no longer sounds like one long sneeze.
4. You are stunned when you learn your uncle played in a band with someone named Kinky Friedman and sang backup on a song entitled "Ride 'Em Jewboy."
5. The fact that you love *The Chosen* is a shameful secret.
6. You are embarrassed to wear a big phat gold Jewish star round your neck in public.
7. You would never admit you once longed for an authentic Lieberman/Gore campaign swag *kippa*.
8. You own no other *yarmulke* but a little royal blue satin number with a 45-degree incline.
9. From the looks of it, you're not sure if your *bris* took place in a *shul* or a slaughter house.

## And the Ultimate Minyan Maker that proclaims you are NOT a Heebster:

10. You bake challah on Passover and freeze it to eat on Yom Kippur.

# Jewish vs Goyish, a Tribute to Lenny Bruce

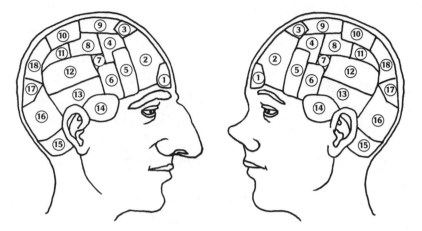

Radical Jewish comedian Lenny Bruce brought down the Torah on Jewish versus *goyish*. All the rest is commentary. As Rabbi Hillel taught, "Go and learn it."

| JEWISH | GOYISH |
|---|---|
| 1. mustard | 1. mayo |
| 2. brisket | 2. beef Stroganoff |
| 3. noodle *kugel* | 3. tuna casserole |
| 4. potato *kugel* | 4. scalloped potatoes |
| 5. *shmaltzy* | 5. Crisco |
| 6. kosher dills | 6. sweet gherkins |
| 7. *matzah* balls | 7. Hostess Sno Balls |
| 8. *mandelbrodt* | 8. biscotti |
| 9. blintzes | 9. crepes |
| 10. liver mold | 10. Jell-O mold |
| 11. Philadelphia Cream Cheese | 11. Velveeta |
| 12. Bazooka | 12. Double Mint |
| 13. hand-rolled Cubans | 13. Dip aka Skoal Chewing Tobacco |
| 14. He'Brew | 14. Coors |
| 15. Manischewitz | 15. Almaden Burgundy in a box |
| 16. Covenant Cabernet Sauvignon | 16. Lefite-Rothschild Napa Valley Pauillac Bordeaux |
| 17. overcooking | 17. undercooking |
| 18. Mama Cass* | 18. Karen Carpenter** |

You do the math!

*Jewish?
She died eating.

**Goyish?
She died starving.

# Jews Who Outgoy the Goyim

Sometimes, Jews aren't so Jewish. They stray far away from the Mosaic time-space continuum and come out the other side very un-Jewish. This is called *goyish*. This type of Jew is not a Heebster. He is not even just any *goy*. No, this is a super *goy, a complete and total goy,* known in Hebrew as a *goy gamur*. The famed Torah scholar Nechama Leibowitz taught, "A *goy gamur* is always a Jew." A *goy gamur* is someone who is so good at being *goyish* that he or she is *more goyish than the goyim*. Take fashion designer Ralph Lauren, who represents the height of the WASP luxury lifestyle. His lead brand is Polo—not exactly a Jewish hobby. Will the real Ralph Lifshitz please stand up?! Or actress Lauren Bacall, an ultimate symbol of Hollywood glamour, known for her husky voice and sultry gaze. Her true *Yiddishe* identity? Betty Perske, cousin of former Israeli Prime Minister Shimon Peres. And then there is Zsa Zsa Gabor, who epitomized the lifestyle of the white rich and famous. Lo and behold, her maternal grandparents were killed in the Holocaust and some biographers speculate that her paternal line was also Jewish but converted to Catholicism in order to assimilate. Poor Zsa Zsa . . . No wonder her theme song had her wanting to get the heck out of TV's *Green Acres*. Ancestral fears must have been screaming within as she was forced to contemplate settling amongst the Kossacks of Ku Klux Klan Kountry, far far away from Jew York City. As Zsa Zsa sang in the show's theme song: "Dahling, I love you but give me Park Avenue!" Indeed.

## Heeb vs Dweeb

| | |
|---|---|
| concerned with *kreplach* | concerned with crunches |
| wandering Jew | Lord Waterloo |
| funny, warm, self-deprecating | a *bissel* sauerkraut |
| loves being Jewish | perpetually flu-ish |
| knows it's okay to believe | shuns spirituality |
| understands this world is merely a corridor* | huh? |

*As Matisyahu croons, Jewish mysticism teaches that this world is merely an entryway to the world to come.

# SHEEBSTER, MEET HEEBSTER

*so smart, she could start her own Mensa chapter*

*her hair has a life of its own, which can be quite helpful*

*Bubbie's retro frames retooled with prescription lenses*

*379 bffs programmed into speed dial*

"Havana Nagila" *ring tone*

*notebook and blue gel pen, her constant companions*

*requisite* bendel *(red string bracelet)*

*hips genetically programmed for childbirth*

*vintage Swiss Army backpack contains* Tractate Bava Kama, *notes for her defense of her PhD in religion at Columbia,* The Heebster Handbook, *Latke Chips, Diet Coke with Lime, $2.53, three credit cards (two with mileage points), yoga pants,* Hamsa *key chain, two Band-Aids, hair clip, and twisty tie from last night's nosh: Green's babka*

*naturally, she shops blue and white bling by Michal Negrin, shoes by Naot*

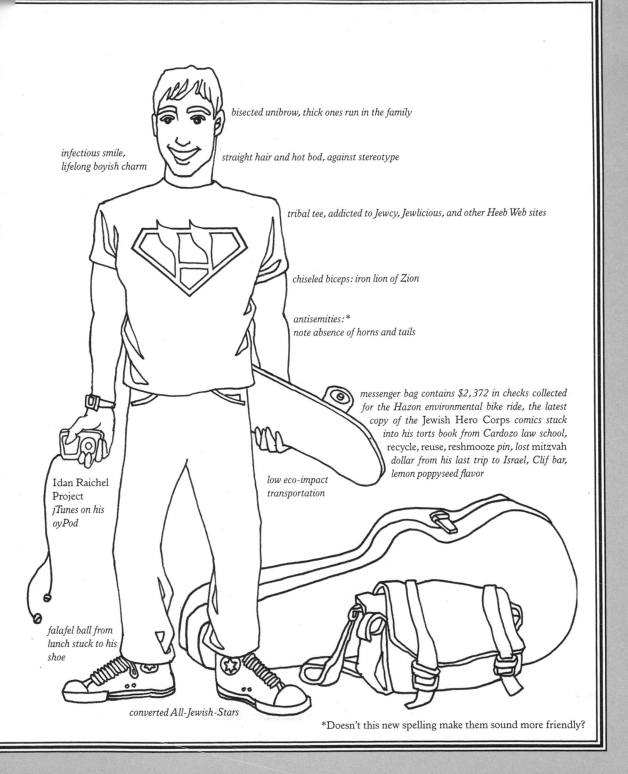

bisected unibrow, thick ones run in the family

straight hair and hot bod, against stereotype

infectious smile,
lifelong boyish charm

tribal tee, addicted to Jewcy, Jewlicious, and other Heeb Web sites

chiseled biceps: iron lion of Zion

antisemities: *
note absence of horns and tails

messenger bag contains $2,372 in checks collected
for the Hazon environmental bike ride, the latest
copy of the Jewish Hero Corps comics stuck
into his torts book from Cardozo law school,
recycle, reuse, reshmooze pin, lost mitzvah
dollar from his last trip to Israel, Clif bar,
lemon poppyseed flavor

Idan Raichel
Project
jTunes on his
oyPod

low eco-impact
transportation

falafel ball from
lunch stuck to his
shoe

converted All-Jewish-Stars

*Doesn't this new spelling make them sound more friendly?

# Heebster Evolution

Becoming a Heebster isn't something that happens overnight. It usually takes years if not generations. But don't let that make you feel bad. You've got your irrepresible Aunt Bessie and Uncle Irwin to take care of that. Besides, it took the ancient Israelites forty years of wandering in the desert after they left Egypt before they got it right. On the other hand, by the time they got to the Promised Land, they had nearly all died off. So scratch that example and take inspiration instead from all the Heebsters who came before you.

| PERSONALITY | TALENT | PRINCIPLES | VOILÀ! |
|---|---|---|---|
| **Matisyahu** | Sing inspirational reggae hits | Never Lose Da Jew | *First Hasidic artist on VH1* |
| **Primo Levi** | Pen Holocaust memoirs | Never Forget | *Revered as national Italian treasure* |
| **Fran Drescher** | Produce hit sitcom | Protect obnoxious New Yawk accent | *Sexy, saucy Jewess* |
| **Madonna** | Sing/share the gospel in children's books | Attempt to become Kabbalistic master | *Superstar target of endless ridicule* |
| **Sarah Jessica Parker** | Produce/star in massive hit | Shun the knife | *Mega actress, fashion icon* |
| **Barbra Streisand** | Yodel like nobody's business | Never gentile-ify your *shnoz* | *Showbiz legend* |
| **Werner Klemperer, of blessed memory** | Portray Colonel Wilhelm Klink on *Hogan's Heroes* | Insist the bumbling fool always fail | *Two Emmys, comedic justice, and triumph over a refugee past!* |
| **Lubavitcher Rebbe** | *Shmear* Yiddishkeit 'round the world | Empower every Jew | *From Laos to Las Vegas, minyans heard 'round the world!* |

זשאָרזש דער נײַגעריקער
*George der Naygeriker*

ה. אַ. ר"י
*H. A. Rey*

ייִדיש: שלום בערגער
*Yidish: Sholem Berger*

*Curious George* by H. A. Rey in Yiddish translation

*Curious George* in Yiddish

# Curious Jews

Did you know Curious George is a Heebster? It's true. The "parents" of *Curious George*, Hans Augusto Rey and his wife Margret Rey, first met in their native Hamburg, Germany. They remet and married in Rio de Janeiro. Later, the happy couple moved to Paris and there, they conceived their story about a lovable, inquisitive monkey. As the Nazis began their advance on Paris, Hans realized they were in danger. Much like their beloved George might, Hans cobbled together spare parts into two bicycles. And in the early hours of June 14, 1940, he and Margret started pedaling. Within hours, the Nazis occupied Paris but the Reys had already escaped to safety. Four days later they reached the Spanish border, bringing their precious manuscript with them. From there, they traveled on, to Lisbon, Brazil, New York City, and finally, Cambridge, Massachusetts, where they lived out the rest of their days. Like Babar, Bambi, Pippi Longstocking, Oliver, and other fictional childhood heroes, George is an orphan. And much like the Reys, he, too, is a refugee from another world. Echoing the Reys' escape to freedom, each of the seven George books includes an antic chase scene, helping sell millions of books in many languages. *Naturlich,* naturally, there is a Yiddish version entitled, *George der Naygeriker*. A Heebster collectible: the Curious George *dreidl*.

No Curious Georges were harmed in the photographing of this dreidl.

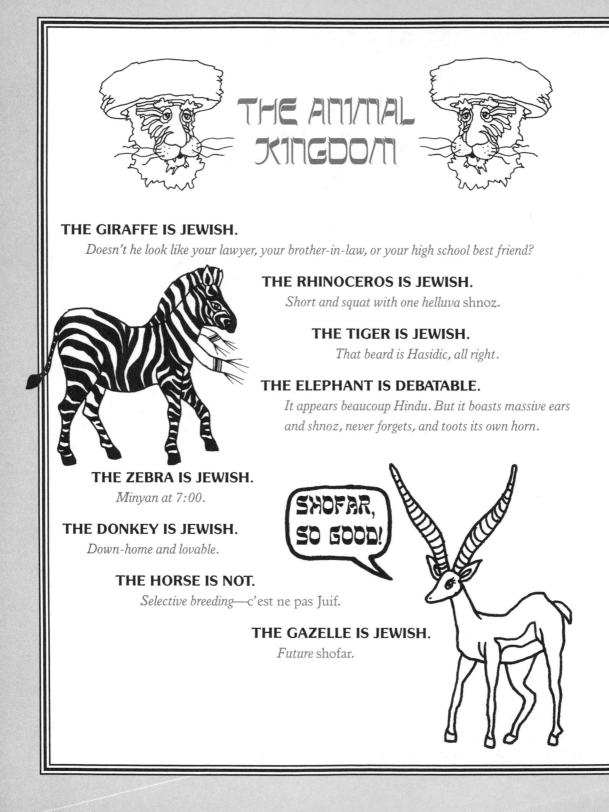

# THE ANIMAL KINGDOM

**THE GIRAFFE IS JEWISH.**
*Doesn't he look like your lawyer, your brother-in-law, or your high school best friend?*

**THE RHINOCEROS IS JEWISH.**
*Short and squat with one helluva shnoz.*

**THE TIGER IS JEWISH.**
*That beard is Hasidic, all right.*

**THE ELEPHANT IS DEBATABLE.**
*It appears beaucoup Hindu. But it boasts massive ears and shnoz, never forgets, and toots its own horn.*

**THE ZEBRA IS JEWISH.**
*Minyan at 7:00.*

**THE DONKEY IS JEWISH.**
*Down-home and lovable.*

**THE HORSE IS NOT.**
*Selective breeding—c'est ne pas Juif.*

**THE GAZELLE IS JEWISH.**
*Future shofar.*

SHOFAR, SO GOOD!

### THE PONY IS NOT.

Goyish *and manicured.*

### THE MOOSE IS JEWISH.

*Wild and awkward.*

### THE ELK IS NOT.

*Evokes the Good Old Goys, the hunting lodge, and the very unkosher taxidermy.*

### THE KOALA IS JEWISH.

*Short and fuzzy, like Grandpa.*

### THE MONKEY IS, OF COURSE, JEWISH.

Curious George *says it all.*

### THE GORILLA IS NOT.

*Fierce, angry, and threatening.*

### KING KONG, HOWEVER, IS JEWISH. *Rejected, alienated, and a wee bit hairy.*

### THE SEAL IS JEWISH.

*Sleek, dark, and graceful.*

### THE PENGUIN IS JEWISH, TOO.

*National Geographic presents "March of the Hasidim."*

### THE CHICKEN IS JEWISH.

*In a word: soup.*

### THE PARTRIDGE IS OBVIOUSLY NOT.

*In a pear tree . . .*

### THE PUSH-ME-PULL-YOU* IS SO JEWISH.

*One body, two opinions: the Tevye of the jungle.*

*The two-headed marvel featured in *Dr. Doolittle.*

# Jew? Or Not a Jew?! An Homage to *Saturday Night Live*

Scarlett Johansson? Jew!

Beck? Even if you turn Scientologist, once a Jew, always a Jew!

Avril Lavigne? Only phonetically!

Adam Goldberg? His mom is Roman Catholic, but he plays
　　one on TV!

Lou Reed? Jew!

Al Franken? Jew!

Pink? Jew!

Gwyneth Paltrow? A Jew, not a Jew, a half Jew, whatever.
　　Related to thirty-three rabbis!

Elvis? Jew!

Adam Goldberg stars as
Mordechai Jefferson Carver aka
"The Hebrew Hammer."

# The (Other) King

"In Jewish," G-d is the true king. The (other) king, of rock 'n' roll fame, is, of course, Elvis Aaron Presley. In the believe-it-or-not category, as a child, Elvis Presley often visited his upstairs neighbor, a rabbi, for whom he would turn on and off lights on the Jewish Sabbath. This is called a *Shabbos goy*. Only in this case, the *goy* wasn't so *goyish*. Turns out, Elvis descended from a Jewish woman, his maternal great-great-grandmamma, Martha Tackett. Nancy begat Martha who begat Dolly who begat Gladys who begat Elvis. Yes, Elvis. It's true. The King of Rock 'n' Roll officially qualifies as a Member of the Tribe. Technically speaking, Elvis was a *Yid*. As the documentary *Schmelvis: Searching for the King's Jewish Roots* explains, Elvis's Jewish identity rests on three pillars: Elvis loved *matzah* ball soup. Elvis's mother wanted him to be a doctor. And Elvis's *shnoz* went under the knife. *"If that doesn't prove that he's Jewish, nothing will. What more proof do we need?"*

　　The King actually knew about his Jewish roots, but his parents reportedly suggested he hide them. When his mother, Gladys Love Presley, passed away in 1958, however, Elvis proudly engraved a Jewish star on her tombstone. Elvis was also a philanthropist. This is known in Hebrew as a *ba'al tzedaka,* one who exhibits righteousness. He gave generously to the Memphis Hebrew Academy and Jewish Community Center. And throughout much of the 1970s,

Elvis donned a *chai* necklace. Spelled with the Hebrew letters *chet* and *yud, chai* is the Hebrew word for life. As Elvis explained, he didn't want to "miss out on going to heaven on a technicality." Spoken like a true Heebster!

# Jewish Inventions

One of the greatest Jewish inventions of all time is not the Barbie doll, which Ruth Handler invented; the egg cream, which Louis Auster invented; the shopping cart, which Sylvan Goldman invented; blue jeans, which Levi Strauss and Jacob Davis invented; the infomercial, which Ron Popeil invented; the remote control, which Robert Adler invented; the flexi-straw, which Joseph Friedman invented; vinyl records, which Peter Carl Goldmark invented; Valium, which Leo Sternbach invented; rent control, which Lillian Wald invented, or countless other invaluable contributions to society. No, one of the greatest Jewish inventions of all time first appears in the Talmud. It's the footnote!*

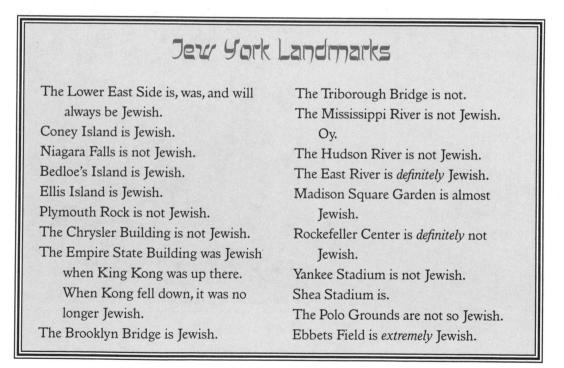

## Jew York Landmarks

The Lower East Side is, was, and will always be Jewish.

Coney Island is Jewish.

Niagara Falls is not Jewish.

Bedloe's Island is Jewish.

Ellis Island is Jewish.

Plymouth Rock is not Jewish.

The Chrysler Building is not Jewish.

The Empire State Building was Jewish when King Kong was up there. When Kong fell down, it was no longer Jewish.

The Brooklyn Bridge is Jewish.

The Triborough Bridge is not.

The Mississippi River is not Jewish. Oy.

The Hudson River is not Jewish.

The East River is *definitely* Jewish.

Madison Square Garden is almost Jewish.

Rockefeller Center is *definitely* not Jewish.

Yankee Stadium is not Jewish.

Shea Stadium is.

The Polo Grounds are not so Jewish.

Ebbets Field is *extremely* Jewish.

*This page wouldn't be complete without one!

# A MINYAN OF HIGHLY EFFECTIVE HEEBSTER HABITS

1. **CREATE A COUNTERCULTURE** *like Abbie Hoffman, Jerry Rubin, and Allen Ginsberg.*

2. **PROTEST FOR SOCIAL CHANGE** *like Rabbi Abraham Joshua Heschel, who marched with Dr. Martin Luther King Jr.*

3. **COMPOSE/PERFORM BELOVED TUNES** *like Irving Berlin, Burt Bacharach, Mama Cass, Bob Dylan, Art Garfunkel, Jerry Leiber, Paul Simon, Carly Simon, Mike Stoller, Carole King, Arnold Schoenberg, Stephen Sondheim, Felix Mendelssohn, Leonard Bernstein, Jerome Kern, George Gershwin, and . . .*

4. **RUFFLE SOME FEATHERS** *like visionary Theodor Herzl, who promoted the idea of Jews creating the modern state of Israel. The Montefiores and Rothschilds sponsored early settlements and Henrietta Szold rallied women to join the cause.*

5. **LOVE THE LAW** *like U.S. Supreme Court Jewstices: Louis Brandeis (on the bench 1916–1939), Benjamin Cardozo (1932–1938), Felix Frankfurter (1939–1962), Arthur J. Goldberg (1962–1965), Abe Fortas (1965–1969) and two still kickin': Ruth Bader Ginsburg (1993–), and Stephen Breyer (1994–).*

6. **DO GREAT THINGS WITH CASH** *like the disproportionate number of prize-winning Jewish economists and those* machers *at the National Reserve Bank.*

7. **SET AN EXAMPLE** *like the sixteen* Yiddelach *who have won the Congressional Medal of Honor, innovators Bella Abzug and Betty Friedan, and elected officials Barbara Boxer, Diane Feinstein, and Joe Lieberman. Who can forget former Secretary of State Henry Kissinger, Milwaukee-born Israeli PM Golda Meir, and former New York City Mayor Ed Koch? That Jew's got Yidi-tude to spare.*

8. **MEMORIALIZE JEWISH LIFE** *in Anatevka and beyond like Sholom Aleichem, Joseph Stein, Wendy Wasserstein, Philip Roth, Herman Wouk, Chaim Potok, Marge Piercy, Michael Chabon, Emma Goldman, the Kluggerebbie, and . . .*

9. **FLEX YOUR GRAY MATTER FOR GOOD** *like Dr. Jonas Salk, who developed a vaccine for polio in '55, Albert Einstein, and legions of Nobel Prize winners.*

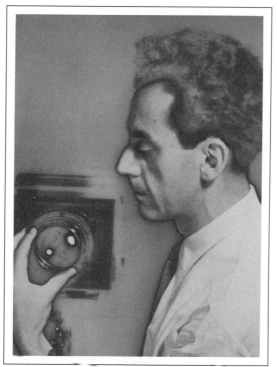

Man Ray (1890–1976), self-portrait

10. **CREATE BRILLIANT WORKS OF ART** *like Yaacov Agam, Diane Arbus, Richard Avedon, Friedl Dicker-Brandeis, Marc Chagall, Frida Kahlo, Roy Lichtenstein, Jacques Lipchitz, Annie Liebovitz, Amedeo Modigliani, Man Ray, Ben Shahn, Art Spiegelman, Alfred Stieglitz, Roman Vishniac, and Diego Rivera. Si señor, Diego descended from Conversos, Jews forced to convert to Catholicism during the Inquisition.*

# HEEBSTER CHALLAH FAME

Jewish history is filled with legions of Stars of David who have left their mark on that other Western Wall, the Wall of Fame. Here is but a *shtickl*.

### BIBLICAL HEEBSTER HEROES

Adam
Eve
Noah
Abraham
Sarah
Joseph
Moshe Rabbenu
    (Moses)
Miriam
Aaron
Pinchas
Nachshon
Joshua
King David
King Solomon
Elijah the Prophet
Daniel
Ruth
Judith
Yael
Abigael
Deborah
Samson
Hulda the
    Prophetess
Channah
The Maccabees

Queen Esther
Mordechai

### HA HA HEEBSTERS

The Three Stooges
Walter Matthau
Don Adams
Jack Benny
Milton Berle
Mel Blanc
Mel Brooks
Red Buttons
George Burns
Eddie Cantor
Sid Caesar
The Marx
    Brothers
Danny Kaye
Jerry Lewis
Gilda Radner
Carl Reiner
Gene Wilder
Billy Crystal
Henny Youngman
Ilan Gold
Adam Sandler
Lenny Bruce
Larry David
Sarah Silverman
Jerry Seinfeld

Mark Weiner(ville)
Triumph the Insult
    Comic Dog

### HEE HAW HEEBSTER

Barbi Benton

### CELEBRITY HEEBSTERS

Sarah Bernhardt
Zach Braff
Adam Brody
Kirk (Issur Demsky)
    Douglas
Adam Goldberg

Jacob Benjamin
    Gyllenhaal
Maggie Ruth
    Gyllenhaal
Dustin Hoffman
Natalie Portman
    (née Hershlag)
Amanda Peet
Sarah Jessica Parker
Elliot Gould
Sarah Michelle Geller
Harry Houdini
    (Erich Weisz)
Isaac Liev Schreiber
Kyra Sedgwick
Jerry Stiller

### MUSICAL HEEBSTERS

Bob Dylan (né
    Robert Allen
    Zimmerman)
Adam Duritz (lead
    singer/songwriter
    of Counting
    Crows)
Perry "Peretz" Farrell
Barbra Streisand aka
    the incomparable
    Babs
Gustav Mahler

## LITERARY HEEBSTERS

Judah ha-Levi
Walter Benjamin
Arthur Miller
Anne Frank
Philip Roth
Henry Roth
Bernard Malamud
Chaim Potok
Saul Bellow
Herman Wouk
Marge Piercy
Cynthia Ozick
Heinrich Heine
Franz Kafka
Boris Pasternak
Marcel Proust
Gertrude Stein
King David
King Solomon

## BIG-BRAINED HEEBSTERS

Albert Einstein
Albert Michelson
The Vilna Gaon
Robert
  Oppenheimer
Sigmund Freud
Anna Freud
Karl Marx
Franz Boas
Philo Judaeus
Baruch de Spinoza
Moses Mendelssohn
Niels Bohr

Emile Berliner
Henri Bergson
Maimonides
Nachmanides
Rashi
The Baal Shem Tov
Franz Rosenzweig
Martin Buber
Emile Durkheim

## DESIGNING HEEBS

Ralph Lauren
  (Lifshitz)
Calvin Klein
Isaac Mizrahi
Marc Jacobs

## HOLLYWOOD HEEBSTER MOGULS

William Fox
Samuel Goldwyn
Carl Laemmle
Jesse L. Lasky
Marcus Loew
Louis B. Mayer
The original Warner
  Brothers
Adolph Zukor

## ATHLETIC HEEB HEROES

Gidget
Lenny Krayzelburg
Mark Spitz
Gal Fridman

Sarah Hughes
Oksana Baiul
Sasha Cohen
Irina Slutskaya
Yael Arad
Oren Smadja
Max Baer

Benny Leonard (né
  Benjamin Leiner)
Kingfish Levinsky
  (né Harris Krakow)
Dmitry Salita
Barney Ross
Harris Scott Barton
Hank Greenberg
Sandy Koufax
Grandpa Lefty's
  cousin Itzhik who
  outran the Kossacks
  all the way from
  Yekaterinoslav to
  Hong Kong

## FAMOUS HEEB CONVERTS

Abraham
Sarah

Kate Capshaw
Nell Carter
Sammy Davis Jr.
Anne Meara
Marilyn Monroe
Elizabeth Taylor
Jim Croce
Walter Sobchak,
  *The Big Lebowski*
Charlotte York
  Goldenblatt,
  *Sex in the City*

## HONORARY HEEBS

Ray Charles
  (he's got soul)
Napoleon Dynamite
  (love the Jewfro)
Woody Guthrie
  (Hanukah
  Grammy)
Bob Marley
  (got Zion?)
The Munsters
  (Grandpa)

## HEEBSTER WANNABEES (AT ONE POINT IN HISTORY)

Madonna
Paris Hilton
Ashton Kutcher
Demi Moore
~~Britney Spears~~

# SALAD BAR

The plant kingdom has both Jewish and non-Jewish representation.

| CONTENDER | VERDICT | RATIONALE |
|---|---|---|
| Artichoke | Undoubtedly Jewish. | *Bristly outside. Yummy inside.* |
| Carrot | Borderline. | *Gefilte-friendly, but tight with the Easter Bunny.* |
| Parsnip | Jewish. | *Just has that ring to it: snip, snip.* |
| Rhubarb | Not Jewish. | *No tribal associations.* |
| Celery | Jewish. | *Snaps at you when you bend it.* |
| Iceberg Lettuce | Jewish enough. | *Iceberg, Goldberg, whatever.* |
| Spinach | Jewish. | *Parentally advised.* |
| Green Asparagus | Jewish. | *Ethnic.* |
| White Asparagus | Not Jewish. | *Aryan.* |
| Onion | Very Jewish. | *Pungent and layered.* |
| Shallot | Not Jewish. | *Upper crust.* |
| Garlic | Very Jewish. | *Heavy shtetl.* |
| Pomegranate | Duh. | *So Jewish, they're biblical.* |
| Olive | Ditto. | *Ditto.* |
| Prickly Pear | Ditto. | *The Israeli national fruit: brutal outside, juicy inside* |
| Passion Fruit | Not. | *The wrong passion, as in you know who.* |

| CONTENDER | VERDICT | RATIONALE |
|---|---|---|
| **Persimmon** | Jewish. | *Terrifically sweet or horribly bitter!* |
| **Kiwi** | But of course. | *Short and fuzzy, a fruity koala.* |
| **Strawberry** | Goes both ways. | *Short and sweet but very preppy.* |
| **Blueberry** | Jewish indeed. | *Round and robust.* |
| **Pink Grapefruit** | Naturally. | *Tart and flavorful.* |
| **Navel Orange** | Not Jewish. | *Engineered to get that way.* |
| **Star Fruit** | Of course. | *The name says it all.* |
| **Prune** | Definitely. | *Ugly, helpful, unexpectedly delicious.* |
| **Watermelon with Seeds** | Jewish. | *The original.* |
| **Seedless Watermelon** | Not Jewish. | *Disturbs the natural order.* |
| **Macintosh Apple** | Jewish. | *Short and sour.* |
| **Red Delicious Apple** | *Goyish.* | *The nose job of apples.* |
| **Golden Delicious Apple** | Need we say more? | *You fill in the blank!* |

# Super-Powered Heebsters

Superheroes reflect the Talmudic injunctions to do good for its own sake, seek justice, and pursue peace. They also embody the Jewish ideal of repairing the world: *Tikkun Olam*. Who cares if superheroes don't really exist, they're Jewish! Try these on for size: Atom Smasher, Colossal Boy of the Legion of Super-Heroes, Doc Samson, The Escapist, Gertrude Yorkes of the Runaways, Iceman, Justice, Magneto, Masada, Monolith, Moon Knight, Nite-Owl,  Nyssa Raatko, Prime, Ragman, Sabra, Sandman, Scarlet Witch, Seraph of the Global Guardians, Shadowcat of the X-Men, Songbird of the Thunderbolts, Sublime, Ben Grimm aka The Thing of the Fantastic Four, Quicksilver, and Volcana. Not to mention Menorah Man, Magen David, Dreidel Maidel, and Shabbat Queen.

CafePress.com

## SUPERMENSCH

Two Jewish teenagers from Cleveland, Jerry Siegel and Joe Shuster, invented the greatest superhero of them all, Superman, the ultimate symbol of "truth, justice, and the American Way." Unbeknownst to most, he's got a Heebro heritage!

Back in 1933, Siegel wrote a science fiction story, "The Reign of Superman." His pal Shuster drew it up. The original Superman was an evil genius inspired by the German philosopher Nietzsche. But after Hitler distorted Nietzsche's ideas, our real-life teenage heroes converted their man Clark into a force for good. Five years later, an editor at D.C. Comics finally backed the first issue of Action Comics.

Like many American Jews, Superman hailed from another world: Krypton. His ancestors sported a mystical Jewish surname, El, which is Hebrew for L-rd. A bunch of geniuses, Super's ancestors survived a flood reminiscent of the biblical epic and invented compasses, telescopes, and other brainy devices. But they couldn't prevent a holocaust-like disaster that blew up Krypton and wiped out the entire race.

Only one survivor remained: Superman. His peeps launched him to Earth in the hope he might somehow survive—just like baby Moshe sent adrift in the Nile. And true to the biblical story line, Clark Kent became a hero. He could do what disenfranchised American Jews could not: save the innocent from the death grip of the Nazi war machine. After the Japanese attack on Pearl Harbor, the Caped Crusader doubled as a combat hero, destroying Nazi armor, Japanese submarines, and virtually any enemy of democracy. Dude had *chutzpah*. Superman even cornered Hitler and Tojo by the collar on the cover of a 1944 issue.

### SPIDEY

Like Superman before him, when Spider-Man burst onto the comic book scene of Cold War 1963, he was a perfect antidote for the zeitgeist. The bite of a mutant spider gave this unpopular teen nerd superpowers. But unlike his confident predecessor, cynicism and self-doubt plagued poor Spidey.

True, Spider-Man had a *goyish* name, Peter Parker. But his inventor was the very Jewish Stan Lee, who had circumcised his own original moniker, Stanley Martin Lieber. For all we know, Peter might have descended from a Farfel Piasatsky detained for tuberculosis at Ellis Island. What's more, Stan rooted Spidey in that can't-get-much-more-Jewish 'chood of Forest Hills, Qveens. And he gave the crime fighter motivation born not of patriotism or innate goodness, but that old Jewish favorite: guilt. In this case, guilt for the death of his beloved uncle. Spider-Man won the hearts of Jewish kids everywhere. The bullied underdog, he mustered up every ounce of street cunning, wit, and irreverence toward authority to put the bad guys exactly where they belong, in *Gehenna*.*

*Yiddish for hell.

## Jew Glue

As a Heebster, you're naturally endowed with Jew Glue. This is your innate ability to bring your breadren together. And bring them together thou shalt over *challah,* rye, pumpernickel, pita, bagels, bialys, *matzah,* and oh so many other carbs. Jew Glue doesn't create the bond between *Yidden.* It simply cements it . . . like a brick rock in your stomach you can complain about for the next forty-eight hours.

Spread your Jew Glue in the Talmudic spirit of *Ahavat Yisrael,* love for your fellow *Yid.* You make the Tribe so much more "jew-tiful" when you're *shmearing* Jew Glue!

### FLAVORITES

**Brunchy** Kraft Philadelphia Cream Cheese

**Crunchy** Adam's All Natural Peanut Butter

***Bubbie's*** homemade *shmaltz* (Yiddish for chicken fat)

**Bris-y** Smoked white fish salad

**Israeli** Osem Kosher for Passover Orange Marmalade

**Deli** Batampte Delicatessen Style Mustard

**Old World** Herring in cream sauce

**New World** Manischewitz Wasabi-flavored Horseradish

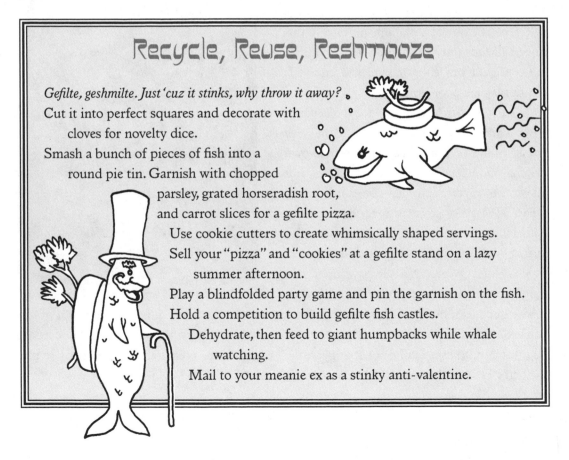

## Recycle, Reuse, Reshmooze

*Gefilte, geshmilte. Just 'cuz it stinks, why throw it away?*

Cut it into perfect squares and decorate with cloves for novelty dice.

Smash a bunch of pieces of fish into a round pie tin. Garnish with chopped parsley, grated horseradish root, and carrot slices for a gefilte pizza.

Use cookie cutters to create whimsically shaped servings.

Sell your "pizza" and "cookies" at a gefilte stand on a lazy summer afternoon.

Play a blindfolded party game and pin the garnish on the fish.

Hold a competition to build gefilte fish castles.

Dehydrate, then feed to giant humpbacks while whale watching.

Mail to your meanie ex as a stinky anti-valentine.

BET

2

FROM BRIS TO BEYOND

# BOYCHICKS AND MAIDELACH, TOO

When you're born Jewish, it's a whirlwind of *l'chaims* from your first snip onward. Naturally, the line up includes a cast of friends and family to emulate, avoid, celebrate, and mourn. Because when you're *of the Tribe,* ritual is nothing short of habitual. And the day you choose to leave this world is as important as the day you enter it. Heebster, this is your life. And this manual covers everything you need to know from womb to tomb ... and how to have a rockin' good time in between!

# The Heebster Life Cycle All-Purpose Playbill

## BRIS/BABY NAMING aka
## ENTERING THE COVENANT

| "NO TURNING BACK NOW!" | WHAT TO EAT | WHAT TO DO | WHAT TO SAY | WHAT TO WEAR |
|---|---|---|---|---|
| Star of the Show | Breastmilk. | Weep. | Waaah! | Silver dollar-sized *yarmulke* or a frilly outfit. |
| Guest | Lox and bagels. | Bring gifts. | *"Mazal tov!"* Think "Ouch!" | Dress clothes among the suit-and-tie set; whatever in Israel, California, and other outlying areas. |

**INSIDER'S TIP:** If it's your *bris,* just keep crying for more Manischewitz. If you're the g-dparent, the *sandak* who holds the baby on his lap during the circumcision, or the hormonal mother, and you can't stand to watch, just keep toasting with more Manischewitz.

## SHABOT 6000 by Ben Baruch

© Ben Baruch

## *BAR/BAT MITZVAH* aka COMING OF AGE

| "BYE BYE GOOD OL' DAYS!" | WHAT TO EAT | WHAT TO DO | WHAT TO SAY | WHAT TO WEAR |
|---|---|---|---|---|
| **Star of the Show** | Candy pelted at you with love after reading from the *Torah!* | Chant from the *Torah* and give a speech that makes you sound brilliant! | "Thanks, Mom and Dad!" | Your first tallit or prayer shawl; light blue tuxedo or eye shadow. |
| **Guest** | Everything. | Give fat checks. | *"Mazal tov!"* | Free souvenir *yarmulke.* |

**INSIDER'S TIP:** If it's your *bar* or *bat mitzvah,* and you've totally screwed up chanting your *Torah* portion, just keep sipping more Manischewitz. If you're a non-Jewish guest and have no clue what's going on, just keep accepting more Manischewitz.

### FYI: FOR THE YIDDISH IMPAIRED

A *mitzvah* is a commandment. A *bar* or *bat mitzvah* comes of age and is responsible for fulfilling the commandments. Doing so earns spiritual bonus points for the World to Come. At a *bar* or *bat mitzvah,* the parents say a blessing, *baruch sh'patrani* aka "Thanks G-d, now ve're off da hook!"

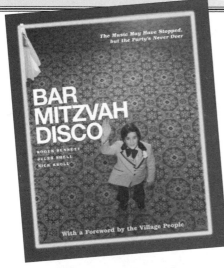

## *CHUPPAH*/WEDDING aka
## CREATING A "FAITHFUL HOME AMONG ISRAEL"

| "LAST RESORT: GET OUT" | WHAT TO EAT | WHAT TO DO | WHAT TO SAY | WHAT TO WEAR |
|---|---|---|---|---|
| **Stars of the Show** | Nothing on this "mini *Yom Kippur.*" Besides, once the ceremony concludes, your face will ache from all that pinching. | Pray it all goes smoothly; not just the wedding, but your years of unbiding devotion. | "You are consecrated to me according to the laws of Moshe and Yisrael." | If you're the bride, pure white. If you're the groom, it doesn't matter. No one will notice you anyway. |
| **Guests** | The entire smorgasbord. | Bring *shtick* galore and do a goofy dance to entertain bride and groom. | *"Mazal tov!"* Think "Soon by me!" | In Orthodox settings, cover arms to the elbow and legs to the knees. In Israel, wear sandals. |

**INSIDER'S TIP:** If you're the bride or groom, and you can't believe you're actually marrying this *shlemiel,* just keep gulping more Manischewitz. If you're the guest who has been in love with the bride or groom since the third grade of Hebrew school and can't stand to watch, just keep sneaking more Manischewitz.

## SHIVA aka SEVEN DAYS OF MOURNING

| "BURY 'EM WHOLE!" | WHAT TO EAT | WHAT TO DO | WHAT TO SAY | WHAT TO WEAR |
|---|---|---|---|---|
| Star of the Show | Hard-boiled eggs and bagels to symbolize the cycle of life. | Weep, pray, and "process." | The favorite joke of the deceased. | A shirt you tear in mourning. |
| Guest | Your favorite cake. | Bring your your favorite cake; give to charity in memory of the departed. | "I'm so sorry … He told the best jokes ever!" | Dark clothing. |

**INSIDER'S TIP:** If you're sitting *shiva*, just keep longing for more Manischewitz. If you can't bear the loss of your old pinochle partner, just keep downing more Manischewitz.

## THE WORLD TO COME/GARDEN OF EDEN aka
## ETERNAL PARADISE!

| "HEAVEN CAN WAIT NO LONGER" | WHAT TO EAT | WHAT TO DO | WHAT TO SAY | WHAT TO WEAR |
|---|---|---|---|---|
| **Star of the Show** | Everything; look mahvelous, and never gain an ounce. | Anything you've ever dreamed of. | Any joke … Here everyone will laugh! | Wings and fab retro Adidas tracksuits you could never afford on Earth. |
| **Guest** | Not permitted except in dreams, hallucinations, drug trips, and George Burns *Oh, G-d!* movies | | | |

# Good-bye Ghetto

Back in the day, the arrival of Jews at Ellis Island led to the bleaching of heavy *shtetl* names. Piasastzki became Post. Shlomovitz became Sloan. And even later, due to antisemitism, some families, like the Radnitzkys of Da 'Burg, joined the trend, changing their surname to Ray. Son Emmanuel took it a step further, eventually becoming known as the modernist artist, Man Ray. The same thing happened in Hollywood. Ol' skool celebs aplenty circumcised the Jew right out of their names in order to play to a wider audience. Emmanuel Goldenberg became Edward G. Robinson. *Baruch Hashem,* thanks G-d, those days are over.

# Name That Jew

Match the star to the stage name!

1. **The (original) Three Stooges: Moe, Larry, and Shemp**
2. **The Marx Brothers: Chico, Groucho, Gummo, Harpo, and Zeppo**
3. **Jack Benny**
4. **Milton Berle**
5. **George Burns**
6. **Eddie Cantor**
7. **Howard Cosell**
8. **Kirk Douglas**

a. Benjamin Kubelsky
b. Mendel Berlinger
c. Leonard, Julius, Milton, Adolph, and Herbert
d. Harry Moses Horwitz (Moshe ben Reb Shlomo Natan ha-Levi), Louis Feinberg, and Samuel/Shmuel Horwitz.
e. Edward Israel Iskowitz
f. Nathan Birnbaum
g. Issur Danielovitch Demsky
h. Howard Cohen

*Answers:* 1. d, 2. c, 3. a, 4. b, 5. f, 6. e, 7. h, 8. g

# Extreme Name-Over

Are you walking around as Justin or Samantha? Not that there's anything wrong with it, but if you zap your moniker with a Hebraic vibe, in seconds, you'll go from *goyish* to ghetto gorgeous!

| GOYISH | HEBREW | YIDDISH | LADINO | GHETTO GORGEOUS |
|---|---|---|---|---|
| George | Avraham | Avrohum | Avramiko | Avrumi |
| Tiffany | Shoshana | Bluma Sheindel | Shoshanika | Bloomie |
| Marshall | Moshe Mordechai | Moisheleh Mersheleh | Moises/Moshiko | Momo |
| Myrtle | Hadassah | Estee | Estercita | Dassie |
| Preston, IV | Yonatan | Yonasan | Julio | Sunny |
| Mackenzie | Malka | Malkalah | Regina | Rej |
| Juanita | Yehudit | Yehudis | Yoodeet | Joojz |
| Nikolai | Natanel | Nosonel | Natan | Natoosh |
| Satchel | Micha'el | Michil | Miguel | Micky |
| Magdalena | Miriyam | Miralah | Miriam | Yummy |
| Roscoe | Reuven | Ruhvin | Ruben | Rashi |
| Dakota | Da-veed | Dovid | David | Dudu |
| Wilhelm | Efraim | Feivel | Efraím | Effie |
| Spencer | Shmuel | Shmillik | Shmuelik | Shmu |
| Gloria | Gila | Golda | Corazon | Cory |
| Joe | Yosef | Yussel | José | Yoyo |
| Gladys | Aliza | Frayda | Alegre | Ale (AH-lay) |
| Judd | Yehuda | Yidl | Yehuda | Yoda |

# Who Are Jew?

Every Heebster has an alias. If you haven't discovered yours yet, never fear. Shred that bland ID into *matzah* meal and groove a new vibe to reveal your inner Jew.

1. Circumcise a long surname into a nickname. Pearlmutter decapitates into Pearl, which is a cool *tranny* name, even for a straight guy. Also heard, Muttke.

2. Play with the suffix for endless prosifunkifying possibilities. Klug (pronounced *kloog*, which, of course, means "clever" in Yiddish) morphs into Klugovitch and other lovabilities.

3. Take the first syllable of your first and last names and combine. Yoav Potash becomes Yopo. Nurit Kirsch becomes Nuki. (Works great for e-mail!)

4. Turn a dorky physical trait into a proud "aka." Take your lead from "The *Shnoz*," a Talmudic term (of sorts) for one of the nation's greatest ancient sages. Rabban Gamliel was known by the Hebrew word for a prominent beak, *khotem*.*

---

## Fun, Fabulous, and Nonfiction!

These Heebsters rock the moniker Jewniverse:

1. The Biale Rebbe serves up wholesome wisdom.
2. Professor James Kugel is named for a *Shabbos* delicacy.
3. He's friendly with Professor Lokshin—"a noodle" in Yiddish.
4. Professor Yom Tov Assis of Hebrew University translates to "juicy holy day."
5. His colleague, Professor Ilana Pardes, translates to "tree of the orchard."
6. The late philanthropist Mortimer Fleishhacker's surname means "butcher."
7. And then there's Rabbi Basil Herring. Yum!

---

*As the saying goes, Jews have big noses to keep their heads in the Five Books of Moses.

# Rover Do Over

Forget Fido. Bust a Heebster moniker for your furry friends.

**The Bible**—The possibilities are nearly endless: Zeek (Ezekiel), Meth (Methuselah), and Shmoo (Shmoolikel). Not to mention Machli, Mooshi, and Vashi, the Jewish Flopsy, Mopsy, and Cottontail.

**Liquor**—Arrack, Schnapps, Slivovitz, and Sabra (an Israeli orange aperitif) spell out "L'Chaim, everybody!"

**Yiddish**—Feivel is the perfect mouse moniker à la the film, *An American Tail.* Fartzendik fits the gassy one in the corner.

**Food**—Farfel is a delectable Yiddishe risotto that meows. Kasha, Yiddish for buckwheat, goes well with *varnishkes,* bow tie noodles. And Adam Sandler is partial to his four-legged friend, Matzoball.

**Compliments**—Express your softer side with Shayna Punim, pretty face in Yiddish. Ditto for Shatzie. Motek, Hebrew for sweetheart, circumcises to Mo. Loving-kindness, *Chesed* in Hebrew, morphs to Kessy.

**Translations aka The Literal Label**—Kelev is Hebrew for dog. Khetzeleh is Yiddish for kitty. Fishel is your baby gefilte. And Arnevet, Hebrew for bunny, shortens gracefully to Arnie.

---

## FYI: FOR THE YIDDISH IMPAIRED

The name Cowznofski was a frequent spoof at *MAD* magazine—the satirical publication, not the late-night *MADtv* show. Coupled with Melvin, Lance, or Irving, Cowznofski also doubled as a pseudo-unit of measure.

# Leaving Home

When it comes to your early schooling, you're at the mercy of your parents. Whether you attend *yeshiva,* Jewish day school, public school, afternoon Hebrew school, Sunday school, or Hebrew high, you're very likely going to have to accept your parents' decisions if you want them to pay for college. At that point, though, it's time to flex your Heebster muscles, at least a *shtickl.* Who cares about the "Old Goy Network" when you can have your gefilte and eat it, too?!

# Entrance Exam

1.   Look for a college that offers
     a.   Solomonic Wisdom 101 (that prof's gotta be a *Yid*)
     b.   The annual "*Latke-Hamantaschen* Debate"
     c.   A comforting "Knishmas Eve Party"
     d.   All of the above

2.   Your college choice is acceptable if
     a.   Your SAT score helps you score a Jewish hottie at Hillel House
     b.   On Saturday afternoon, the nearest Chabad serves *cholent*
     c.   Students crowd into lectures by the rabbi-priest team known as the "G-d Squad"
     d.   All of the above

3.   Even better is a university that also offers
     a.   The study abroad program at Hebrew University known as the "One-Year Party"
     b.   Soul Patrol boycotts of all lectures on *Yom Kippur* and *Rosh HaShanah*
     c.   An annual alumni weekend called "Caring, Sharing, and Herring"
     d.   All of the above

4. Apply to institutions whose faculty vacation in Miami during Passover—just like you!
   a. Albert Einstein College of Medicine
   b. Brandeis University
   c. Yeshiva University
   d. Touro College
   e. All of the above

5. When preparing for a future profession, nearly every career is suitable for a Heebster, as long as it does not involve
   a. An actual pimp coat
   b. Italian, Israeli, Russian, or any other mafia
   c. Trafficking anything but yourself on the freeway
   d. All of the above

*Answers: All of the above!*

# The Art of the *Shnorr*

Moving away from home is the perfect time to perfect the *Art of the Shnorr*. This is the Yiddish term for freeloading. When you snooze, you lose. But when you *shnorr,* you score!

1. Look up friends of your parents and grandparents who live near your college. Make sure they know you're new in town. If they don't get the hint, invite yourself over for *Rosh HaShanah* dinner, *Yom Kippur* break-the-fast, and Thanksgiving.

2. During dorm move-in week, identify the bereaved mother grieving the "loss" of her only child. She'll be the bag lady *schlepping* tons of food. Befriend that kid and be sure the mom knows your room number. You, too, will be receiving care packages in no time.

3. Learn exactly what time nearby synagogues start *kiddush,* a midday snack

you can consider lunch! (For the kiddush freeloading menu, see page 94.)

4. Dog-sit for wealthy synagogue members and store up fat with delectables from the pantry.

5. Befriend the nearest hip Hasidic family. They all have eleven kids and make huge meals. They'll hardly notice another mouth at the table.

6. When you go home for winter break, remember, you can't count on your anorexic *shiksah* roommate for nourishment. *Schlep* along an extra piece of luggage to fill with leftovers.

# UNBEARABLE FAMILY GET-TOGETHERS

Like any human being, as a Heebster, you may be frequently challenged by those who brought you into this world: your family. Counting the minutes until you can get out of another intolerable gathering of those who came before you? Try these Heebster Escape Strategies . . . there's one for every miserable day of the week!

### SUNDAY
### Make Them Laugh

Liven things up with an impromptu stand-up comedy routine. Channel your inner Billy Crystal to make *700 Sundays* pass like nothing flat. Because when you're the entertainment, you're always entertained!

### MONDAY
### Semitic Cinematic Challenge

Forget your personal dramas! Play charades in the basement. Get the ball rolling with super Jew movie titles. Better yet, bring along the DVDs. Press PLAY and you'll barely need to interact with anyone. An added bonus: temporary relief from your own dysfunctional family by watching the truly *farkakte!*

### TUESDAY
### Games Yidden Play

Gather up all the kids. Take them to a nearby park with lots of cookies, chalk, jump rope, bubbles, *matkot* (Israeli beach paddleball) . . . anything that promotes a frolic in the sun. Instead of looking like an asocial loser, all the boring grown-ups will love you for getting the kids outside. And all the kids will love you for acting their age!

## Video Therapy

*Annie Hall*

*Nina's Tragedies*

*The Chosen*

*Chutzpah, This Is?*

*Everything Is Illuminated*

*Exodus*

*Fiddler on the Roof*

*Frisco Kid*

*The Hebrew Hammer*

*The Jazz Singer*

*Keeping Up with the Steins*

*The Life and Times of Hank Greenberg*

*Life Is Beautiful*

*Marjorie Morningstar*

*Rochelle, Rochelle: A Young Girl's Strange, Erotic Journey from Milan to Minsk*

*The Ten Commandments*

*Unstrung Heroes*

*Ushpizin*

*Yentl*

Why play any ordinary game when you can get your game on and turn it into a Jewish one?! Go on now, play matchmaker!

| | | | |
|---|---|---|---|
| 1. | **Go Fish** | a. | *Melech Shlomo* (King Solomon) |
| 2. | **Hopscotch** | b. | Pin the *Shtreiml* on the Rebbe |
| 3. | **Pick Up Sticks** | c. | Rabbis and Sinners |
| 4. | **Simon Says** | d. | Hopschlep |
| 5. | **Red Rover** | e. | Not Jewish, but sure sounds it! |
| 6. | **Cops and Robbers** | f. | *Shticks* |
| 7. | **Marco Polo** | g. | *Shimon Omer* |
| 8. | **Pin the Tail on the Donkey** | h. | Go(filte) Fish |
| 9. | **Yahtzee!** | i. | Big *Shnorrer* |

*Answers:* 1. h, 2. d, 3. f, 4. g, 5. i, 6. c, 7. a, 8. b, 9. e

## WEDNESDAY

### Bookworm with a Mission

Even the most dysfunctional Jewish families respect education. Everyone will be so impressed when you tell them you've got to catch up on your reading for your "B.S." degree in Jewish Studies. No one has to know it's from inventyourownuniversity.com.

Forget about learning about Jewish life by dealing with reality. Learn about it the fun way: with fiction. When you think about it, it's really a perfect match. Graphic novels aren't true, just like your degree!

---

### Hammock Companions

*The Adventures of Rabbi Harvey: A Graphic Novel of Jewish Wisdom and Wit in the Wild West,* Steve Sheinkin

*A Contract with G-d,* Will Eisner

*Isaac the Pirate: The Capital* and *Isaac the Pirate: To Exotic Lands,* Christophe Blaine

*The Jew of New York,* Ben Katchor

*The Rabbi's Cat* and *Klezmer: Tales of the Wild East,* Joann Sfar

*Tintin au Pays de l'Or Noir,* 1950 edition, Herge aka Georges Remi

---

## THURSDAY
### *L'Chaim,* Everybody!
Mix up a generous batch of Mani(schevitz)tinis and get shnookered. Repeat.

---

## MAKING A MANI
Blend a splash of Rose's sweetened or fresh lime juice with ½ cup orange juice and ½ cup vodka—or whatever proportions work for you! Pour over ice. Add a tablespoon or more of Blackberry Manischewitz. Add seltzer, champagne, or lemon-lime soda. Garnish with a fresh lime wedge or blackberries.

---

## FRIDAY
### It's a Small World
Start a game of Jewish Geography. Aren't we all only six degrees away from Jerry Stiller?

## *MOTZEI SHABBOS* AKA SATURDAY NIGHT
### Bonding with Bubbie and Zayde*

1. Ply them with Manis.
2. Smoke a cigar together.
3. Compare shared family quirks and anatomical anomalies.
4. Write down their favorite no-measurement recipes.
5. Swap your worst nightmare date or vomiting stories.
6. Videotape them singing their favorite songs.
7. Before you turn off the camera, record them sharing embarrassing stories about your parents as kids. Keep these in a safety deposit box as potential ammo.

*That's your grandparents, *Saba v'Savta* in Hebrew.

# Finding a Match

According to the ancient sage, Rabbi Yochanan, making a match is as difficult for G-d as splitting the Red Sea. But that shouldn't put a cramp in your style.

## ADVICE YOU DIDN'T ASK FOR

So you're single. Heebsters don't let this get them down. Besides, they're not really alone. G-d is single, too! And according to the Talmud, so is one day of the week. Every day of the week has a partner except for one. Sunday has Monday, Tuesday has Wednesday, Thursday has Friday, and *Shabbat,* well, *Shabbat* is single, just like you. So who is *Shabbat*'s date? Millions of *Yiddelach* around the world. So what if you've already gone out with every friend of your Facebook friends? No matter how long you're single, when you're a Heebster, you've always got a date! Sure, it's not exactly what you'd hoped for, but at least you're not a polytheistic loser, a cynical atheist, or some other pathetic ingrate at the end of this sentence!

## LAUGH-FIRMATIONS

Finally going out with another live being? Think Heebster positive to boost yourself pre-date.

- *Why dwell in self-pity, when you're so Jew pretty!*
- *I'm good enough, Jew enough, and gevalt, do I like me!*
- *Feeling blue? It's your color. You're a Jew!*

© *Hamsa* by Josh Baum

# BETROTHALS ACCORDING TO THE

**1.** Outdoor wedding canopy surrounded by requisite foliage. In Israel, cedars of Lebanon. In Northern California, towering redwoods. On the East Coast, flowering dogwood.

**2.** A tallit or prayer shawl traditionally doubles as the wedding canopy or chuppah *(clear your throat with a /ch/ as in Bach). Groovy types sew a quilt or handpaint a piece of silk that will reappear in the boudoir.*

**3.** The bride and groom honor four die-hard bachelors holding the chuppah *poles. This is considered good luck. They need it.*

**4.** The groom is known as the Chatan *in Hebrew or the* Chossen *in Yiddish (with a / ch/ as in Bach). Note: If the groom is Reconstructionist, she is pregnant.*

**8.** Rabbi.
Note: If the rabbi is Reform, she is pregnant.

**9.** Mother of the Bride.
Note: If the mother of the bride is Orthodox, she is pregnant.

**10.** Manischewitz is naturally an integral part of the ceremony. It is sipped slowly to avoid staining the bride's dress.

**11.** The ketubah, *the Jewish marriage contract, written in ancient* Aramaic in beautiful Hebrew calligraphy, surrounded by decorative art groovy types create themselves.

**12.** Shtick, *merrymaking props at the ready for the reception.*

# LAWS OF MOSHE AND YISRAEL

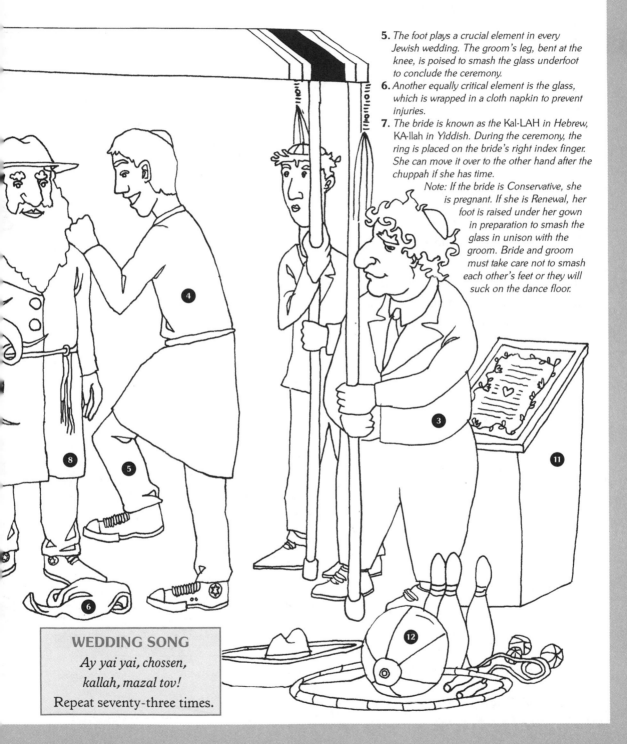

**5.** The foot plays a crucial element in every Jewish wedding. The groom's leg, bent at the knee, is poised to smash the glass underfoot to conclude the ceremony.

**6.** Another equally critical element is the glass, which is wrapped in a cloth napkin to prevent injuries.

**7.** The bride is known as the Kal-LAH in Hebrew, KA-llah in Yiddish. During the ceremony, the ring is placed on the bride's right index finger. She can move it over to the other hand after the chuppah if she has time.

Note: If the bride is Conservative, she is pregnant. If she is Renewal, her foot is raised under her gown in preparation to smash the glass in unison with the groom. Bride and groom must take care not to smash each other's feet or they will suck on the dance floor.

**WEDDING SONG**
*Ay yai yai, chossen,*
*kallah, mazal tov!*
Repeat seventy-three times.

## A Minyan of Wedding Dos

1. Earth-friendly (free) evites.
2. Homemade art on invitations and *ketubah*.
3. Wedding dresses borrowed from the local *gemach*, the pocket-and-planet friendly bridal co-op of Orthodox communities.
4. Wedding dresses bought on eBay, at thrift stores and factory outlets.
5. Ruffled-shirts-and-light-blue-tuxedo looks recycled from bar mitzvahs.
6. *Schmaltzy* slide shows of the bride and groom growing up accompanied by dorky muzak.
7. Piles of *shtick* for crazed circle dancing.
8. Disposable cameras for backup candid shots.
9. Performing friends and relatives.
10. More than enough food.*

## Making the Bride and Groom Happy

The Talmud teaches it is a great *mitzvah* to make the bride and groom happy. At Heebster wedding receptions, friends and family pull out the stops to celebrate the couple. This includes pulling out chairs from someone about to sit down. This is also the time to bust your best dance moves, break out party favors saved from the last wedding you attended, whip out your seventh-grade magic tricks, and zip around in your favorite sneakers. You know, the ones with the retractable wheels!

PERFECT FOR
BAR MITZVAHS,
WEDDINGS,
AND CIRCUMCISIONS.
HE BREW THE CHOSEN BEER.

* Why should this night be different from all other nights?

## THE ULTIMATE *SHTICK* LIST

During the marathon of Jewish circle dance aerobics at weddings and bar mitzvahs, Heebster hosts-in-the-know provide guests with party favors a-go-go.

Balloons, no-stain bubbles, confetti*

Sparklers

Nerf balls, beach balls, inflatable *matzah* balls

Royal scepters, crowns

Butterfly wings

Hula hoops

Noisemakers, horns, and tambourines

Animal masks

Giant sunglasses, Blues Brothers sunglasses, and Groucho Marx glasses

Plastic derby hats, cowboy hats, striped Cat-in-the-Hat hats

Grass skirts, faux flower leis, and coconut bras

Inflatable guitars, saxophones, and oversized clown shoes

Glow-in-the-dark necklaces—snap and glow

Any other goofy thing you can think of

Shoppers' Note: The best day to snag discounted goodies is the day after Halloween!

## MERRY MAKING

Tie cloth napkins into a giant jump rope

Act out a pretend bullfight between matador and bull with a cloth napkin cape

Dance with a bottle of water on your head, then serve the bride a drink

Dance with a lit candle stuck into the bottle on your head

Dance with a hat on fire

Fire-eaters

Juggle, belly dance, do the splits

Pirouette to the point of nausea

Tap dance

Dance the Limbo, The *Katzatzka,* the "Elaine"

Do cartwheels, handstands, backflips, and capoeira

Run and hop over another person's shoulders

Spin a human windmill: Four people lock arms in a circle. Every other person runs. The other two hold on, pick up their feet, and fly!

The classic: hoist the couple up in chairs as they hold a cloth napkin between them

The *Rebbe Tanz*: a Hasidic rabbi dances the finale at the wedding's end

* Yidden don't throw rice at weddings. We throw confetti!

# I Gave Birth to a *Hasid*
## A Personal Confession Based On Actual Events

Exactly nine months after standing under the *chuppah,* I gave birth to a beautiful baby boy. Eight days later, my husband and I fulfilled the *mitzvah* of entering him into the covenant of Abraham. Afterward, as he sucked on Manischewitz on his Zaydie's thumb, we were filled with pride and emotion. We looked forward to blissful years of little league, skateboards, burgers and milkshakes, but our little boy soon expressed other interests. He treasured every Jewish ritual item in our home and at two, recited the Four Questions at Bubbie's Passover *seder.* At three, we gave him his second circumcision: his first haircut. And from then on, he insisted on wearing Zaydie's *yarmulke* every day. That *Purim,* he asked for a long black coat and *shtreiml* as his costume. He claimed my great-grandfather's old prayer book as his own, faced an eastern wall, and stood swaying and mumbling like the old bearded *Yid* in the oil painting in our hallway. When we asked what he was doing, he answered in a word: *"Shuckling."*

After *Purim* ended, he said he was now a *hasid* and would only wear black and white. He asked for his own set of ritual fringes, which he wore under his coat. He refused cheeseburgers, beef Stroganoff, and other dishes containing milk and meat. He ate fresh fruits and vegetables on paper plates and drank hot tea from a glass with a sugar cube between his front teeth. He answered only to his Hebrew name and peppered his speech with Yiddishisms out of nowhere.

The other children in the neighborhood were quite happy playing and watching cartoons Saturday mornings. Our boy asked instead to go to *shul.* He took up a regular seat in the front row. When he learned he would soon be starting kindergarten, he asked to visit *yeshivot* where he engaged the rabbinic faculty in Talmudic discourse.

The first few years with our son have been a spiritual experience. We have now bought him his own George Foreman Grill, mini refrigerator, and milk and meat dishes. Every night at dinner, he gives a brief class on what he learned that day at *yeshiva.* We've taken to calling him our little rabbi. We expect he will be ordained at his *bar mitzvah.* Somehow, he has already grown a full beard.

# Party On (and On!)

Just because you've never heard of these parties, doesn't mean they don't exist! Heebsters make a party out of everything. Match these events to their (so-called) occasion.

1. **Lay'l Shishi**
2. **Melave Malka**
3. **Shabbos Kallah**
4. **Aufruf**
5. **Farbrengen**
6. **Upshurin/Honey Lickin'**
7. **Tish**
8. **Pidyon HaBen**
9. **Chanukat HaBayit**
10. **Siyyum**
11. **Henna**
12. **Mishmar**

a. pre-wedding in-*shul* candy toss at the groom
b. pre-wedding *Shabbat* party for the bride, no tossing allowed
c. anniversary of a Lubavitcher *rebbe* getting out of jail
d. Thursday night warm-up for *Shabbos*: singing, stories, food
e. boy's first haircut at age three, eating the Hebrew *alef bet* written in honey
f. Saturday night *Shabbat* bye-bye: singing, stories, food
g. pre-wedding celebration among Sephardi Jews in which hands are decorated with henna
h. symbolic redemption of the first-born son on a silver platter
i. nailing the *mezuzah* into the doorpost aka Heebster housewarming
j. "table" of celebration at a *farbrengen* or pre-wedding reception or any other good excuse
k. pre-*Shabbos* Torah study all-nighter with copious coffee breaks, popular with the *yeshiva* set
l. completion of the study of an entire mind-bending text like a Talmudic tractate

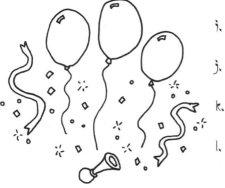

*Answers:* 1. d, 2. f, 3. b, 4. a, 5. c, 6. e, 7. j, 8. h, 9. i, 10. l, 11. g, 12. k

---

### FYI: FOR THE YIDDISH IMPAIRED

The only proper Jewish toast is *"L'chaim/*To life!" For a people with a history of persecution, forced out of their homes at a moment's notice and threatened with annihilation, there is simply nothing else to say!

# Cork-Free Tasting

While it is entertaining for corks to fly unexpectedly into open mouths and select body parts, it does present an unfriendly challenge to arthritic tribal members and Crackberry addicts with repetitive thumb strain. When throwing a party, it is perfectly Heebster acceptable to serve screw-cap-only vintages. These Judaica Juices wisely avoid the cork. *L'chaim,* everybody. It's five o'clock somewhere!

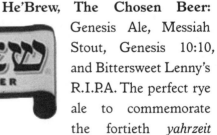

**Manischewitz Concord Grape:** Full-bodied, like a jar of jam left in your basement to ferment to 11 percent. Boasts a certain foxiness with slight whiskers. A home-less favorite. Also available in Blackberry, Cherry, and Elderberry. Ideal for circumcision guests and main attractions. Doubles as an intoxicating adult cough syrup or topping for Sunday morning *matzah brei* (see page 180) or leftover *challah*-turned-French toast.

**Mogen David:** All the bite without the sugar. Only the traditional Red Grape label packs a whopping 18 percent alcohol content. MD is sold under two labels: the classic dark red Passover rendition and the trendy, rainbow-colored MD 20/20. An excellent substitute for Novocain, "Mad Dog" is yet another street fav'.

**J&B Scotch:** A popular *l'chaim* for all occasions; also known as Jew Booze or Jew Boy.

**Vodka:** The preferred libation among Lubavitchers.

**Arrack:** Anise-flavored Sephardi liqueur. Delish with ice water.

**Slivovitz:** Classic plum brandy; offers temporary relief for sore throats.

**He'Brew, The Chosen Beer:** Genesis Ale, Messiah Stout, Genesis 10:10, and Bittersweet Lenny's R.I.P.A. The perfect rye ale to commemorate the fortieth *yahrzeit* of Lenny Bruce aka Leonard Alfred Schneider. Naturally brewed with "obscene amounts of malts and hops."

# You Got a Problem with That?

There is no man like Manischewitz. But when a Heebster's cuppeth runneth over a little too ofteneth, how do you know when you've had too much of a good thing?

True or false: You know you're addicted to Manischewitz when,

1. Going to your third *bris* this week trumps getting a free shiatsu massage.
2. "Friday Night Live" means crashing the local Jewish Home for the Aged Fridays at 5:30 P.M.—just in time for the complimentary refreshments.
3. You cancel your weekend getaway to attend Temple Emanuel's Wine and Cheese Singles' Mixer and taste a rare Manischewitz Special Reserve from 1936.

*Answers:* If you answered true to any question, you're on a black diamond slope toward tooth (and liver) decay.

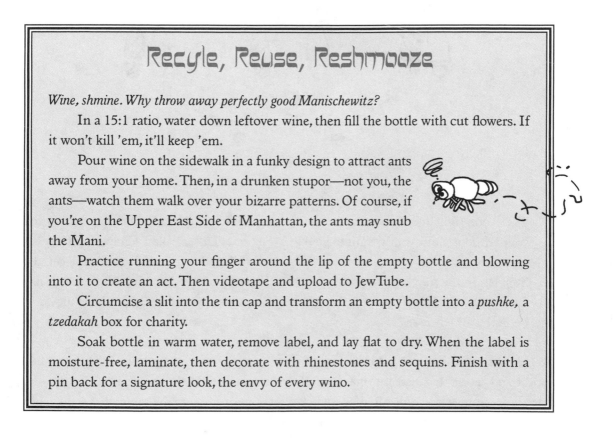

## Recyle, Reuse, Reshmooze

*Wine, shmine. Why throw away perfectly good Manischewitz?*

In a 15:1 ratio, water down leftover wine, then fill the bottle with cut flowers. If it won't kill 'em, it'll keep 'em.

Pour wine on the sidewalk in a funky design to attract ants away from your home. Then, in a drunken stupor—not you, the ants—watch them walk over your bizarre patterns. Of course, if you're on the Upper East Side of Manhattan, the ants may snub the Mani.

Practice running your finger around the lip of the empty bottle and blowing into it to create an act. Then videotape and upload to JewTube.

Circumcise a slit into the tin cap and transform an empty bottle into a *pushke,* a *tzedakah* box for charity.

Soak bottle in warm water, remove label, and lay flat to dry. When the label is moisture-free, laminate, then decorate with rhinestones and sequins. Finish with a pin back for a signature look, the envy of every wino.

# KOSHER CARDIO

Despite the old stereotype that Jews aren't athletic, any wedding reveals otherwise. The requisite dance at every Heebster wedding or *bar* and *bat mitzvah* party is the *hora*. And the requisite song is "Hava Negila." Combined, the workout kicks kickboxing.

## THE MOVES

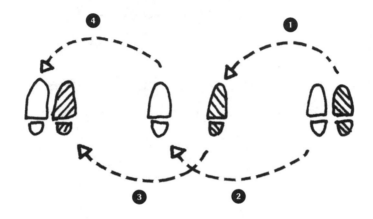

1. Take your right foot and cross it over your left foot. Shift your weight to your right foot.
2. Step left to the side.
3. Take your right foot and step to the side behind your left foot.

4. Shift your weight and step left to the side. This is called a grapevine step. It's called that because until you get the hang of it, it kinda makes you look like you've been hanging out in a vineyard.

To help keep your balance, hold hands with the clammy person next to you and repeat. Then repeat and repeat and repeat some more. Keep repeating until the song ends. That may be forty-five minutes later. For variation, switch directions or run into the center and slam dance the person opposite you.

## THE LYRICS

This heartfelt melody conveys a message astounding in its depth and meaning. Impress your friends and family by singing the oh-so-rare English translation.

| | |
|---|---|
| *Hava nagila. Hava nagila.* | Let us get happy. Let us get happy. |
| *Hava nagila v'nis'mecha.* | Let us get happy and we will be really glad. |
| | |
| *Hava nagila. Hava nagila.* | Let us get happy.  Let us get happy. |
| *Hava nagila v'nis'mecha.* | Let us get happy and we will be so glad. |
| | |
| *Hava neranena.* | Come and we will rejoice. |
| *Hava neranena.* | Come and we will rejoice. |
| *Hava neranena* | Come and we will rejoice |
| *v'nis'mecha! (repeat verse)* | and we'll be really glad! (repeat verse) |
| | |
| *Uru! Uru achim!* | Wake up! Wake up brothers! |
| *Uru achim belev same'ach.* | Wake up brothers with a happy heart. |
| *Uru achim belev same'ach.* | Wake up brothers with a happy heart. |
| *Uru achim belev same'ach.* | Wake up brothers with a happy heart. |
| *Uru achim belev same'ach.* | Wake up brothers with a happy heart. |
| *Uru achim! Uru achim!* | Wake up brothers! Wake up brothers! |
| *B'lev same'ach!* | With a very happy heart! |

Repeat from the beginning and continue again and again until your very happy heart requires attention from your cardiologist cousin who flew in for the occasion.

### CINNAMON TOAST!

The more Hasidic you get, the more celebrations lend themselves to boisterous singing and dancing. A very far cry from the decorum of Westminster Abbey, breaking out in song and dance in the aisles of your local *shul* is a perfectly welcome interruption to the usual sequence of prayers. And it doesn't even matter why! Whatever the celebration, the song is always the same. *Siman tov u'mazal tov!* literally means "A good omen and good luck!"

    If you can't pronounce these Hebrew words fast enough when the ruckus cuts loose, just keep repeating "Cinnamon toast!" as you sing along. No one will even notice.

# Jewish Geography

MINNY HYAMOWITZ lives in FAR ROCK-AWAY and winters in MIAMI BEACH. Her dear friend is ROCHELLE FINKELSTEIN, who is actually her third cousin once removed. Their grandparents and their grandparents all came from the OLD COUNTRY.

MINNY and ROCHELLE play MAH-JONGG in their MIAMI condo league. MINNY loves to bake for her weekly games but she can't eat any of her delicacies. She suffers from diabetes and, while playing, enjoys drinking decaffeinated ICED COFFEE when it doesn't bother her gastritis. ROCHELLE prefers RASPBERRY SELTZER (no ice).

MINNY very much wants to see her granddaughter CHAYA YISKA aka JANE get married. JANE lives on the UPPER WEST SIDE and just graduated with a degree in occupational therapy. So when MINNY and ROCHELLE meet with ESTHER and SARALEH for a game on Wednesday afternoon at MINNY'S lovely two-bedroom, MINNY lets her intentions be known.

Turns out, ESTHER'S cousin SARALEH is visiting from PASSAIC, where she can barely stand the heat. And her cousin's son's math tutor is a brilliant guy from TEANECK. He just graduated with a bachelor's degree in astrophysics and is applying to graduate school at the TECHNION in Haifa. DOVID is his name.

Intuition tells MINNY that DOVID is the perfect match for JANE. Immediately, her hosting becomes strategic. She brings out her best china, specialty RUGELACH and infamous POPPY-SEED CAKE with the LEMON GLAZE. She was saving it for *SHABBOS* but she can always make another. MINNY insists that her grand-daughter JANE is a real catch. She even brings out a photo of JANE visiting "last summer" when she did a CHESED project by volunteering at the FIRST HEBREW CONGREGATION'S SENIOR CENTER. JANE was actually only sixteen at the time, but she looks so pretty in that picture, MINNY feels justified in taking a little creative license. MINNY convinces SARALEH to ask her grandson if he's dating anyone serious—right then and there. Without a minute to lose, MINNY pushes her phone on SARALEH insisting she call DOVID immediately. After all, she has unlimited long distance. SARALEH catches him just as he is "about to go to MINYAN."

"What?" MINNY asks. "He's religious?" JANE says she isn't so religious but MINNY knows better. Now MINNY is more determined than ever. She grabs the phone out of SARALEH's hands and drones on and on about how fabulous JANE is until DOVID yells, "I've got to go!"

ROCHELLE is so embarrassed for poor JANE. Besides, she thinks, what's her grandson, CHOPPED LIVER? ROCHELLE leaves MINNY'S upset but the next day, when her visiting grandson SHMUELIK finally admits he's gay, ROCHELLE realizes she better step in to help JANE. She is her MISHPOCHA, after all. Although ROCHELLE doesn't like to boast, she has already made eighty-three MATCHES. She's got a reputation to uphold. Besides, it will help her get a killer seat in HEAVEN.

When ROCHELLE flies into NEW YORK CITY the following week for an appointment with DR. ARIK SCHULMAN, THE HEART SPECIALIST, she calls up JANE. ROCHELLE invites JANE, DOVID, and a large group of singles for *SHABBOS* DINNER that FRIDAY NIGHT at her UPPER EAST SIDE apartment. Reluctantly, JANE accepts the invitation. Just to shake things up a bit, she wears a LOW-CUT TOP.

ROCHELLE's intoxicating BRISKET works like a Jewish Cupid's arrow and cuts straight to the heart. DOVID is completely entranced by JANE. He can hardly believe JANE is actually all the things MINNY bragged about. Plus, she has a gap between her teeth, which DOVID finds endearing because it reminds him of his favorite camp GAN IZZY counselor when he was eight. JANE really likes the way DOVID speaks through his nose like a *fonfer*. It reminds her of her uncle SEYMOUR. And all the YIDDISH words DOVID throws around are totally hot. She even digs that ratty *yarmulke* with his name on it.

When JANE tells him she thinks his *kippa* is adorable, DOVID tells her his favorite camp counselor, DENA LEWINSKY, made it for him when he was eight. "No way!" JANE says. She knows DENA from her summer learning at PARDES. DENA made ALIYAH and got married to an Israeli-born American named AVIV TANNENBAUM. They have three kids and live in BAKA, right near PARDES.

DOVID can't believe it. He studied at SHAPELL'S with AVIV. And DOVID'S roommate, YANKI GREEN, was AVIV'S study partner.

Actually, YANKI and DENA are distantly related. So are AVIV and the former director of PARDES.

DOVID and JANE start dating. Before you can say PASTRAMI ON RYE, they're engaged. DOVID asks his Hasidic uncle in Antwerp for a good deal on a 2.8-carat rock for JANE. DOVID and JANE plan to get married at the ATRIUM in MONSEY.

They serve STUFFED CHICKEN BREAST WITH MUSHROOM-INFUSED KASHA as the main dish. JANE'S parents, MORRIS and SHAYNDIE ROSENBLATT of TEANECK are so proud. DOVID is a fine boy, a real *mensch*. They actually heard DOVID read TORAH at *shul* three years ago when his parents, HYRAM and SHARON, moved into the neighborhood. DOVID *leins* like a bird. *Mamash* a nightingale. They just wish they could find someone *heimish* for their daughter, MIRIAM, a shrink, who is five years older than JANE.

During the reception, MINNY and ROCHELLE realize that their gay grandsons should meet. Meanwhile, MIRIAM is drawn to the Sephardic drummer. He's a real looker. But DR. SCHULMAN, who lost his wife three years ago to "the wrong answer," has his eye on MIRIAM. He mentions it to ROCHELLE and she tells him, "Leave it to me." ROCHELLE figures, once MIRIAM and DR. SCHULMAN get a taste of her BRISKET, *that* will take care of *that!*

# Guide to Marital Bliss

*Mazal tov!* You're married. Good luck with the in-laws. These are your *machetaynestes.* There is no advice for dealing with them. But you should at least get the terminology straight. The *mechutan* is the father-in-law. His wife is the *machataynesteh.* Together, they are the *machatonim.*

As they say in Yiddish, "You've fluffed your pillow. Now sleep on it." Or something like that!

# The Day of Rest, but Not From Sex!

The rumors are true. It's a double *mitzvah,* when you're married, to get down on *Shabbos,* especially Friday night. What's more, the husband is obligated to satisfy his wife. "In Jewish," his failing to get her groove on is actually grounds for divorce. You can't divorce *farkakte* family, but you can get out of eternal misery.

# Gotta Get a *Get*

Jews are not monks. We have no celibacy tradition. We are supposed to get married and get it on. That is, unless it becomes impossible to get along. Then it's time to get divorced. Or as we say "in Jewish," get a *get.*

A *get* is a Jewish bill of divorce. You can get married again after a Jewish divorce. But first, you gotta get a *get.* To get a *get,* you meet with a Jewish court. This is called a *Beit Din,* or House of Judgment. Three bearded ZZ Top *rebbeim* hear your testimony. They want to make sure your marriage is 150 percent kaput before they do the honors. It's a fair deal. Now that you have a *get,* you can get another. But first you gotta get married again.

# The Sunset Years

Hard to accept but true: everyone gets old, even the Matisyahu *Youth.* In the Talmud, having white hair was a sign of distinction. Even if you're not yet gray, you can channel that special mature feeling by learning how to *krekhtz.*

*Krekhtzen* is Yiddish for emitting sounds from deep within that convey physical discomfort, national angst, and other worrisome expression. The preferred sounds are *"uch"* and *"ach."* Both are acceptable, although each has its own adherents. Take two *"achs"* and you get three *"ichs!"* And ichy and icky are also, for the record, Yiddish.

# Wailing 101

A good lament is a cherished form of Jewish expression. At the end of life, as in the beginning, your tears may increase as you attend one funeral after another. Some Jews are quite skilled in mourning. The cry may be punctuated by a snort, chortle, or bountiful *"Oy veys."* If your health is, G-d forbid, declining, and you've alienated all your friends and relatives by criticizing their children, you may consider hiring professional wailers for your own funeral in advance of your demise. On your deathbed, coach your support team in your preferred form of weeping. Be sure to videotape for posterity, your children's children, or your own twisted enjoyment before it's too late.

# Jewish Duck Duck Goose

The essence of Old World Jewish reasoning may be summed up in this authentic version of Duck Duck Goose, *Dos Kaddish Shpiel,* aka the Mourning Prayer Game. Because, after all, a little dark humor never *hoirt* nobody.

To begin, players sit on the ground in a circle. The one who is "It" digs a hole in the ground with a stick. A gloomy conversation ensues.

### DOS KADDISH SHPIEL

PLAYERS: Why do you dig a hole?
   IT: To put stones.
PLAYERS: Why to put stones?
   IT: To sharpen knives.
PLAYERS: Why do you need knives?
   IT: To slaughter geese.
PLAYERS: Why do you need geese?
   IT: To eat.
PLAYERS: Why do you need to eat?
   IT: To live.
PLAYERS: Why do you need to live?
   IT: To have children.
PLAYERS: Why do you need children?
   IT: To have someone say *kaddish* (the mourner's prayer) for me when I die.

Players jump up and run away. It runs after them. It tags the next It.

## THE KLUGGEREBBIE SAYS

When Jews visit the cemetery, we don't put flowers on the grave. We put stones. The rationale behind this is noteworthy. Our losses don't fade as wilted blooms. Our sacrifices have lasting significance. Besides, rocks are free.

# Recycle, Reuse, Reshmooze

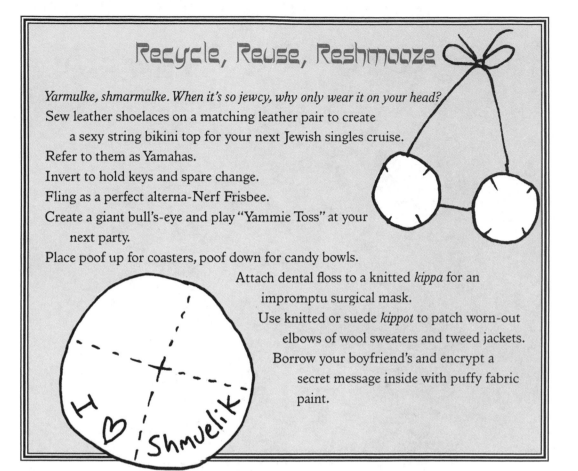

*Yarmulke, shmarmulke. When it's so jewcy, why only wear it on your head?*
Sew leather shoelaces on a matching leather pair to create
   a sexy string bikini top for your next Jewish singles cruise.
Refer to them as Yamahas.
Invert to hold keys and spare change.
Fling as a perfect alterna-Nerf Frisbee.
Create a giant bull's-eye and play "Yammie Toss" at your
   next party.
Place poof up for coasters, poof down for candy bowls.

Attach dental floss to a knitted *kippa* for an
   impromptu surgical mask.
Use knitted or suede *kippot* to patch worn-out
   elbows of wool sweaters and tweed jackets.
Borrow your boyfriend's and encrypt a
   secret message inside with puffy fabric
   paint.

## ALEF

### UNTIL WE EAT AGAIN

Like fellow Heeb Harry Houdini before us, every Heebster goes through life with a bag of tricks. To work a little Mosaic magic, sometimes what you need most are totally tangible tools, from holy headgear to the just-right ritual item. But just as every *bubbie* knows, sometimes the true fix is simply a toasted boreka, bagel or bialy smothered in buttah.

As an organic outgrowth of Chapter Alef aka the Heebster Heart Plan, and Chapter Bet aka the Heebster Life Span, Chapter Gimel aka the Heebster Gear Can includes everything and a *kreplach*. So why not start out right? With an appetite! Because haven't you always known the best accessory is food?

# Heebster Food Pyramids

Perfect symmetry offers the ultimate balanced diet.

1. *challah*
2. gefilte fish, horseradish
3. herring in wine sauce
4. lox and bagels*

5. chicken soup
6. *hamantaschen,* macaroons, *rugelach,* and manna
7. seconds and thirds of everything

* Some say the essence of the bagel is the hole. The dough is only there for emphasis.

# Mystery Eats

Sometimes Jewish food is, well, just plain weird. Do you even know what gefilte fish is? How about *shav, charoset, hummus, baba ghanoush, gehakte ayer, gribenes, kreplach? Charoset* we know has a ritual significance, to remind us of those antiunion days slave laboring in Egypt. But the rest? It's all stuff mushed up beyond recognition, morphed into something else, hardly recognizable from its pure state.

As a MOT with the M-O-S-T, you'll expand your culinary capabilities with this brief guide to Jewish mystery foods. Don't bother with exact quantities. Summon the Jewish mother within. She'll pat your chest gently and remind you, "All you need to know is right here, *bubbeleh.*"

***

**Shav** Pureed spinach, turnip greens, or sorrel grass, and water. Served cold, this is one famous Jewish version of creating something from nothing. See *gribenes.*

**Baba ghanoush** Eggplant pâté. Salt, roast, puree, and spice up eggplant with abundant amounts of olive oil, garlic, salt, and lemon. Shmear on pita, challah, and other doughy foundations.

**Charoset** Ashkenazi *charoset* is made of chopped apples. It gets mushy. It turns colors. The *charoset* of kings, however the Sephardic variety, relies on dried apricots, cherries, dates, almonds, pine nuts, ginger, cardamom, and other spices for real panache. Experiment with your own blends, "process," and add generous amounts of Manischewitz for an east-west blend with a kick.

---

### FYI: FOR THE YIDDISH IMPAIRED

The term *charoset* is used alternatively among some Yiddish speakers as a synonym for any *shmear*-able, even when you can't eat it. This includes antibiotic ointment, Vick's VapoRub, or Bengay (not that there's anything wrong with that). For shock value, say "charosh-t" instead.

---

**Hummus** Cousin to *baba,* this paste begins with cooked or sprouted garbanzo beans mashed into smithereens and flavored with crushed garlic, lemon juice, olive oil, salt and *techina* (known outside Israel as tahini, sesame seed puree). In a pinch, doubles as grout.

**Gehakte ayer** If you can pronounce it, your doing *qvite vell. Ayer* means egg and *gehakte* is, well, just what it sounds like, hacked up into tiny pieces. Chop hard-cooked eggs and add mayo or olive oil, salt n' peppa, and shove into a mold. *Invoirt* and *soirve.*

**Gefilte Fish** This slightly sweet, slightly savory dish is an acquired taste unbeknownst to *goyim*. Gefilte contains different kinds of "Filet O' Fish," pike, carp, whitefish, and more, ground with eggs, onions, and spices, then cooked. Originally, it was stuffed back into the empty fish skin and then baked. Best of all, gefilte contains no bones, avoiding the Sabbath restriction of separating bad from good and helping prevent any accidental loss of Tribal members. You can update this classic by using cookie cutters to create fish-shaped gefilte cookies and decorating them with hot mustard, wasabi horseradish, or wasabinaise!

**Gribenes** This is one Jewish food that threatens rather than nourishes survival. It consists of hunks of chicken skin and onions fried in chicken fat. Not recommended if you plan on living past seventeen. But then again, without *gribenes,* why would you want to?

**Kishke** Stuffed derma (beef intestinal casing) filled with savory spices, flour, chicken fat, ground carrots, celery, and onions. Vegetarian versions made with oil or nondairy (pareve) margarine and Tam Tam crackers are a classic substitute. Process, spice with S&P, form into sausages, smother with foil, and bake. Add parsley, sage, rosemary, and thyme for Thanksgiving stuffing.

Note: *Kishke* is also a synonym for guts. As in, "I'm *plotzing* with that *kishke* rotting there in my *kishkes.*"

**Gehakte Leber** With its near lethal cholesterol count, authentic chopped liver is passé. But mock liver, now we're talkin'. Made with walnuts, green beans, and spices, it's less likely to put Uncle Melvin into cardiac arrest.

**Manna** This heavenly miracle food was something akin to coriander seed covered with a crystal-like dew that glimmered in the sun. The *Midrash,* ancient commentary on the Bible, says *mahn* could be baked into any shape to taste like any other food. But it only stayed fresh for one day, until Friday, when a double portion came down in preparation for *Shabbos.*

Alas, manna is no more. The contemporary equivalent may be strawberry marshmallow fluff. Soak the label off a jar and replace with a handcrafted one that reads MAHN HOO (that's manna) as a gift to impress with minimal mess. Alternate plan: Grab a box of Krispy Kremes and a Sharpie. Edit.

# Jewish Food IQ

Can you tell *knaidelach* from *lokoom*? Test your gastronomical intelligence.
Match the foods to the right definition.

1. **babka**
2. **falafel**
3. **gribenes**
4. **kishke**
5. **knaidelach**
6. **knish**
7. **kreplach**
8. **latkes**
9. **rugelach**
10. **shmaltz**

a. stuffed *derma*
b. potato pancakes
c. rolled yeast cake filled with chocolate or cinnamon
d. fried chicken skin and onions
e. chicken fat
f. *matzah* balls in Yiddish
g. Jewish pot stickers stuffed with meat or potato and added to soup
h. doughy pockets filled with potato, kasha, spinach, and other fixins
i. deep-fried balls of mashed garbanzo beans and spices aka the Israeli hamburger
j. mini *babkas,* perfectly pocket-sized

*Answers:* 1. c, 2. i, 3. d, 4. a, 5. f, 6. h, 7. g, 8. b, 9. j, 10. e

**Score:** Give yourself 1 point for every correct answer, 2 points for every answer you almost got right, 3 points for the ones you missed entirely, and 4 points for running out and grabbing a falafel because reading this list made you so hungry.

# Jewish Food IQ Bonus Round

1. **biskocheetos**
2. **chamin**
3. **chareef**
4. **khilbe**
5. **fuoul**
6. **jachnun**
7. **jala**
8. **lafah**
9. **lokoom**
10. **mandelbrodt**

a. flavorful fava beans served atop hummus

b. Sephardic stew, cooked overnight and served *Shabbat* day

c. a massive pita-like contraption used to wrap *shwarma* and/or falafel

d. an ancient artform, Ladino biscuits and crackers made by hand

e. Jewish biscotti, stuffed with almonds

f. Hebrew for hot spicy condiments, including a doozy called *schoog*

g. Turkish delight, a gelatinous candy stuffed with pistachios or other nuts and dusted with powdered sugar—weird, gooey, and gooood

h. plates of seeds, nuts, and candies aka Yemenite dessert

i. Yemenite *Shabbat* bread cooked overnight, served with *techina,* hard-boiled egg, *schoog,* and sour cream

j. cooked fenugreek, a Yemenite condiment, slimy and delicious

*Answers:* 1. d, 2. b, 3. f, 4. j, 5. a, 6. i, 7. h, 8. c, 9. g, 10. e

**Score:** Give yourself 200 points for every correct answer. You, my friend, are a Sephardi, an Ashkenazi boundary crosser, the multicultural Ashkephardi, an ally to all . . . or just someone with a darn good vocabulary and possibly a belly to boot! Whatever your score, *mazal tov!* It doesn't really matter how much you know. If you read this list and start salivating, that's solid evidence you're in!

# Kosherspiracy

The rumors are true. Well, sort of. There actually is a kind of a Jewish "conspiracy" afoot. Contrary to popular antisemetic opinion, however, ours is not a mission to dominate the world. (We already do *that*!) No, the real Jewish "conspiracy" is a *kosherspiracy*. We are not out to control the global economy. We're out to control what we eat. As every *bubbie* has always known, our primary concern is not stock markets. It's stomachs! As part of the global Jewish kosherspiracy, hundreds of symbols designate tribal-friendly food world over. *Trayfe* be gone!

Achdut Israel
Buenos Aires

Atlanta Kashruth Commission
Atlanta, Georgia

Beis Din of Crown Heights
Vaad HaKashrus
Brooklyn

The Beis Din Tzedek of Agudas
Israel Moetzes HaKashrus
Jerusalem

Calgary Kosher

Chief Rabbinate of Quebec
Kashruth Commission

Cyprus Kosher

Earth Kosher

HKK Kosher Certification Service
Hong Kong

Hoshgoche Charedis of Mexico

Kosher Australia

Kosher Kiwi Licensing
Authority of New Zealand

KoLA
Los Angeles

Kosher Supervision of America

Mehadrin Kashrus of Texas

The Orthodox Council of
Kashruth "MaHaRal"
Prague

Ufficio Rabbinco DiTrieste
Italy

Vaad HaKashruth of Omaha

Vaad HaRabanim of Greater
Seattle

Vaad of Lancaster
Congregation Degel Israel
Lancaster, Pennsylvania

# Recycle, Reuse, Reshmooze

*Matzah ball, shmatzah ball. When it's this delish, why only eat it with soup?*

Select perfect specimens. Remove excess moisture in a salad spinner. Encase in Lucite as paperweights. Mass-market on eBay.

Forget frozen peas. Freeze a dozen of various sizes in a Ziploc bag as an emergency ice pack.

Soak in water with cucumber slices. Place on eyelids to alleviate dark circles.

Marinate overnight in a blend of balsamic vinegar, garlic, Bragg's Amino Acids, and extra virgin olive oil. Finely chop, toast, then top a stir-fry or salad. Challenge dinner guests to identify your mysterious, confetti-like croutons.

Smother with marinara sauce to recycle into faux meatballs: a Judeo-Roman delicacy.

Drop floaters and sinkers from your rooftop and time their descent to test theories on mass and velocity. *Warning:* Do not conduct this experiment from New York high-rises and in other potentially litigious venues.

Insert a steel pin into *matzah* ball. Let dry. Using a pair of needle-nose pliers, form loops to create unique earrings. Every compliment is further validation you should duplicate and mass-market.

# The Great Egg Cream Debate

The hot Jewish cure-all is chicken soup. Its warm weather equivalent is the very cold egg cream. Naturally, the Jewish egg cream contains neither egg nor cream. Furthermore, it is drunk not from the sickbed, but while standing.

Purists contend the authentic Brooklyn egg cream relies on three ingredients and three ingredients alone:

1. almost frozen, real, whole milk
2. very cold, authentic seltzer, preferably from a $CO_2$-charged seltzer bottle
3. chocolate syrup made with sugar, such as Fox's U-Bet Kosher for Passover Chocolate Syrup.

This hot commodity is generally available pre-*Pesach*, right alongside the wasabi horseradish and the canned macaroons.

## HOW TO POUR AN EGG CREAM

Pour three to four fingers of milk into a chilled tall glass. Add plenty of seltzer to produce a thick, foamy, egg white–like head. Pour several tablespoons of chocolate syrup in a thin stream into the head. Using a long spoon, stir from the bottom.

Or, add the chocolate to the glass first. Then add the milk. Then the seltzer. Depending on your stirring technique, this may produce a chocolate head.

Like the old saying goes, two Jews, three arguments. A third group of EC lovers argue not about the chocolate but the seltzer. The only acceptable method for seltzer delivery, they say, is to place a long spoon about halfway down the inside of the glass and bounce the fizz from the seltzer off the head of the spoon—yet another critical step for ultimate froth. For extra panache, forgo the spoon and adorn the egg cream instead with a long pretzel stick.

The moment you've been waiting for:

Drink. Wipe foam off upper lip. Belch. Repeat.

# On the Side

The black-and-white cookie is another legendary contradiction popular within Da Tribe. Despite its name, the black-and-white cookie is, in fact, not a cookie. Nor is it truly black and white. Divided down its middle, half is frosted with dark chocolate icing and half with vanilla. In plain black-and-white language, the "cookie" is actually a dark brown chocolate-and-white cupcake that has been sat on.

## Heimishe Homespun Labels

Batampte Delicatessan Style Mustard
Max Brenner's Chocolate by the Bald Man
Bubbie's Pure Kosher Dills
Flaum Herring in Cream Sauce
Hebrew National
Foulds Wacky Mac
Gold's Horseradish
He'brew, The Chosen Beer
It's Delish
Maccabeans
Manischewitz
Meshuggamints
Meshuga Nuts
Mrs. Mintz's Blintzes
Shalom, the Chosen Gum
Schlitz Malt Liquor Beer
Shlomo's Matzoball Soap
Soy Vay
Star of David Brand Kosher Soap
Tabatchnick Soup
Thou Shall Snack
Vita Nova Salmon
Zwack Slivovitz

# Recycle, Reuse, Reshmooze

*Challah, shmallah. When Shabbos tastes this good, why throw the leftovers away?*

Brush loaf with beaten egg yolk. Decorate with rainbow sprinkles and bake on a very low heat until the egg yolk dries. Horizontally, slice off the top. Scoop out the innards to create a unique serving dish for a massive ice cream sundae or faux baked Alaska.

Slice *challah* thin. Drizzle with olive oil, a touch of rosemary, and crushed garlic. Toast to create flavorful crostini. Top with Philly and Nova or Philly-filled Nova or whatever combo floats your feely.

Beat eggs and mix *mit a bissel* milk, Cointreau orange liqueur, cinnamon, and orange juice. Soak thick slices in batter, then fry in butter for French toast with a kick. Substitute Manischewitz for the blackberry-inclined. Shellac whole loaves for decorative bookends. Or, substitute for *Torah*-Yoga blocks to express the HinJew in you.

# BET
## IS FOR BLING, GOTTA GET THIS THING
## AKA NON-EDIBLE HEEBSTER MUST-HAVES

## Attitude

When it comes to outlook, the *goyishe* optimist sees the glass *half full*. And the *goyishe* pessimist sees the glass *half empty.* But not if you're Jeeeeewish!

The Jewish optimist sees the glass as *only* half empty. It could, after all, always be much worse.

"They might not have filled it up at all!"

The Jewish pessimist sees the glass as only half full.

"What, they couldn't have filled it up all the way?"

## Soundtrack

The words to the Israeli national anthem, *Hatikvah* (The Hope) in Hebrew, are a rousing call to the actualization of Jewish identity and the dream of a homeland despite more than two thousand years of exile. Hands down, it's a must-have at every Hebrew school assembly. *Hatikvah* still produces goose pimples. And now that we have a homeland, it's time to adopt a twenty-first century ballad to parody all those nasty Jewish stereotypes. Award-winning singer/songwriter Rav Shmuel is a beer-drinking Hasidic rabbi with six kids, a predilection for the Grateful Dead and a cartoon music video that puts antisemities to shame.

# PROTOCOLS
## by Rav Shmuel*

Some people ask me if I'm Jewish.
Some people look at me and know.
Some people want to know if I believe in
   Jesus and have trouble when the answer
   is "Well, no."
Some people think that that's my right.
Some people think that I am damned.
Some people think that I'm a part of a
   conspiracy to take over the world and
   rule with an iron hand.

*Chorus*

*You see The Protocols of the Elders of Zion*
   *are true. And I am a member of standing.*
   *Our goal is to milk all the money from you.*
   *It's world domination we're planning.*
*Not long ago I've let the cat right out of the bag.*
*Will you please keep my secret, I pray.*
*'Cuz I'm undercover as a singer/songwriter*
   *right here*
*At the Sidewalk Café.*


Some people ask if I'm Middle Eastern.
Some people stare at me with hate.
Some people want to know if I pick up
   every penny so they toss them at me
   and quickly drive away.
Some people think that that's my right.
Some people think that I am damned.
Some people think that I should pack
   up all my bags and get out of the
   Promised Land.

*Chorus*

Some people ask if I speak English.
Some people stare at me when I pray.
Some people want to know if I know the
   Kabbalah and have trouble when
   the answer is "Why don't you ask
   Madonna?"
Some people think that that's my right.
Some people think that I am damned.
Some people think that I'm a real threat to
   world freedom and that I will
   turn their oil into sand.

*Chorus*

Some people ask me if I'm Amish.
Some people think I'm a big joke.
Some people think that we would make up
   a big lie
And say that Hitler sent our people up
   in smoke.
Some people think that that's my right.
Some people think that I am damned.
My next assignment in our quest to rule
   this world will be as front man in a
   heavy metal band.

*Chorus*

Cuz I'm undercover as a singer/songwriter
   right here
At the Sidewalk Café.

*Reprinted with permission of Jewish Music Group and Rav Shmuel.

# COLOR-BY-NUMBER

The classic black-and-white uniform of Hasidim is a surefire way to identify male ultra-Orthodox Jews. No one else in his right mind would sport the telltale *shtreiml, kapota,* and *gartel* combo, let alone the distinctive hair growth smothering the face, especially in 98 degree heat! Naturally, not just any black-and-white garb will do. No, hundreds, if not thousands of dollars are spent to procure the perfect (fur-lined) brim and extended frog coat. The beauty of the Hasidic uniform is long renowned. And the look is widely imitated by the Blues Brothers, penguins, and squad cars everywhere. Even fashion designer Jean Paul Gaultier once designed a Hasidic-inspired ensemble for the Paris catwalk—complete with the requisite black silk caftan—that has never since seen the likes of Fashion Week!

The benefits of the B&W uniform are unparalleled. Hasidic Jews never have to worry about trends, mixin' and matchin',

**THE ORIGINAL MEN IN BLACK**

Hasidic ain't cheap.
*Shtreiml?* $4,000
Deluxe "tux"? $650
Hand-braided silk *gartel?* $300
Borsalino? $200
*Tzitzit,* four-cornered garment with fringes? $30
Black velvet *kippa?* $5
Total: priceless

Some things in life are free.
For everything else, there's the diamond trade.

or mistaken identity. Granted, they may be temporarily confused with Abe Lincoln, the Amish, the "cough drop guys," and, that rare breed, the urban lumberjack. But the beard, sidelocks, and yarmulke trifecta is unique to the Tribe and the Tribe alone. And while Hasidic threads resemble those of medieval Polish gentry, biblical precepts dictate the wild and free facial hair.

If thou wisheth to experience this exceptional combination, pop into Boro Park for a fitting. Alternatively, study these figures carefully. *Then, using a black felt-tip pen, fill in all the spots marked number 1. Refrain from coloring all sections marked number 2. Leave those white.* Depending on your age, or the age you determine for your Hasidim, you may decide to color the beard and sidelocks black, white, or an appetizing salt-and-pepper combination. Experiment with your friend's copy of *Cool Jew.* Remember, with age, redheaded rabbis fade to pink.

shtreiml

short or no sidelocks
requisite beards

Borsalino

kapota *aka* rekel,
tzertuk *or*
beckesher

gartel *(belt)*

stockings

Bostoner

Lubavitcher

★ = ❶
☆ = ②

# HEADWEAR DECODER

| STYLE | WHO WEARS IT | SPIRITUAL CONVICTION |
|---|---|---|
| 1. Black Fedora | *Litvitsh*/yeshivish | *It's all according to the book—the Good Book.* |
| 2. Black Borsalino | Lubavitch *Hasidim* | *We want* Moshiach *now!* |
| 3. Black Velvet Yammie | *Yeshivish*/Ultra-Orthodox | *I believe in formal wear.* |
| 4. *Shtreiml* | *Hasidish* | *In this heat, I'll take a sombrero!* |
| 5. *Spudik* (vertical fur) the brimless alterna-*shtreiml* | *Hasidish* | *What's that you say about SPF?* |
| 6. *Toka* | Old World Ladino | *The Jewish version of "Rock the Casbah!"* |
| 7. Black Knitted *Kippa* | Fence Straddler | *Bipolar* Yarmulke *Disorder.* |
| 8. Black Leather *Kippa* | Modern Orthodox | *Wannabe Hell's Angel.* |
| 9. Personalized Knitted *Kippa Sruga* | Modern Orthodox/Zionist | *I've been labeling my clothes since I first went to sleep away camp!* |
| 10. Oversized Knitted *Kippa* | Carlebach *Hasidim*, hippie Jews, residents of Bat Ayin, Israel | *I'm spiritual and bald.* |
| 11. Crocheted *Kippa* with a mystical chant in dark blue letters *"Na, Nach, Nachman, Nachman M'Uman"* | Breslov *Hasidim*, followers of the legendary Nachman from Uman | *Rebbe Nachman taught that repeating one word brings spiritual bliss!* |
| 12. Embroidered Oversized Bucharian *Kippa* | Sephardic, hip, underaged, and . . . | *Officially bobby pin intolerant (quite often bald).* |
| 13. Mickey Maus Ears | Mausketeer | *Art Spiegelman's my hero.* |
| 14. Beanie with propeller | Jughead | *I'm just another Jew in the comic book biz.* |
| 15. Baseball Cap (double duty, covers your head and a secret Yammie underneath) | Anyone and everyone | *So what if I can't wear a yarmulke at work? Go Yankees!* |
| 16. Toupeé (not shown) | No one who will admit it! | *The furry yarmulke.* |

# What the Lid Says About the Yid

# THE JEWESS CONTEST

Being a Jewish woman is somewhat akin to be a contestant in the Ms. Shebrew Contest. Will you wear a crown? What kind? And when? In *shul,* every day, or only on special occasions like the spring closeouts at Loehmann's? On the menu, a *minyan* of choices:

1. **Tiara**—Worn in some Hasidic circles on *Shabbos,* adapted from the original "Jerusalem of Gold," a gold headband worn by the daughters of ancient Israel.

2. **Wig**—Aka *sheitl,* works well with a tiara. All the rage in Orthodox circles.

3. **Fall**—A hipper version of the *sheitl.*

4. **Kerchief**—Aka *tichel* in Yiddish, the scarf may be tied a myriad of ways, including the Cinnamon Bun, Dutch Crown, Rapunzel, Settler, Rasta, Marge Simpson, and more.

5. **Snood**—Although it sounds like Hebrew, this twelfth-century English term refers to a decorative knitted shopping bag worn by Orthodox women. Used to effectively conceal ponytails, bald patches and the Jewfro.

6. **Hat**—Worn primarily by the Modern Orthodox and conservative Conservative; styles range from the beret and cloche to hipster knit caps and more elaborate brimmed varieties.

7. **Baseball Cap**—Preferred by soccer moms; flip backwards or side spin for added sassiness.

8. **Bandana**—A hit with Sheebster hippies and hikers. Also popular, the convertible "Buff" brand.

9. **The Synthetic Lace Doily**—In black, white, or cream, the doily is worn mostly by Reform and Conservative women of a certain generation; either flat atop the head or folded in three and clipped to the back of the head like a fancy napkin.

10. **The She-pa**—A girly kippa with beads, sequins, sparkles, and the occasional found object. Warning: resembles a shimmery bird's nest. Feathered friends may come to roost.

# Crazy and Fabulous!

1

2

3

4

5

6

7

8

9

10

# SHMATTE LAND

As a Jew, it's not so important what you wear. It's who you are inside that counts. Every self-respecting Heebster, however, still maintains a growing T-shirt collection, with the occasional pair of sweat pants, "Look-at-Me" belt buckles, "I ♥ *Hashem*" messenger bags, and "Wandering Jew Must-Travel" totes. Few if any restrictions apply to style, as long as the design expresses abiding affection for the Yiddishe complexion.

**Threaded Heritage**
**getthreaded.com**

In a word
jewcy.com

Kitsch culture
popjudaica.com

On newstands everywhere
heebmagazine.com

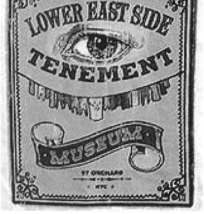

History has its eye on Jew @
**tenement.org**

An ensemble befitting a Shebrew from
**rabbisdaughters.com**

*Sephardilicious*

Yummy
**rotemgear.com**

HEBREW SCHOOL

Established Since Mt. Sinai

In G-d We Trust

DROP OUT.com

Messenger bag doubles as *tallit* bag
**cafepress.com/jewlicious**

BUBELEH

TUSH

I ♥ HASHEM

# Heebster Bling

*Hamsa* hands against the evil eye and other amulets
*Bendels* aka red strings, blue and other colored eye-
    like beads with the
    same mojo
*Asimon,* retro Israeli
    public phone token,
    dipped in sterling and
    personalized with a
    Hebrew name
Name in gold or silver Hebrew letters
*"Teshuv Hey"* necklace by Avraham Lowenthal
*Chai,* Star of David, and mini *mezuzah* necklaces

Israeli jewelry containing Eilat stones or Roman
    glass retrieved from archaeological digs
Israeli designs by Adaya,
Ayala Bar, Laly Cohen,
Dganit Hen, Leetal
Kalmanson, Talma Keshet,
Michal Negrin, Maya Ofir,
Chaim Paz H. Stern, and
others
*Tehillim*/Psalms key chain
Serious ice: diamonds
The cover of this book

# The Jewish Week of Shopping

Besides thrift stores, Urban Outfitters, eBay, H&M, Steve & Barry's for BITTEN Sarah Jessica Parker, Loehmann's, Nordie's Rack, sample sales, farmer's markets, Costco, Trader Yo's, and Tarzjeh (aka Target), where does a Heebster shop every day of the week?

| Monday | chosencouture.com | "Let my people go" *matzah* print toilet seat cover, sports *yarmulkes,* *"MAZEL TOV"* candles, mah-jongg *maven* baskets, T-shirts, and much more. |
|---|---|---|
| Tuesday | funkyfrum.com | For the Ortho-Sheebster femme fatale, all the styles without all the skin. |
| Wednesday | heebmagazine.com | Purveyors of the JEWBOY belt buckle and Super Jew, Honorary Heeb, and "Jesus saves . . . Moses invests" T-shirts. |
| Thursday | jewcy.com | *Hasid* Double Dutch, Manischewitz Kosher, Jewcy, and other tees, and the "Let's Go *Schlepping*" board game. |
| Friday | michalnegrin.com | Fantasy bling and très girly things from the granddaughter of Israel's first prime minister. Stores worldwide, but Sheebsters gravitate to the duty-free shop at David Ben-Gurion Airport. |
| Shabbos | rabbisdaughters.com | Shebrew gear for the young, old, *goyish,* and their pets from three daughters of you guessed it. Yes, your little *matzah* ball deserves a *Shayna Punim* T-shirt. |
| Sunday | shmaltz.com | Dedicated to "creating quality beer and quality *shtick* for the Jewish community and beyond," this tchotchke Emporium is *the* place for all things He'Brew. |

# LOVE THE LOOT

At celebratory events, Heebsters always rake it in. Prior to the event, savvy celebratees register at da local sista'chood gift shop or Jewish bookstore. After all, if strategic Heebsters play their cards right, they may never need to purchase another piece of Judaica again!

Although gift-giving practices vary somewhat within communities and from event to event, they do follow general guidelines that can be reduced to a basic scientific formula.

1. *Shabbat* candlesticks
2. *Chanukah* menorah and *dreidls,* wooden, silver, and "retired" Waterford crystal
3. Seven-branched candlebra, a symbol of the Jewish nation
4. *Havdalah* set
5. Silver tray for candlesticks and/or *havdalah*
6. *Shabbat* candles, *havdalah* candles, *yarhzeit* candles, *Chanukah* candles, and decorative match box
7. *Mezuzah,* tiny scroll containing hand-scribed biblical verses hung at an angle on doorposts in pretty, protective cases
8. *Kiddush* cup, in silver, Venetian glass, ceramic, or wood
9. Wine decanter, decorative corks, and *kiddush* distribution system aka *pisher* in silver or handpainted wood by Israeli artists
10. Bible, commentary, *Midrash,* and other beloved Judaica books
11. Popular Jewish books
12. Jewish calendars, cards, and music
13. Full set of Talmud aka *Shas*
14. *Tallit* prayer shawl, decorative bag, and *yarmulkes*
15. *Tefillin* (phylacteries), leather ritual straps* and boxes containing biblical verses, decorative bag
16. *Pushke,* Yiddish for charity box
17. Fragrance decanter, sprinkle friends with rosewater in a Sephardic custom for *havdalah* and happy occasions
18. *Shofarot*
19. *Benchers,* personalized booklets filled with songs and prayers for *Shabbat* and holidays

*You think leather is big now, it's been "in" for thousands of years!

20. Sabbath and holiday tablecloths
21. Ritual hand washing cup, optional basin for pre-meal cleansing, and *mayim achronim* set in miniature for a post-meal replay
22. Decorative *challah* cover, cutting board, knife, and salt dish
23. Passover *seder* plate
24. *Matzah* cover
25. *Haggadot,* Passover prayer books, complete with directions on how to adorn the *seder* plate, conduct the *seder,* and traditional Passover songs
26. Honey decanter for High Holiday meals
27. *Etrog* and *lulav* cases for *Sukkot*
28. *Yad,* a "pointer" for reading *Torah*
29. *Megillat Esther,* the Scroll of Esther, for Purim
30. Heck, why not ask for a *Torah* and rescue one from eBay!

## Games Heebsters Play aka Steal the *Kiddush* Cup!

"It" sits down in a chair, blindfolded, with a *kiddush* cup resting on the floor. The other players align their chairs facing "It." One by one they sneak up ever so quietly and try to steal the cup without "It" getting a whiff of them. If "It" hears anyone approaching, "It" shouts "Good *Shabbos!*" and the players return their tushes to the chairs. Then they try again. The one who successfully steals the cup is the next "It!"

# HEEBSTER SHPEEDSTER, TRANSPORT THYSELF

Why bother living large, living Jewish if you're not cruisin' in style?

## OPTION *ALEF*: ADOPT A SEDATE PLATE

Vibe your ride with a vanity plate. Shout out that you're down with all things Hebraic. And test your wits with this translation twister!

**PLATE**

1. ETROG18
2. GDSHBOS
3. SHMAYAL
4. MSH1ACH
5. JKSHRJKSS
6. JEWCREW
7. HEEBBRO
8. CRCMSZD
9. SHEBSTR
10. MATZBAL

**TRANSLATION**

a. Now!

b. You in?

c. Yah mahn!

d. Kosher kiss? Deelish!

e. A *Sh'mantra* to y'all!

f. The perfect label for lemon-colored VW Beetles.

g. Good *Shabbos*!

h. She is your shero!

i. Beige Beetles are beautiful.

j. Beware of *bris*.

*Answers:* 1.f, 2.g, 3.e, 4.a, 5.d, 6.b, 7.c, 8.j, 9.h, 10.i

## OPTION *BET*: ROLL OUT DA BIG WHEELS

Some cars just have that Jewish *je ne sais quoi*.

**Audi TT**

*Totally Tribal, oyPod compatible*

**Mini Cooper**

*Manny Kupferstein, circumcised*

**Cadillac DeVille, Chevy Impala, Chevy Malibu, all early models**

*Homage to* "The Hebrew Hammer"

**Chevy HHR**

*Heebster Holy Roller*

**Chevy Nova**

*Best in Philly*

**Chrysler 300**

*Hasidic stylin'*

**Chrysler PT Cruiser**
*Honorary courier of* Pakn Treger (PT) *magazine.*

**Honda Element**
*Built-in Heebster logo. Shine your Hebraic on the highway!*

**Any hybrid or convertible**
*These are, by definition, Jewish.*

**Any Jeep**
*For forty years you wandered in the desert . . .*

**Retired ice cream or postal truck**
*Perennially hip, pre-*Borat*.*

**Scion xB**
*Traveling tefillin box.*

**Tesla Roadster**
*Any roadster, Heebster.*

**Toyota Rav 4**
*Rav, rebbe, rabbi: variations on a theme.*

**Toyota Yaris**
*Sounds like Yiddish.*

**Zap! Obvio 828**
*So happy, so Heebster, it practically hurts.*

**Zap! Xebra Sedan in Zebra Flash**
*Matching traveling tallit.*

**Zenn 100% Electric Hatchback**
*Zero emissions and no noise. A Heebster enigma.*

## OPTION *GIMEL:* GO WHOLE HOG

Pimp your ride like the Hebrew Hammer. Express your personality and "recycle, reuse, and reshmooze" junk you can't bear to part with. Live wise, Hebraicize, Judaize, customize!

**Go-Filte Mobile** Collect unwanted CDs. Plaster in overlapping patterns to create shimmery fish scales. Hot glue an orange pylon to the top of the trunk as a rear fin, a bottle of horseradish on the dash for extra flash, and faux incisors on the front end to show you mean business. Paint a large Styrofoam disk orange, hot glue on a few green branches, and attach it all to the roof as garnish.

Slap a fish sticker that spells out GEFILTE in faux Hebrew letters on the rear bumper.

**Super Jew** Hang a massive fuzzy Jewish star from the rearview window. Prop up this book in the rear window, cover facing out. Paint biblical verses on the side of your van. Broadcast Matisyahu from your speakers.

*Alter Kocker* (**Off Your Rocker**) Hunt for swatches of wacky fabrics at Goodvill. Apply squares of clashing patterns on massive, gas-guzzling sedans. Drive crazy-tush slow until everyone honks at you repeatedly.

**Pass-Over** Squirt ketchup along your vehicular doorposts—the top edge and sides of the windshield—for Passover-inspired clearance from the ~~Angel of Death~~ "Angel of Bad (Road) *Car*ma."

**Homeland Homies** Slap bright blue racing stripes down the sides of a white convertible. Blast the Idan Raichel Project and the Israeli national anthem, "Hatikvah." Forget ticker tape. Instead, toss falafel balls to your friends and scream *Shalom chaverim!*

---

### Low Eco-Impact Wheels
Electra Karma Cruiser Bicycle
Koa Blunt Sustainable Skateboard
Razor Scooter
Rollerblades
Heelys
(sneakers with retractable wheels)
Segway

# GIVING NEW LIFE TO ANCIENT HEEBSTER WAYS

The Heebster rhythm of life has a ba-dump-bum all its own. Not to be outdone by anyone, we have our very own calendar with its very own months. Actually, we borrowed a bunch of Babylonian names but the rest of it is all ours! Why stop at adding one extra day on a leap year when you can add a whole month! Better yet, a heaping host of holidays keep Heebsters celebrating *and* overfed . . . Ready for the next Yom Kippur at a moment's notice! Think of it as a self-regulating system, your internal Yehudis Leah Katzowitz (the Jewish Jenny Craig). But with the way Jews cook and the ways Jews eat, it's largely a losing battle. Might as well milk it for every *knish* it's worth . . . And if the thought of that combination gives you *shpilkes* in your *gazektagazoink,* you're in!

# Feast, Fast, Fun!

Anorexics beware! The Jewish Dietary Cycle consists of binging and starving. Where do you think the saying "feast or famine" comes from anyway?

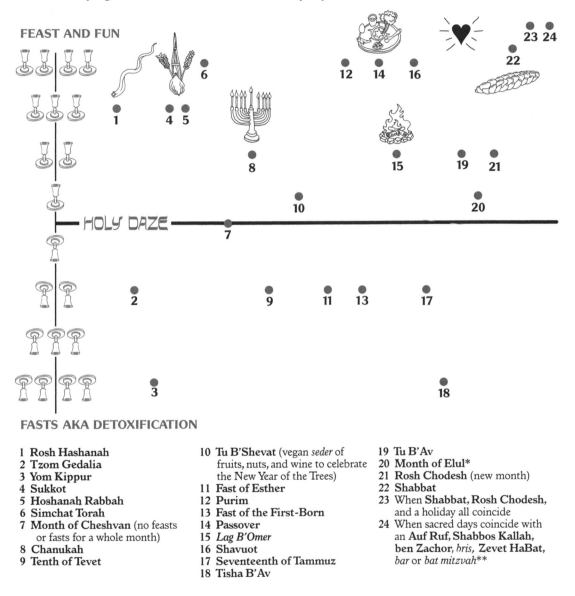

**FEAST AND FUN**

HOLY DAZE

## FASTS AKA DETOXIFICATION

1 **Rosh Hashanah**
2 **Tzom Gedalia**
3 **Yom Kippur**
4 **Sukkot**
5 **Hoshanah Rabbah**
6 **Simchat Torah**
7 **Month of Cheshvan** (no feasts or fasts for a whole month)
8 **Chanukah**
9 **Tenth of Tevet**

10 **Tu B'Shevat** (vegan *seder* of fruits, nuts, and wine to celebrate the New Year of the Trees)
11 **Fast of Esther**
12 **Purim**
13 **Fast of the First-Born**
14 **Passover**
15 *Lag B'Omer*
16 **Shavuot**
17 **Seventeenth of Tammuz**
18 **Tisha B'Av**

19 **Tu B'Av**
20 **Month of Elul***
21 **Rosh Chodesh** (new month)
22 **Shabbat**
23 When **Shabbat, Rosh Chodesh,** and a holiday all coincide
24 When sacred days coincide with an **Auf Ruf, Shabbos Kallah, ben Zachor,** *bris,* **Zevet HaBat,** *bar* or *bat mitzvah***

*Spiritual preparation for the year to come. Daily blowing of the shofar. Breathe deep and repeat!
** Honoring a groom on the *Shabbat* immediately preceding his wedding, honoring a bride on the *Shabbat* immediately preceding her wedding, Friday night gathering to celebrate the birth of a son, ritual snip, baby naming of a daughter

# ROCK OF AGES

Harmonize your Hebraic and jewce up your Judaic with this Heebster holiday mix!

| WHAT AND WHEN* | COMMEMORATION | THE MIX |
|---|---|---|
| *Rosh HaShanah*<br>1st and 2nd of *Tishrei* | **Jewish New Year**<br>Why two nights?<br>Why not! | *New Year's Day*<br>U2 |
| *Yom Kippur*<br>10th of *Tishrei* | **Day of Atonement**<br>Dust bust the *shmutz* from<br>your soul. | *(You've Got to*<br>*Change Your) Evil Ways*<br>Santana |
| *Sukkot/Sukkos*<br>15th of *Tishrei* | **Festival of Booths**<br>Another excuse for a party<br>Vhat, you've never heard<br>of Jewish camping? | *Turn! Turn! Turn!*<br>*(To Everything There Is a*<br>*Season)*<br>The Byrds |
| *Sh'mini Atzeret &*<br>*Simchat/Simchas Torah*<br>22nd /23rd of *Tishrei* | **Rejoicing in Torah**<br>When else can you break-<br>dance with a little animal<br>parchment and some<br>wooden scrolls | *Shiny Happy People*<br>R.E.M. |
| *Chanukah*<br>25th of *Kislev* | **Rededication of the**<br>**Temple in Jerusalem**<br>No Limit Texas Dreidl™* | *Hanukkah Song*<br>Adam Sandler |
| *Tu B'Shvat*<br>15th of *Shevat* | **Birthday of the Trees**<br>Jewish Earth Day; gefilte<br>fish *is* biodegradable. | *It's Not Easy Being Green*<br>Kermit the Frog |

* ModernTribe.com

| WHAT AND WHEN | COMMEMORATION | THE MIX |
|---|---|---|
| *Purim* <br> 14th of *Adar* | **Hidden miracles** <br> The original Esther was not Madonna! | *Miracle* <br> Foo Fighters |
| *Pesach (Passover)* <br> 15th of *Nissan* | **Passover sacrifice** <br> Means eight days of constipation. | *Exodus* <br> Bob Marley |
| *Shavuot/Shavuous* <br> 6th of *Sivan* | **Receiving the Torah** <br> 1,000 B.C.E. is calling your name! | *White Wedding*** <br> Billy Idol |
| *Tisha B'Av* <br> 9th of *Av* | **Destruction of the Temple, exile from Israel** <br> Game over! | *Bad Day* <br> Daniel Powter |
| *Tu B'Av* <br> 15th of *Av* | **Jewish Day for Lovers** <br> When Nice Jewish Girls pursue Nice Jewish Boys. | *Stay With You* <br> Goo Goo Dolls |

## FYI: FOR THE YIDDISH IMPAIRED

In the Gregorian calendar of the Western world, the point of reference is the birth of Yashkie. But what could be more *goyish*? Instead, Heebsters use the terminology B.C.E. to refer to "Before the Common Era." Also referred to as "Big Chocolate Eclairs" and "*Bubbie* Craves *Engelach*" (grandkids).

** The holiday is likened to a marriage between Da Boss and Da People

# THE *SHULCHAN ARUCH* AKA THE SET TABLE

Every Jewish festivity worth its salt serves up piles of food . . . so much you can't imagine it will ever disappear. But it will. In record time. Like a *hamantaschen* on an anthill, shaved down to nothing in nothing flat. Naturally, every Heebster happenin' calls for a *l'chaim,* but booze always ranks second to *essen.* At a Jewish party, the food will die out. The bar will live on. Although menus vary from region to region and holiday to holiday, the Jewish *shpread* follows basic guidelines resembling this scientific formula.

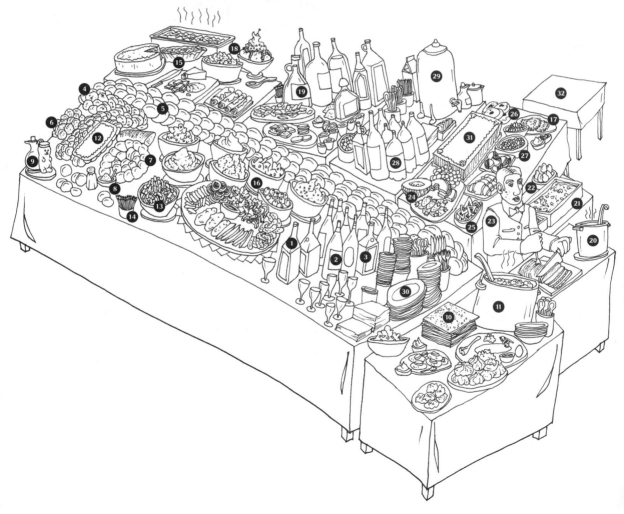

1. **Wine.** The classic choice: Manischewitz.

2. **For the softer palate, any kosher fine red or white wine.** Crowd pleasers include Golan, Herzog, HaGafen, organic Four Gates, and Bartenura Moscato D'Asti or Rashi.

3. **Kosher Grape juice for teetotalers and children.** Organic in Berkeley, Boulder, West Mt. Airy (Philly), Sharon, Massachusetts, and other hip(pie) areas. Kedem and Manischewitz nearly everywhere else.

4. **For Friday night *Shabbat* dinner, *Shabbos* lunch, and every holiday meal, add traditional braided egg *challahs*.** Two loaves are customary, plus rolls for late comers. Seeds, including sesame and poppy, are optional. Poppy seeds are not recommended for those with the intention to flirt (they muck up a smile in seconds) or get drug-tested immediately following ingestion. Chocolate chips, rainbow sprinkles, or raisins are optional decorative elements.

5. **For *bar* and *bat mitzvahs* and weddings, extend the *challah* until it covers the length of the head table.**

6. **In Berkeley, California, and other groovy territories, substitute spelt and other alternative *challot*.**

7. **On *Rosh HaShanah*, substitute round *challah* turbans for traditional braids to symbolize the cyclical nature of life.**

8. **To recall the sacrifices in the Holy Temple in Jerusalem, sprinkle *challah* with salt before eating.** Among foodies, substitute Celtic. Consider a rainbow of specialty salts, including pink, green, and other colors, as its very own course.

9. **Swap honey for salt during the first year of marriage and from *Rosh HaShanah* through *Simchat Torah*.**

10. **On Passover, substitute *matzah* for *challah*.** Alternates include whole wheat, spelt, oat, and handmade *shmurah*, which looks three thousand years old!

11. **At the Passover seder, add *maror, charoset, karpas,* shank bone, roasted egg (these two items are purely decorative), *matzah* ball soup, gefilte fish, horseradish, macaroons, and *matzah* meal cakes.**

12. **Cover all breads (and *matzah*) with decorative cloths embroidered or hand-painted with Jewish themes.** Since the wine blessing is recited first, this tasteful draping avoids embarrassing the *challah*.

13. **For Saturday morning *kiddush*, add pickled herring.**

14. **When adding pickled herring, add toothpicks.**

15. **At dairy meals, add quiche, cheeses, and herring in sour cream.**

16. **At all meals, add side dishes.** These may include egg salad, tuna salad, chopped liver, *hummus, tehina,* roasted eggplant, *baba ghanoush,* guacamole, vegetable salads, and platters of raw veggies, olives, pickles, and other accoutrements.

17. **On *Chanukah*, add *latkes* and applesauce.** At dairy meals, add sour cream.

18. **On *Shavuot*, remove all meat dishes. Load up on dairy.** Serve blintzes, cheesecake, and ice cream sundaes with all the fixings. Lasagna, pizza, and pile-your-own tostadas are optional. Lactaid is essential.

19. For the groom's wedding *tish,* remove all food except for crackers, herring, and toothpicks. Add Scotch, whiskey, vodka, arrack, Amaretto, and other inebriants. In Miami, and other party places, add tequila, kosher salt, and limes.

20. For the elaborate *kiddush,* add steaming hot *cholent,* the classic Sabbath stew.

21. When adding *cholent,* add noodle *kugel.* Varieties include sweet noodle, potato, and sweet and spicy "Yerushalmi."

22. At Yemenite meals, add *jachnun, hilbe,* hard-boiled eggs and sour cream or, with meat meals, a *pareve* (neutral) tofu-based substitute.

23. At weddings, add a staffed smorgasbord of "appetizers." Pasta with sauces to order, customized omelets—depending on the hour, carved brisket, turkey, sushi, shwarma and a mashed potato "sundae" bar.

24. For desserts and at *Yom Kippur* break-the-fasts, add melons, strawberries, grapes, poppy seed cake, *rugelach,* brownies, cookies, sorbet, baklava, and other blood sugar boosters.

25. On *Purim,* add *hamantaschen.* Options include poppy, prune, apricot, peanut butter, and chocolate.

26. On *Chanukah,* add jelly doughnuts for Ashkenazim and *sfenj* for Sephardim.

27. At Yemenite events, add *jala,* raw and roasted nuts, seeds, dried fruits, and candies.

28. Mineral water (e.g., San Pelligrino, Crystal Geyser, Arrowhead), seltzer, plain and with fruit essences, fresh juices, Scotch, and sodas.

29. Tea and coffee. Sweet N' Low, Equal, and Spelnda required. Honey, stevia, and agave nectar optional.

30. Dinner plates, napkins, cutlery, and a variety of cups for hot and cold drinks and endless *l'chaims.*

31. For birthdays, retirements and other "kiddush occasions" add a personalized sheet cake, cupcakes, or pizza-sized chocolate chip cookie.

32. On *Yom Kippur* and *Tisha B'Av,* omit all foods. Ditto for all minor fast days: *Tzom Gedalia,* Tenth of *Tevet,* Fast of Esther, and Seventeenth of *Tammuz.* On these days, no foods are served until after sunset when the fast formally concludes and mayhem breaks loose.

---

## FYI: FOR THE YIDDISH IMPAIRED

*Kiddush* is where the action is. As the saying goes, *nicht Shabbos gerecht,* certain topics are not appropriate for the Sabbath—primarily those involving financial transactions. So nothing is ever fully *formalized* at *shul.* But over all that noshing, plenty of essential *shmoozing* takes place: deals, tips, matchmaking, and more. Note: *Kiddush* is not a meal. It is a snack. After *Kiddush,* everyone goes home to eat lunch.

## Return Again

The Jewish New Year is not the time for partying in Times Square. *Rosh HaShanah* is the time for recalling the creation of the Jew-niverse. The holiday's peak moment is the blowing of the *shofar*. This exotic Jewish ritual item is created from the horn of a kosher mammal such as the antelope, Big Horn sheep, buffalo, gazelle, gemsbok, goat, ibex, kudu, ram, or Rocky Mountain goat. To make your own, see page 98. But first things first.

## Learn the Lingo & Toot Your Own . . .

**TEKIAH**—A trumpet blast signifying kingship.

*The Jewish foghorn, an excellent ring tone.*

**TERUAH**—Nine staccato notes in rapid succession; short bursts of crying.

*Really bad cell reception.*

**SHEVARIM**—Three "broken" notes of equal length, each three beats long.

*Your battery needs recharging.*

**TEKIAH GEDOLAH**—Concluding each set of blows during the *Rosh HaShanah* and *Yom Kippur* prayers is "The Great Blast," one gigantic toot.

*The original cry of Tarzan.*

# Make-a-Shofar

1. Boil in a mixture of water and baking soda for two to five hours to remove all the cartilage. (Barf.) Keeping with the theme of the High Holidays, throw away the bad and keep the good! Place on a counter or in the sun to dry.

2. Use pliable wire from a coat hanger or a plastic Flexi-straw to measure the inside of the horn, from the hollow end to the smaller, closed-off tip. Mark it with a pen.

3. To open the horn, saw off the small end perpendicularly at a point 1½" away (in the direction of the smaller end) from the hollow point you've just marked. Then using a 3/16" drill bit, drill from the small tip into the empty cavity. With a knife, carefully carve a trumpetlike depression as a mouthpiece. Smooth the edges with a mechanical sander. Consult the local Chabad or an experienced trumpet, tuba, bugle or *shofar* blower for help.

4. To keep the *shofar* kosher, thou shall not drill holes in the length of the *shofar*. Thou shall not paint it. Thou shalt ensure it is longer than the palm of your hand. Thou mayest carve decorative verses about *shofarot*, such as Numbers 29:1 or Psalm 98:6. Thou mayest also carve a crown-like border along the large opening.

If you're vegan or just plain grossed out by the idea of gutting an animal horn, shop for a *shofar* in Israel, on the Lower East Side, or in any Judaica store.

Word to the wise: don't choose a *shofar* online. Before you buy, it's best to know how thy horn doth blow. Pucker up!

Al Jolson croons
"Kol Nidre" on
Yom Kippur in
the first talkie, the
1927 film, *The Jazz
Singer.*

# *Yom Kippur* Dos and Don'ts

The Day of Atonement is also the day of At-One-Ment, the day of repentance and, sometimes, The Pennant. Pronounced *YAHM Kipp'er* in Yiddish or *Yohm Kee PUR* in Hebrew, Yom Kippur is associated with one of the most legendary Jewish baseball players. In the first game of the 1965 World Series, the legendary Sandy Koufax refused to play ball because it was the holiest day of the Heebster year. Koufax understood that on Kippur, all the rules change.

| **Dos** | **Don'ts** |
|---|---|
| feast on a celebratory meal before *and* after | *essen o'trinken'* (eating or drinking) |
| praying | nookie |
| sleeping | bathing |
| reading | wearing leather shoes |
| studying | anointing (and annoying) |
| soul accounting | pitching in the World Series |

On this day, traditional Jews also refrain from using electricity, cooking, writing, shopping, surfing (the Net or gnarly waves), driving, phoning, typing . . . There's one more thing Jews do on *Yom Kippur*. While praying, we beat our chests to feel the pain of every failure, every broken promise, every wrong. Even if you don't think you screwed up, you did. Besides, it's a team effort. You're praying for every other Jew in the entire world. And so are they. Best of all, if somebody hits one out of the park, everyone scores!

# YK Oy Vey!
# Common Interruptions During
# Yom Kippur Prayers

Sometimes, G-d really tests us. Fasting is hard enough. But on *Kippur*, brace yourself for more. Oy! Even in the holiest of *shul*s you may hear

1. Rumors of the next American Idol
2. Crackberry dings from stockbrokers
3. Pocket broadcasts of World Series scores
4. Buzz saws and jackhammers from nearby construction
5. Next-door fraternities playing "Stairway to Heaven" and barbecuing pork ribs
6. Pipes bursting and toilets backing up
7. Text messages with photos of Sacha Baron Cohen arriving in *shul*

# Sukkot

Five days after *Yom Kippur* comes the holiday of *Sukkot*. You may have never heard of *Sukkos*, but those *Mayflower* pilgrims sure did. In fact, they modeled Thanksgiving after this fall Jewish harvest festival. Special for *Sukkot* are the Four Species, your once-a-year holiday bouquet. Sure it costs a sweet *shekel*, but it's the original spiritual light saber. You get to wave it around as if you're defeating Darth Vader. Where do you think George Lucas got it from anyway? "Yes, Obie One. *Hashem* Be One."

The tallest of the Four Species is the center palm branch, the *lulav,* which represents the human spine. The fragrant myrtle branches, *hadassim,* have leaves shaped like human eyes. The willow branches on the left, *aravot,* resemble human lips. And the fragrant *etrog* fruit, aka a citron in Da Qveen's English, looks like a lemon, costs like a Land Rover! It represents the heart. Tradition says pregnant women who eat *etrogim* will give birth to sweet-smelling babies . . . anything for *Yiddishe kinder!*

# Recycle, Reuse, Reshmooze

*Sure, your Four Species were holy. Now they're not. But why toss them away after the holiday?*

Play bookie and collect bets on whose *etrog* stays yellow the longest.

Poke holes in the peel and stuff with whole cloves for potpourri.

Decorate with a miniature hat, eyes, nose, lipstick, and mini Manolo Blahniks borrowed from Barbie. Make Mrs. Etrog prank Mr. Potato Head.

Collect *etrogim* from your friends. Cut them up, and add to a bottle of vodka for *etrog* liquor or add fruit slices to heaps of sugar and a *bissel vasser.* Simmer for hours for jam.

Play mock wiffle ball. Hit your dried up *etrog* with your *lulav.* Use with caution in residential areas.

Challenge frenemies to a *lulav* duel.

Beware: the best *lulavim* have sharp tips.

# Chanukah

Did you know, the Festival of Lights actually celebrates the victory of Jewish zealots riding on ancient mastodons? Elephants are long gone from the Holy Land, but we're not! Using those massive tusks, and more than a smidgeon of guerilla warfare, the Maccabees defeated the evil Syrian-Greeks. Oh yeah, and the oil miraculously burned in the ancient Temple in Jerusalem for a few extra days. Make that eight.

To commemorate all these miracles, each night we light the *Chanukah* menorah, aka the *Chanukiah*. We recall the miracle becoming even greater each day by increasing the number of lights each night, from one the first night to eight on the last. And we use a "helper" candle, called the *"Shamash,"* which loosely translates to janitor in Hebrew, to do all that lighting. So it's really two on the first night and nine on the last. The math may be confusing but the message isn't. *Chanukah* embodies the old adage that sums up nearly all Jewish holidays, *They tried to kill us. We survived. Let's eat!*

On *Chanukah*, that means eating oil in latkes and doughnuts. We also slather latkes with sour cream not only 'cuz it's yummy, but also because dairy foods recall the bravery of Judith. This shero fed the no-goodnik King Holofernes salty cheese, quenched his thirst with wine, and, once he fell into a drunken doze, chopped off his head. Those medieval painters loved her.

The best reason to adore *Chanukah* is obvious! Everyone knows how to spell Christmas. But no one can decide how to spell *Chanukah, Chanukka, Channukah, Khanukah, Hanukah, Hannukah.* Win big and put your own spin on it!

# And the *Dreidl Will Rock*

To play the traditional *Chanukkah* game of *dreidl*, at least one top is needed along with copious quantities of "currency." Use pennies, raisins, hazelnuts, tasteless chocolate *Hanookah* coin *gelt,* shekels left over from your last visit to the Holy Land, spare undergarments … whatever works for your crowd.

On each *dreidl*, the Hebrew letters *Nun, Gimmel, Hey* and *Shin,* stand for the message of *Khanuka:* A great miracle happened there/*Nes gadol haya sham.* In Israel, this phrase is abbreviated with the letters *Nun, Gimmel, Hey,* and *Peh*/A great miracle happened here. This also makes for a slogan across the rear of an innovation occasionally found on eBay: panties from the company formerly known as Jewish Fashion Conspiracy. To play *dreidl*, give that top some top spin. Then decode, fork up or cash in!

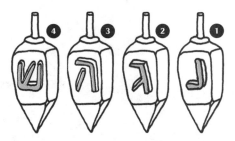

1. *Nun* stands for *nisht,* nothing in Yiddish. If you're looking to collect, sorry. If you're playing Strip *Dreidl* and looking to stay dressed, hallelujah!

2. *Gimmel* means *gantz,* Yiddish for all. Take the whole pot. If you're collecting everyone else's undergarments, wear gloves.

3. *Heh* represents half or *halb* in Yiddish. You take half the pot. If there's just one pair of panties, tear it in two.

4. *Shin* stands for *shtel* or put in Yiddish. "Put in," not "put out." No pressure here … Just toss in a spare pair of undies!

# Channuka Kitsch List

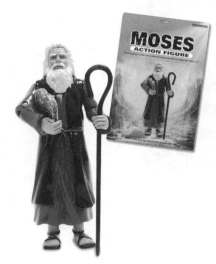

"Chassidic Smiley" candles
*Chutzpah, This Is?* mockumentary DVD
*Moses Is My Homeboy, What Would Babs Do?*,
    and *Yo Semite* T-shirts
*A great miracle happened here* panties
Groucho Marx glasses
*Let's Go Schlepping* board game
Star of David holographic glasses
    (turns every Xmas light into a Jewish star!)
*The Hebrew Hammer* DVD
Hebrew National *mezuzah* in a bun
*Jewish Hero Corps* comics and T-shirts
Moses Action Figure

Rabbi Trading Cards
Rabbi Punching Puppet
Rockin' Jewish music CDs
    (see page 228)
Ruthie and Gussie's "*kvetch* proof"
    Latke Gram (frozen *latke* batter
    with all the fixings)
Shalom, The Chosen Gum
Shlomo's Matzoball Soap
Star of David Brand Soap
Ultra Happy Hanukkah Body Detergent
This book!

The Stropkover Rebbe

The Bobover Rebbe, zt'l

# Test Your *Hannooka IQ*

1. Tradition dictates Jewish women file their nails while the Chanooka lights burn. Kosher or *trayfe*?

2. The Syrian king who wanted to annihilate the Jewish religion ruled Jews in his kingdom must
   a. Stop teaching Torah.
   b. Stop circumcising their sons.
   c. Eat the other white meat.
   d. All of the above.

3. Hasidic reggae superstar Matisyahu shares his name with a Jewish elder who summoned his inner warrior and squashed the nasty no-goodniks. Kosher or *trayfe*?

4. Hannah, a Chanuk-Ahhh Sheebster shero mothered seven sons who were executed because they refused to eat honey-glazed ham. True or false?

5. In the It-All-Comes-from-Us Category, Christians celebrate Xmas on the twenty-fifth of December because of the mystical significance of Hah!Nuka falling on the twenty-fifth of Kislev. True or false?

6. The Talmud states the Chachanookah menorah should be placed
   a. outside one's home
   b. in a window near the street to show the world the miracle of the holiday
   c. on a fire retardant tarp on the hood of your car
   d. all of the above

7. And yet another possibility in the It-All-Comes-from-Us category: the tradition of Xmas lights is based on the tradition of Hannooka lights. Kosher or *trayfe*?

8. In Europe, Xmas Eve was a dangerous time for *Yiddelach* because no-goodniks often made it a night of Jew killing. True or false?

*Answers:* 1. *Trayfe*, but tradition suggests they do kick back! 2. d. 3. Kosher. 4. True—more or less; it was some kind of *trayfe*. 5. Highly likely. 6. a and b are both kosher but c and d also work! 7. Sure seems like it. 8. Tragically, all too true.

# HIP-HOP HA-NEW-KAH

Set up a turntable and invite your rapper friends. If your crowd is not up for free-stylin', screen the world's first Heebsploitation film, *The Hebrew Hammer*. Part man, part street, 100 percent kosher, this Heebster hero saves Hanukkah from the clutches of evil. You know!

## KHANOOKAH ¡TUNES

"Bei Mir Bist Du Schön," The Andrews Sisters

"Chanutronikah,' Laurence Juber and Craig Taubman

"Chanukah's Da Bomb," Chutzpah

"Chanukah, Skanukah (Chag Yafay)," Alan Eder and Friends

"Descarga Ocho Kandelikas," The Afro-Semitic Experience

"Driedel, Driedel," Meshugga Beach Party

"Drey Dreydele," Frank London and CURHA

"Eight Days a Week," The Beatles

"Electranukah," Socalled

"Good to Be A Jew at Christmas," Good for the Jews

"They Tried to Kill Us, We Survived, Let's Eat," Good for the Jews

"Hanu-Calypso," Kenny Ellis

"(I'm Spending) Hanukkah in Santa Monica," Tom Lehrer

"Hanukah with Monica [Lewinsky]," Sean Altman

"The Hanukkah Song I, II and III," Adam Sandler

"Jewish Girls (at the Matzoh Ball)," The Levees

"Lonely Jew at Christmas," Kyle from *South Park*

"Makin' Whoopee (in Yiddish!)," The Barry Sisters

"Ocho Kandelikas," Hip Hop Hoodios

"Oh Hanukkah," Meshugga Beach Party

"Oy Chanukah," James Fuchs

"The Punk Rock Chanukah Song," YIDcore

"Rich Girl," Gwen Stefani

"They Ain't Making Jews Like Jesus Anymore," Kinky Friedman and the Texas Jewboys

"Tradition," Zero Mostel and chorus

"Tzena, Tzena, Tzena," The Weavers

Woody Guthrie's "Happy Joyous Hanukkah," Klezmatics

## THE HEEBSTER HUSTLE

Good for Channeke, *Purim,* or any time of year, the Heebster Hustle conveys essential expression of the Jewish soul, the *Yiddishe neshume.* So crank it up, boogie down, and like a super fresh *latke,* drop it like it's hot, baby!

1. Form a circle, keep the time. Shuckle from the waist like a davening mime.

2. Look to the left, bust out a grapevine. Hip-hop your Hebraic and let it shine!

3. Wiggle your tushy, then bump and grind. Show off your *pupik* 'cuz you look so fine!

4. Shout "Shalom, y'all!" and *katzatzka* just a little. Then click your heels and play air fiddle!

5. Spin to the right, wave your hand "puh-shaw." Toast *l'chaim* to your posse. Slurp a Mani through a straw!

6. Clap three times and pretend to scribble. Hyperventilate, then act *farshimmeled.*

7. Put a bottle on your head. Shake hands with your Pa. Be a Super Jew and blow a kiss to your Ma!

## Purim

If you've always wanted to lead services after sucking on a helium balloon, *Purim*'s your chance! This holiday, too, is all about the eternal struggle between good and evil. Break it down: Once again, *They tried to kill us. We survived. Let's eat!* Only this time, we add a P.S., *"Let's drink!"*

It's a *Purim* tradition to get so intoxicated you confuse the good guy, Mordechai, with Shushan's bad guy, Haman (booooo!). Everything turns upside down, making it a perfect time for dressing in drag, or mimicking *shul machers* with a riotous Purim *shpiel*. With costumes a go-go, and unlimited *l'chaims, shul*s everywhere transform into one big par-tee. So pack a flask, grab a *gragger,* and rock a new identity!

## Masquerade Menu

### HASIDIC POP CULTURE ICON

**The Look:** Rent a costume and throw a traditional prayer shawl over it. Add a *shtreiml* or black hat. Any recognizable character works. Not recommended for tropical climates.

**The *Shtick*:** Pretend you're constantly praying or studying. Carry a book of Jewish wisdom. **The requisite *gragger*** (GRAHger aka *Purim* noisemaker): Harpo Marx horn.

**The Lingo:** If anyone can actually hear you in that get-up, quote incessantly in a Yiddish accent. Or communicate silently using Disneyland-inspired gestures like Mickey Mouse or Goofy!

## OVER-PARTIED GIRL

**The Look:** Get glammed up but instead of high heels, wear slippers and ripped stockings. Throw on a bathrobe. Let last night's eye make-up run wild.

**The *Shtick*:** Rock a Mani glass filled with aspirin. Boast about having too much fun the night before. **The *gragger*:** *Sex in the City* cell phone ring tone.

**The Lingo:** Speak with a slur as if you're terribly hungover.

## CONFUSED HITCHHIKER

**The Look:** Wear a beach outfit or hula skirt with a lei and your "coconut shell" *kippa* bra (see page 57). Put a flower behind your right ear if you're single; left ear if you're attached. *Shmear* zinc oxide aka *charoset* on your nose.

**The *Shtick*:** Carry a sign that reads "Waikiki or Bust" no matter where you live. In cold climates, add a flesh colored bodysuit. Bust a Mai Tai or another umbrella drink. Serve kosher macadamia nuts to friends and desirable strangers. **The *gragger*:** battery-operated boom box.

**The Lingo:** Speak like you're wasted and keep asking, "Dude, can I borrow your sex wax?"

## SHUSHAN AIRLINES SEXY STEWARDESS

**The Look:** Wear a '70s-style polyester dress. Add tall boots or leg warmers. Throw on a platinum blond or neon-colored mod wig. Using a peel-and-stick-on label, draw a creative SA logo for Shushan Airlines and attach it in a prominent spot above your

bosom. (Stuff it if you're not yet blessed like Bubbie.)

**The *Shtick*:** Using a tray in one hand, pose repeatedly like Vanna White and serve Black Mani Shpritzers to help prevent Purim hang-overs. **The *gragger:*** handheld PA system.

---

### Black Mani Shpritzers
Mix two shots of Blackberry Manische-witz with a splash of lemon-lime soda and two Alka-Seltzer in a *yahrzeit* glass.

---

**The Lingo:** Roll a feline purr under every word, coming on to everyone. Remind passengers to "Please buckle up and remain seated during flatulence."

## SHOE SHINE *PURIM*

**The Look:** Grow a beard or draw one on. Fill apron pockets with shoe polish, giant shoehorns, and other *shtick*. Pack a faux photo album with images of celebrity Jews like David Lee Roth, Zack Braff, and Jeremy Piven and mock autographs that read, "Rock on Shoe Shine!" Sign a Charleton Heston portrayal of Moshe Rabbenu with, "Thanks for the great sandal shine. I'd cross deserts for it."

**The *Shtick*:** Ply everyone with your "yearbook" of the good ol' days. **The *gragger*:** two containers of metal polish you clang together like tiny cymbals.

**The Lingo:** Affect a Tom Waits-ish, jazz-like baritone, Wolf Man Jack or Scatman Crathers.

### SHUSHAN NEWS

**The Look:** Sport a khaki-colored safari vest, mirrored sunglasses, and a microphone. Keep a small spiral pad, pens, and a bunch of cords poking out of other pockets. If you're hard-core, slap on some camouflage face paint.

**The *Shtick*:** Recruit a sidekick who refuses to dress up as your camera person. **The *gragger:*** boom mic or megaphone.

**The Lingo:** In an annoying "this-just-in" TV tabloid tone, greet everyone with "Live from (wherever the heck you are)." **The *gragger:*** If your camera actually works, record drunken messages to post on JewTube. Remember, dork is the new macho.

## Purim Pairs

Got a jDate? Re-create these famous Jewish partners in history.

| PERSONALITIES | PERSONAS |
|---|---|
| Abraham and Sarah | Pious Idol Smashers |
| King David and Bathsheva | Royal and Sexy |
| King Solomon and Queen of Sheba | Hot Know-It-Alls |
| Samson and Delilah | Studly and Seductive |
| Moshe Dayan and Golda Meir | His and Hers Macho |
| Woody Allen and Diane Keaton | Neurotic Meets *Goyishe* |
| Jerry Stiller and Anne Meara | Loud and Proud |
| G-d and Da Sabbath Queen | The Super Holy One and Only |

## SHABOT 6000   by Ben Baruch

I WANT A PASTRY SHAPED LIKE THE HAT OF A GENOCIDAL ANTI-SEMITE WHO WAS EXECUTED BY PUBLIC HANGING.

YOU MEAN *HAMENTASHEN,* TO CELEBRATE *PURIM!*

I HAVE NO IDEA WHAT YOU ARE TALKING ABOUT.

WWW.SHABOT6000.COM

© Ben Baruch

# DON'T PASS OUT, PASSOVER!

One night every spring, traffic everywhere picks up at an inordinate pace. It's the annual "Running of the Jew" to the *Pesach* seder! Still relevant after all these years, this pivotal Passover programming calls upon us to see ourselves as if we were each redeemed from bondage. (Not that kind of bondage!)

In Hebrew, the word *Pesach* literally means "the mouth speaks." So, naturally, we relive our liberation by *shmoozing* and eating all night long! As an encore, once more we celebrate national triumph over our enemies. *They tried to kill us. We survived. Let's eat!*

Only this time there is a little P.S. And that is, you must eat unleavened bread and suffer innumerable gastrointestinal afflictions . . . Hence the standard *Pesach* phraseology: "This is the bread of affliction our forefathers ate in Egypt." Hurt your tummy though it may, thou shalt eat it anyway!

## The Four Questions in Four Tongues

Traditionally, the youngest present asks the pivotal Four Questions of the Passover *seder*. As a user-friendly event, every Passover prayer book aka *Hagaddah* includes them. But what if you don't yet read the Holy Tongue? Or you're busting a multicultural vibe? At the Heebster *seder*, it's aaaaaahll gooooood! And with our handy transliteration guide, you can fake out family and bff's with fabulous faux foreign language skills!

## Hebrew Transliteration

Ma-nishtana halaila hazeh mee-kol ha-lay-lot? Mee-kol ha-lay-lot?

She-b-chol ha-lay-lot, anu ochlean, chamaytz u'matzah, chamaytz u'matzah.

Ha-laila hazeh, ha-laila hazeh kulo matzah. (repeat)

She-b-chol ha-lay-lot anu ochlean she-ar yerakot, she-ar yerakot?

Ha-laila hazeh, ha-laila hazeh maror, maror. (repeat)

She-b-chol ha-lay-lot, ain anu matbilin, afilu pa'am echad, afilu pa'am echad.

Ha-laila hazeh, ha-laila hazeh sh-tay fey-a-meem. (repeat)

She-b-chol ha-lay-lot, anu yoshvin beyn yoshvin oo-veyn mesubean, beyn yoshvin oo-veyn mesubean.

Ha-laila hazeh, ha-laila hazeh kulanu mesubin. (repeat)

## Yiddish, *Die Mama Loshen*

Tatteh, ich vill bei dir fregen fir kashes: Farvos iz andersh di nacht fun Pesach fun alleh necht fun a gants yohr?

Alleh necht essn mir say chometz say matzoh; ober in der doziker nacht, nor matzoh.

Alleh necht essn mir alerley grinzn, ober in der doziker nacht, essn mir maror, bittere grinzn.

Alleh necht tunkn mir nit ayn afileh ayn mol, ober in der doziker nacht, tunken mir ayn tzvay mol.

Alleh necht essen mir say zitzendik glaych say ongelent, ober in der doziker nacht essen mir alle ongelent.

## Ladino, Rare and Romantic

Cuanto differente la noche la ésta más que todas las noches?

Que en todas las noches no nos entiniente tampoco vez una y en la noche la ésta dos veces.

Que en todas las noches nos comientes yebdo o seseña y la noche la ésta todo seseña.

Que en todas las noches nos comientes las demás verduras y la noche la ésta lechuga.

Que en todas las noches nos comientes y bebientes, tanto sentados y tanto rescobdados, la noche las ésta todos nos rescobdados.

## Mandarin Chinese, Increasingly Useful in Pacific Rim Negotiations

为什么今天晚上跟别的晚上都不一样？

别的晚上我们都吃面包和" "干饼，今天晚上我们只能吃" "干饼？

别的晚上我们吃所有的菜，今天晚上我们只吃苦菜？

别的晚上我们连一次都不把菜放在盐水里边，今天晚上我们把菜放在盐水两次？

别的晚上我们坐着吃或者躺着吃，今天晚上我们都是躺着吃？

# Pesach JTunes

The *seder* traditionally concludes in song. Now that you've had four cups of wine, the worst crooner sounds better. That may be you! A little intoxication could be a good because this song makes no sense sober!

Found! Matzah ball timer.

## THEY TRIED TO KILL US (WE SURVIVED, LET'S EAT)
### by Sean Altman and Rob Tannenbaum*

We were slaves to Pharaoh in Egypt.
The year was 1492.
Hitler had just invaded Poland.
Madonna had just become a Jew.
Moses was found on the Potomac.
Then he marched with
    Martin Luther King.
He came back to free us from our bondage
'cuz S&M has never
    been our thing.

They tried to kill us, we survived, let's eat!
    Let's eat!
They tried to kill us. We were faster on
    our feet!
So they chased us to the border,
There's a parting of the water.
Tried to kill us. We survived. Let's eat!
    Let's eat!

Then the Pharaoh, who looked like Yul Brynner,
    heard the Jews were trying to escape.
Charleton Heston came right down from the
    mountain. He said "Pharaoh, you're
    damn dirty ape!"
The menorah was almost out of oil.
Farrakan was planning Kristallnacht.
The gefilte fish was nearing extinction.
It looked like Moses and his flock
    were *farkakt!*

They tried to kill us, we survived, let's eat!
    Let's eat!
They tried to kill us. We were faster on
    our feet!
And we knew how to resist
'cuz we'd rented *Schindler's List.*
Tried to kill us. We survived. Let's eat!
    Let's eat!

* Reprinted with permission.

And so, yay and verily, G-d brought down the Ten Plagues Upon Egypt:
1. Blood
2. Locusts
3. Boils
4. Dandruff
5. Acne
6. Back-ne
7. Piles
8. Cataracts
9. Sciatica
10. Sickle-cell anemia

We fled on foot. There was no time to tarry.
Leavening the bread would take too long.
All we had was egg foo yung and *matzah* while battling the fearsome Vietcong.
And so tonight we gather to remember the ancient Heeeee' Brews who paid the price.
We have a *seder* every year in December to commemorate our savior Santa Claus**

They tried to kill us, we survived, let's eat! Let's eat!
They tried to kill us. We were faster on our feet!
So we never did succumb to the annual pogrom.
Tried to kill us. We survived. Let's eat! Let's eat!

They tried to kill us, we survived, let's eat! Let's eat!
They tried to kill us. We were faster on our feet!
So come on blow the *shofar*
'cuz they haven't nailed us so far.
Tried to kill us. We survived. Let's eat! Let's eat!

---

**FYI: FOR THE YIDDISH IMPAIRED**

When used as a verb, to pass over refers to spending *Pesach* in any place you don't usually rent or own. Achhh, what a relief!

---

** Original lyrics bleeped out by the *farshtunkiner* censors.

# Shavuot aka Shavuos

Don't let Passover fool you. The next holiday on the Jewish agenda offers a lot more to your taste buds than plain *matzah* and bitter *maror*. There has to be a more digestible holiday and *Shavuot* is it—unless you're lactose intolerant like half the Tribe! Anyhoo, fifty days after Passover, synagogues world over celebrate the giving of the *Torah* at Mt. Sinai. And just as mother's milk nurtures the body, the *Torah* nurtures the Jewish soul. So with the festivities come plenty of ice cream, cheesecakes, and blintzes. And while your arteries are hardening, it's the perfect opportunity to review the Ten Commandments—or at least some version of them!

Mix in Manischewitz to slurp up a super *Shavuos!* Mmmm!

### 'SCHEVITZ FLOATS
Top vanilla ice cream and blackberry soda pop with a splash of
Blackberry Manischewitz. Smother with whipped cream and a blackberry.
Calculate the calorie content on your Blackberry.

### MANISCHEWITZ MANNA AKA MT. SINAI CLOUD COVER
Spike whipped cream with your favorite Mani flavor and mix
in pieces of apples, banana, pitted dates, and oranges.
It's so good, who cares about calories!

### SUPER JEW SAUCE
Simmer Blackberry 'Schevitz with fresh berries, lemon juice,
and sugar, honey, or agave to taste. Cool and pour over cheesecake.
Decorate with berries. As the holiday concludes, slurp leftover sauce
to dull the memory of how much you ate!

# The Ten Commandments, Interpreted

| | **What the *Torah* Actually Says** | *What G!d is Really Thinking* |
| --- | --- | --- |
| **Alef** | I am the G-d who brought you out of Egypt. | *You might try using that red string bracelet for something else besides looking cool.* |
| **Bet** | I am a jealous G-d. | *You won the Kabbalottery and Madonna is the one you're going to listen to?* |
| **Gimel** | Thou shall not profane my holy name. | *Those who groove on Me are chill.* |
| **Dalet** | Work is good but all work is not all good. | *I can take time off whenever I want to. I didn't invent this law for My health!* |
| **Hey** | Honor your mother and father. | *It's up to you. I've got enough tzuris with my own family.* |
| **Vav** | Killin' ain't cool. | *Despite the Grammy wins for "It's Hard Out Here for a Pimp."* |
| **Zayin** | No extramarital *shtupping* allowed. | *Having sex with someone else's spouse is just plain stupid.* |
| **Chet** | Keep your hands to yourselves. No stealing. | *Your limbs might be spared but not your karma. The $#*! ain't worth it.* |
| **Tet and** | False testimony ain't where it's at. | *What, did your mother raise a moron?* |
| **Yud makes 10!** | No coveting your neighbor's sweetie or your neighbor's sweet stuff. | *That 500 series does sparkle nicely in the sun. Get a second job or a reality check. The choice is yours.* |

# The Heebster Top Ten

1.   I will not presume any ancient Jewish belief is outdated, join a cult, or take on any other *farkakte* religious practice.
2.   I will shine my Hebraic with its eternally brilliant 5,000-watt bulb!
3.   I will not speak *lashon hora* (disparaging $#*!) about the Jewish people.
4.   I will speak Yiddish—or pretend to—every chance I get. As Billy Crystal says, "Please pass the *chuch*."
5.   I will not hide my Jewishness.
6.   I will hide $250,000 in diamonds in my pocket and then fund a luncheon with stand-up comedians to entertain *and* feed the poor.
7.   I will not internalize the stereotype that Jews suck at athletics.
8.   I will make entertaining JewTube videos celebrating the meaningful moments in life, including the Hebrew School's annual kosher hot dog–eating contest.
9.   I will not join a reality TV series that requires me to eat non-kosher filth like earthworms and rat guts.
10.  I will love my fellow Jew, even if he cashes in big with a movie about Ickystahn before I do!

# Test Your Ethics

Now that you've got the translation, exactly, what part of *Thou shall not* don't you understand? Answer these questions to determine which way your moral compass points.

Kosher or *trayfe?*

1. Make a run for your neighbor's Audi TT Roadster.

2. It's perfectly acceptable to worship that tennis bracelet on page 36 of the "Big Book."

3. Orgies are an ancient Israelite tradition.

4. Food games are permissible in the bedroom.

5. When you swear on the Bible in Judge Judy's court, it doesn't really count.

6. Once your parents fork over the down on your condo, you don't owe them *bubkes*.

7. "Borrowing" juicy peaches from your neighbor's tree or snacking jelly beans from the bulk bin is no big deal.

*Answers:*

1. Kosher. Anything that belongs to your neighbor falls into the coveting category: car, spouse, pool boy, peach tree, mis-delivered Neiman Marcus catalog . . .

2. *Trayfe.* That, my friend, falls into the category of idol worship. In a word: *verboten*!

3. *Trayfe.* Our G-d is into One-ness in more ways than one.

4. Kosher. Plus, married couples score extra *mitzvah* points for *Shabbos* nookie.

5. *Trayfe.* Bearing false witness is a big taboo-boo.

6. *Trayfe.* Jews are on duty through *kaddish*, the mourner's prayer, which comes with an eleven-month sentence. In Aramaic. Mel Gibson, put that in your pipe and smoke it!

7. *Trayfe.* Quite simply, theft is theft, even if you think nobody notices. Somebody-Up-There is always on duty!

# Unparalleled Events

A true Heebster always knows exactly *where* to be *when*.

## ISRAEL

1. **Jerusalem:** *Da bim bom* for the three major pilgrimage holy daze, Passover, *Sukkot, Shavuot;* plus the High Holidays, Chanukah and Israel Independence Day, and *Shabbos* at the *Kotel* (the Wall formerly known as The Wailing).

2. **Mt. Meron:** On Lag B'Omer, 33 days after Passover, legions flock to the mount to mark the end of a devastating plague and the *yahrzeit* of the great sage, Rabbi Shimon bar Yochai.

3. **Tsfat:** *Shabbat* and Jewish holidays in the ancient birthplace of *Kabbalah.*

4. **Eilat:** Winter and spring visits for swimming with the friendly fins at the Dolphin Reef, chillin' deep in on-site serenity pools under moonlight and getting scuba certification in the Red Sea.

5. **Boombamela:** A rockin' festival held at Nitzanim Beach between Ashdod and Ashkelon during mid-week Passover.

6. **Shantipi:** During *Sukkot,* thousands converge on Pardes Hanna for yet another groovy Israeli festival.

7. **The Whole Shebang:** All Israel is a must-see for every living human being of every faith every day of the year. An entire country of Ripley's, you won't believe it until you see it!

## THE REST OF THE WORLD

1. **Miami Beach:** Passover, especially the boardwalk.

2. **Caribbean:** Winter Kosherica cruises for singles and families.

3. **Alaska:** Meet up with hordes of bull moose, boreal chickadees and wandering Israelis in Denali National Park.

4. **Hawaii:** From *shul* to sand in seconds. Plus, incredible winter whale watching, sometimes even from shore.

5. **Camp:** Kid and staff summers at B'nai B'rith, Camp Stone, Ramah, Habonim Dror, Moshava, Tel Yehuda, Young Judea West, Gan Izzy, JCCs, Joe V. Surf Camp …

6. **ALEPH Kallah:** Fourth of July week at various venues every two years, bringing together all ages of Jewish Renewal brothas and sistas.

7. **Burning Man:** The week prior to and including Labor Day at Blackrock City, a temporary and flamboyant community established in the Nevada desert. Heebsters hang with B'nai HaMidbar, Children of the Desert.

8. **Hershey Park:** Summers, plus *Sukkot* mid-week in Hershey, PA, for kosher family day!

9. **New York City:** Weekly *shul* hopping; closing ceremony of the seven-year cycle of daily Talmud study called *Daf Yomi* at Madison Square Gardens; the annual Israel Independence Day Parade on Fifth Avenue.

10. **Jerusalem Camp:** Fourth of July week at the annual Rainbow Gathering, somewhere in the U.S. National Forest.

11. **Jewlicious Festival:** Every March in Long Beach, California.

12. **Berkshires, Borscht Belt aka Catskills, Poconos:** Fire-fly season!

13. **The Ohel:** *Gimel Tammuz,* the *yahrzeit* of the Rebbe.

14. **770:** *Simchat Torah* at the spiritual headquarters of Chabad *Hasidim:* 770 Eastern Parkway, Crown Heights, Brooklyn.

15. **Hong Kong JCC:** Every Sunday night for the community-wide kosher BBQ.

16. **Palm Springs:** Winter. Includes kosher BBQs at the home of the local Chabad rabbi.

17. **Northern Sinai Desert:** Winter and spring va-kays at Dahab and Nueiba beachside villages so filled with Israelis, everyone speaks Hebrew, even the Bedouin and Egyptian soldiers.

18. **Khaosan Road, Bangkok:** *Shabbat* dinners all-year-round at Chabad House, packed with 300 to 500 Israeli backpackers a night.

2007 JEWISH HERITAGE NIGHT

19. **Katmandu:** The world's largest annual Passover *seder* for more than 1,000 Heebsters. Additional super-sized *sedarim* are held in Thailand, Peru, Argentina, and other assorted outposts.

20. **Uman, Ukraine:** *Rosh HaShana* for the annual, massive, spirited pilgrimage to the grave of Rebbe Nachman of Breslov.

21. **The Matzo Ball and Heebonism:** Big City Xmas Eve shindigs.

22. **Shalom Hunan:** Chinese food and the movies, the classic Knishmas past-time.

23. **San Francisco Bay Area:** The annual Chabad Purimpalooza; the all-night/all-denomination *Shavuot* Torah study at the Berkeley-Richmond JCC, and annual Jewish Heritage Nights, when the Rally Rabbi rocks the San Francisco Giants and the Golden State Warriors with tailgate parties and in-stadium shofar blows.

# Those OTHER Holidays

There's one time of year that challenges even the most triumphant tribalists. If only Irving Berlin and those other clever Jewish composers of yore had an idea what kind of *gehackte tzuris* they were creating for future Heebsters when they wrote "White Christmas," "Chestnuts Roasting," and all those other *verkackte* tunes. When that other holiday's endless barrage of nauseating lyrics and sappy melodies gets to be too much, try these quick fixes.

## SELF-HELP FOR THE CHRISTMAS-CAROL INTOLERANT

1. When carolers come to the neighborhood, Heebsters don their preferred favorite *alter kacker* (rhymes with rocker) outfits and light cigars, channeling George Burns.

   Breathe deeply before you open your door. Then scream at the top of your lungs, slam the door, and return to your previously scheduled programming.

2. Toss on your Orthodox transvestite get up to channel Rebbetzin Hadassah Gross.

   Open your door equipped with bountiful servings of gefilte fish, *kishke,* and chopped liver. Insist the carolers dig in. Again. And again. Keep pushing it on them, *shtipin araiyn,* insisting they finish it all. They'll get so sick, they'll never ever return.

3. Work out your aggressions in private.

   With a little practice with a Punching Rabbi Puppet, deliver a stiff upper cut to the Ken in your Barbie doll collection. Given that Ken and Barbie were created by a Jewish woman, Ruth Handler, who named the dolls after her very own children, taking it out on Ken has the double *oneg* (pleasure) of adding self-inflicted insult to injury.

4. Klutzy Heebsters just throw the darn puppet out the door.

   Even if you're no Jose Canseco and miss the target completely, when carolers pick up the toy rabbi and discover his long beard and *payis* they'll get the message and am-scray.

5. Turn Adbuster's "Buy Nothing Day," the day after Thanksgiving, into "Buy Nothing Month."

   Shop for *Chanukah* presents, wrapping paper, and kitschy holiday paper goods long after the un-holidays pass. You'll snag plenty of *metziahs* aka bargains and avoid the Xmas retail season, eliminating prerecorded audio misery from the day after Thanksgiving until after everyone returns their lame presents at the end of December.

6. If you must shop during these danger-ous days, demonstrate.

Carry a protest sign around your neck that reads, "Knishmas-Carol Intolerant." Wear earplugs and hum a Hasidic *niggun* as if you were sitting at the *rebbe's* festive *tish*.

7. Break out your *Purim* getup and go Hasidic.

Carry a boom box blasting Mati-syahu and strut through the mall wearing B&Ws. If more joined the cause, red-and-green tunes would be banned from public places well before *Moshiach* (the Messiah) comes!

## OY TO THE WORLD!

Lenny Bruce once said, "If Jesus had been killed twenty years ago, Catholic school children would be wearing little electric chairs around their necks instead of crosses."

### JEWISH REINDEER GAMES

Take Ellis Island revenge and rename everything in sight. Forget Dasher, Dancer, Prancer and Vixen, Comet, Cupid, Donner and Blitzen.

Now Dovid! Now Dudu! Now Pinchas *und* Velvel! On Chaimke! On Chanan! On Doron *und* Blintzes!

### FYI: FOR THE YIDDISH IMPAIRED

Jews don't knock on wood. That pagan practice aimed to release the good fairies living inside. "In Jewish," this is nonsense aka *narishe meises* aka *nar-ishkeit* aka *meshugass*. Latter Day prac-titioners thought of the cross. Yes, that cross. Could that *be* more *goyish?!*

## SHABOT 6000 *by Ben Baruch*

© Ben Baruch

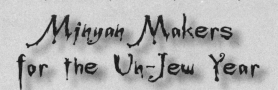

# Minyan Makers
## for the Uh-Jew Year

You know you have the Jeweltide Blues when, the day after Xmas:

1. While everyone else is eating Aunt Felah's *latkes,* you sequester yourself in your Uncle Fishel's office with his treasured *DSM-IV* and hunt for a diagnosis of your strange symptoms, which include a sudden loss of coordination, accidentally leaving the cover *shmeared* with sour cream.

2. You daydream of King Kong wrenching loose the ball in Times Square on New Year's Eve and bonking Ryan Seacrest or some other *schlemiel* on the head.

3. You relish telling every Jew you know that Euro *goyim* call the day Sylvester because it marks the *yahrzeit,* the death anniversary, of a pope named after a puddy tat.

4. You're relieved December 31 will fall on *Shabbos* or *Chanukah* so you have other lyrics to screw up instead of "Auld Lang Syne," which sounds an awful lot like Jewish for "aging giant penis."

5. In the meantime, you start writing *Rosh HaShanah* cards for next fall, and eat apples and honey while watching the *Ten Commandments.*

6. You come in to work early to remove all the mistletoe from your office, then bust the company shredder by trying to dispose of it.

7. You refer to New Year's Rockin' Eve as New Year's F---in' Eve and it's not because you plan on getting lucky.

8. You plan to watch *When Harry Met Sally* for the eighth year in a row. Alone.

9. You are so desperate for a better plan that you spend hours learning *Torah* with the Lubavitchers and actually enjoy it.

## And the Top *Minyan*-Maker reason you know you have the Jeweltide Blues:

10. You finally realize the best way to celebrate life as a Heebster is to ignore New Year's, Christmas, Halloween, Valentine's Day, and every other *goyish* holiday with *farkakte* pagan roots that historically coincided with a pogrom!

KABBA LAH LAH

# NEEDLE IN A HAYSTACK

Hollywood celebs and *People* magazine have popularized Jewish esoteric wisdom among the masses of tired shoppers at grocery stores everywhere. Now you, too, can cut to the fundamentals with this annotated version of Heebster *Kabba Lah Lah.*

Jewish mystical teachings are all about seeing the g-dly in everything, even your belly button lint. This carefully guarded wisdom has been passed down in secret over the ages. Although it remains advisable to find a living, breathing (neo) Hasidic teacher while you contemplate your *pupik,* Mosaic mysticism is more accessible than ever. Right here, right now. It's everything you need to know but are afraid to ask. Or don't know how. Or haven't cared less about until now. Because being an informed Heebster means knowing at least as much as Madonna, Ashton, Demi, and the rest of the red-string gang.

# What They Teach You at Heebster School

*Kabbalah* dates back to ancient Israel.

*Kabba Lah Lah* dates back to Lah Lah Land.

Rumor has it *Kabba Ha Ha* is a forthcoming half-hour sitcom on Comedy Central.

## DAILY PRACTICE

When you're a *Kabba Lah Lah*-ist, there is a Jewish way to do everything. The highly venerated Code of Jewish Law, aka the *Shulchan Aruch,* explains it all, from top to bottom. In fact, let's start there, with a little meditation on your feet.

**Step one:** Put on the right shoe.

**Step two:** Put on the left shoe.

**Step three:** Tie the left shoe.

**Step four:** Tie the right shoe.

When you take them off, reverse the process.

**Step five:** Untie the right shoe.

**Step six:** Untie the left shoe.

**Step seven:** Take off the left shoe.

**Step eight:** Take off the right shoe.

Note: If you're goofy foot, switch it all around.

This may sound like Jewish Hokey Pokey, but it's actually infused with ancient wisdom. You see, *kinderlach,* in *Kabba Lah Lah,* the stronger side represents love or giving. The weaker side represents restraint or discipline. Heebsters harmonize kindness and love over restraint or discipline. Both are important, but love conquers all. Where do you think they got it from anyway?

---

## Shhhh!

As the late great guitar-slinging Rabbi Shlomo Carlebach of blessed memory taught, "If I tell you a secret and now you know, it was never a secret. It was ignorance. If it's a real secret, then even after I tell you, you still don't know!"

That's why the *Kabba Lah Lah* is called the Secrets of the Torah. No one really understands it. Even if they pretend they do. And after you learn it, it's still a secret. So really, when you don't understand, that just makes you an even greater *Kabba Lah Lah*-ist!

# And Let Us Say, "Ahhhhmen!"

True *Kabba Lah Lah*-ists are in constant communion with The One Above. Just like Teyve in *Fiddler on the Roof,* great Heebros talk to The Ultimate Heebster in Heaven in their own words. Yes, *bubbeleh,* you, too can pray throughout the day. Seeking inspiration? Customize this template to express your innermost hopes and dreams. Go on now, speak up and push the pearly gates wide open!

Dear Ultimate Heebster in Heaven,

G-d of our *Zaydes,* Abbie, Izzy, and Jackie,
And G-d of our *Bubbies,* Suri, Rivie, Raykie, and Leilei,
Miraculous provider of all _____.
Please bless me with _____.
Please help me to _____.
Please save me from _____.
Please grant me _____.
And please bless the antisemities
To stay far far away from us!

Thanks again,
Ahhhhmen!

## LEONARD NIMOY'S PRAYER

Dear Ultimate Heebster in Heaven,

G-d of our *Zaydes,* Abbie, Izzy, and Jackie,
And G-d of our *Bubbies,* Suri, Rivie,
        Raykie, and Leilei,
Miraculous provider of all Star Trek royalties .
Please bless me with a new book idea that doesn't
        offend my rabbi .
Please help me to stop speaking Vulcan .
Please save me from William Shatner (he actually
        thinks he's Captain Kirk) .
Please grant me a role in which I am not recognized
        as "The-Name-I-Refuse-to-Pronounce"
        (Mr. Pointy Ears) .
And please bless the antisemities
To stay far far away from us!

Thanks again,
Ahhhhmen!

## BARBARA WALTERS' PRAYER

Dear Ultimate Heebster in Heaven,

G-d of our *Zaydes,* Abbie, Izzy, and Jackie,
And G-d of our *Bubbies,* Suri, Rivie,
        Raykie, and Leilei,
Miraculous provider of all Botox .
Please bless me with another seventy-five years
        on television .
Please help me transition to yet another
        unprecedented position of power for a woman .
Please save me from Rosie O'Donnell .
Please grant me an exclusive interview .
And please bless the antisemities
To stay far far away from us!

Thanks again,
Ahhhhmen!

## BARRY MANILOW'S PRAYER

Dear Ultimate Heebster in Heaven,

G-d of our *Zaydes,* Abbie, Izzy, and Jackie,
And G-d of our *Bubbies,* Suri, Rivie,
        Raykie, and Leilei,
Miraculous provider of all has-been Vegas bookings .
Please bless me with a never-ending supply
        of Rogaine .
Please help me to write the songs that make the
        whole world sing .
Please save me from the Fanilows .
Please grant me repeat appearances on American
        Idol .
And please bless the antisemities
To stay far far away from us!

Thanks again,
Ahhhhmen!

## MEL GIBSON'S PRAYER

Dear Ultimate Heebster in Heaven,

G-d of our *Zaydes,* Abbie, Izzy, and Jackie,
And G-d of our *Bubbies,* Suri, Rivie,
        Raykie, and Leilei,
Miraculous provider of all unpredictable
        Hollywood success .
Please bless me with The Passion II
        costarring Adam Sandler,
Please help me to keep my mouth shut during
        routine traffic stops .
Please save me from myself .
Please grant me a reprieve from South Park parody .
And please bless the antisemities
To stay far far away from us!

Thanks again,
Ahhhhmen!

# Code of Conduct

When you take your prayers to *shul*, certain behaviors are encouraged in and around the synagogue. Others are not.

| IT'S A GO-GO! | IT'S A NO-NO! |
|---|---|
| trudge through the snow | dress like a ho |
| ponytail holders | bare shoulders |
| sexy shawl | bags from the mall |
| gorgeous dress | hair a mess |
| funky skirt | drunken flirt |
| bare leg | port-a-keg |
| ask "Why?" | slimy guy |
| suit 'n' tie | open fly |
| kiss the Torah | speak *lashon hora* (gossip) |
| *Purim* mask | endless task |
| drink "to life!" | grope another's wife |
| dance the hora | trash Dr. Laura |
| daven real slow | inflate ego |
| humble heart | post-*cholent* fart |

---

### FYI: FOR THE YIDDISH IMPAIRED

*Cholent* is a beloved Sabbath stew. From the French for "hot slow," it is pronounced as almost one syllable with a /ch/ as in chair. It contains a smorgasbord in a pot: kidney, navy, lima, aduki, and/or garbanzo beans, potatoes, onion, garlic, spices—and sometimes barley, wheatberries, rice, carrots, yams, whole eggs in the shell, and/or soup mix—and enough paprika to feed a Hungarian village. *Fleish*-lovers add beef ribs known as *flanken* or stuffed *derma* called *kishke*. In Sephardic communities, *cholent* is *chamin* (with a /ch/ as in Bach), from the Hebrew for "hot that will rest"/*chamin sh'yalin*. In Berkeley, *cholent* is meat-free. Every Thursday night in NYC's East Village, it is a namesake event for neo-*Hasidim,* former *Hasidim,* future *Hasidim,* and all their friends. It's also a pre-*Shabbos* yeshiva tradition where all-night study is fueled by a big pot o' *cho'*.

# Cholent 101

*Cholent* is the Cinderella of Jewish foods.

On Shabbat, it is the belle of the ball. Once the party's over, it's below a scullery rat.

By Saturday night, leftover *cholent* has all the appeal of mud.

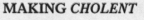

## MAKING *CHOLENT*

To make your very own *cho'*, fill an electric slow cooker with raw ingredients
on Friday morning. Cover completely with water. Plug in and turn to low.
Leave it on overnight and throughout *Shabbat*. Pray for the best.

### *SHABBAT* jTUNE: THAT OTHER JEWISH CUT (OF BEEF!)*

What do we serve on every occasion?
What does *Bubbie* make just right?
What kind of beef spells "celebration"?
Everyone knows it's brisket.
And brisket is quick to make.
Just cover with foil and bake.
Make extra, for goodness sake.
It freezes so well. You can hardly tell.
What makes a vegan Heeb think twice?
What cut of cow is a worth a life?
What really was that manna in the desert?
Everyone knows it's brisket!

*Sung to that '70s tune, "Windy"

# A KABAL (LAH LAH) OF WINNERS

## THE ENVELOPE, PLEASE . . .

In the category of **The *Shul* Where You Can Feel the Grit Between Your Toes**, the winner is the historic St. Thomas Sand Floor Synagogue of the Virgin Islands.

In the category of **The *Shul* You Can Attend in Flip-Flops, Board Shorts, and Hawaiian Shirts**, the winner is the "it's all good" Jewish Congregation of Maui.

In the category of **Most Delicious *Kiddush,*** we have a tie. The winners are the Manhattan Sephardic Congregation and the Edmund J. Safra Synagogue, both on the Upper East Side, New York City.

In the category of **Friday Night TransDance-Boogie-Drum Circle-Davening-Rave**, we have a three-way tie. The winners are the Neo-Hasidic Ortho-Hippydox Carlebach *Shul* of the Upper West Side, New York City;

the unaffiliated B'nai Jeshurun, also of the Upper West Side; and the not-so conservative Conservative Friday Night Live at Sinai Temple of Los Angeles.

In the category of **You'd Swear There's a Church Choir in There Somewhere**, the winner is the egalitarian Orthodox *shul,* Shira Hadasha of Jerusalem.

In the category of **The First Jews to Reach America**, the winners are the Sephardim.

In the category of **The *Shul* Visited by Honorary Heebster George Washington (on Horseback)**, the winner is the Touro Synagogue of Newport, Rhode Island.

In the category of **The Oldest African-American *Shul*** in the USA, the winner is the Commandment Keepers of Harlem, founded in 1919.

In the category of **The Phat-est** *Shul* **Ever,** the winner is the Hasidic Belz Synagogue of Jerusalem, with a whopping six thousand seats.

In the category of **The Most Un-Boorish Moorish** *Shul,* the winner is the Central Synagogue of Midtown Manhattan.

In the category of **The** *Shul* **Between a Rock and a Hard Place,** the winner is the "I Will Survive" Hurva Synagogue of Jerusalem.

In the category of **The Fantastic Four,** the winners are

1. **South of the Equator,** The Great Synagogue of Sydney, Australia;
2. **White Nights** *Shabbos,* The *Shul* in the Park, Giffnock, Scotland;
3. **Grooving a Latin Beat,** The Great Synagogue of Santiago, Chile; and
4. **In Top Hats and Lace Collars,** Congregation Shearith Israel, the Spanish and Portugese Synagogue of the Upper West Side, New York City.

In the category of **The** *Shul* **That Sold Treasures to Save Lives,** the winner is the Great Synagogue of Danzig, Poland, of blessed memory.

In the category of **The Most Beloved Un-**Shul **Ever,** the winner is the Western Wall of the Centre of the Jewniverse, Jerusalem.

In the category of the **Shebrew Who Single-Handedly Turned** *Shul* **into Summer Camp,** the winner is singer/songwriter Debbie Friedman.

In the category of the **Heebro Who Single-Handedly Turned Rock Concerts into** *Shul,* the winner is Rabbi Shlomo Carlebach, of blessed memory.

In the category of **Most Likely Place to Spot Sandra Bernhard with a Shopping Bag,** the winner is the Kabbalah Centre of Manhattan.

In the category of **Most Likely Place to Spy Babs in a Bathing Suit,** the winner is Two Bunch Palms Resort & Spa of Desert Hot Springs, California.

# Congregation Beth Everywhere

Tired of your same ol' Beth Israel? Try another one two states over!

| NAME | LOCATION | URL | ORIENTATION |
|---|---|---|---|
| Congregation Beth Israel | Gadsden, Alabama | bethisrael congregation.org | Reform |
| Congregation Beth Israel | Chico, California | cbichico.org | Non-denominational |
| Congregation Beth Israel Beth Aaron | Quebec, Canada | shul.org | Orthodox |
| Congregation Beth Israel Abraham Voliner | Overland Park, Kansas | biav.org | Orthodox |
| Congregation Beth Israel | New Orleans, Louisiana | ou.org/network/*shuls*/bino.htm | Orthodox |
| Congregation Beth Israel | Bangor, Maine | cbisrael.org | Conservative |
| Congregation Beth Israel | North Adams Massachusetts, aka the Berkshires | cbi.homestead.com | Reform |
| Congregation Beth Israel | Onset, Massachusetts aka Cape Cod | capecod*shul*.org | Orthodox |
| Congregation Beth Israel | Ann Arbor, Michigan | bethisrael-aa.org | Conservative |
| Beth Israel Synagogue | Asheville, North Carolina | bethisraelnc.org | Conservative |
| Congregation Beth Israel | Portland, Oregon | bethisrael-pdx.org | Reform |
| Congregation Beth Israel | Greenville, South Carolina | bethisraelsc.org | Reform |
| Congregation Beth Israel | Colleyville, Texas | congregation bethisrael.org | Conservative |
| Congregation Beth Israel | Milwaukee, Wisconsin | cbimilwaukee.org | Conservative |

# The Very First Superhero

Every Heebster knows the very first human being starring in the *Tanach* was Adam aka *Adam HaRishon*. Not only was Adam the First the world's first human being, he was also the world's first superhero. The Talmud teaches that *Adam HaRishon* (ha-REE-shown) had rad spiritual powers. When he stood up, he reached from earth to heaven. When he lay down, he stretched from east to west. His x-ray vision allowed him to see straight through one end of the globe to the other. His soul knew the entire world and his consciousness encompassed the universe. And yet, G-d made Adam humble as the earth underneath his feet. As every Hebrew speaker knows, Adam means just that: dirt.

*Kabba Lah Lah* teaches that in the natural order of the universe, something created is superior to the ingredients that made it. A *knish,* for example, is superior to the potato it's stuffed with. And so, Adam was superior to the dust he was made of. As great as Adam was, Eve was all dat! She gets a bad rap for that *farkakte* fruit salad story. But she was actually superior to the rib and whom it came from. Now you know why, in the battle of Shebrew vs Hebrew, she wins every time!

---

### FYI: FOR THE YIDDISH IMPAIRED

The preferred term for the Bible among Yidden is, of course, the Jewish nomenclature, *Tanach,* which rhymes with Bach. Heebsters do not use the term Old Testament. That implies a New Testament. For the People of the Book, there is no New Testament. There is only *Tanach.*

# The Power of Prayer

If you really wanna be a *Kabba Lah Lah*-ist, it's essential to know how to pray along nicely with others. At least a *bissel*. And if you're going to learn just one prayer, this is the one. And then, G-d forbid, if you're ever martyred, now you'll know your last words. (These are them.)

Jewish doesn't have a mantra. It has what Rabbi David Aaron calls the *Sh'mantra*. As the Good Book says,

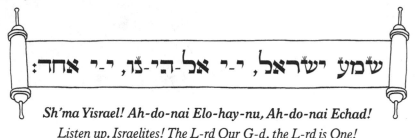

*Sh'ma Yisrael! Ah-do-nai Elo-hay-nu, Ah-do-nai Echad!*
*Listen up, Israelites! The L-rd Our G-d, the L-rd is One!*

Memorize these words and you've got game. The best part is, when everyone is in *shul* saying the *Sh'mantra,* they close their eyes. So no one will know if you're faking!

The *Sh'mantra* is all about recognizing G-d's Oneness. It doesn't just mean there is only one G-d. It also means *all is G-d.* We are all "One" together, Creator and creation. To understand the deep mystical significance of this teaching, call Madonna.

Right after Jews say the *Sh'mantra,* they whisper this line:

Heebsters form the Hebrew letter *shin,* which also stands for G-d, when saying the *Shemantra.*

*Baruch Shem Kavod malchuto l'olam va'ed.*
*Blessed is the Glorious Name of G-d's Kingdom forever more.*

And's that it . . . kind of. Actually, there's another paragraph after that. And then another. And another. Frankly, you could go on for days, with mini bathroom breaks, because that's the one place Jews do not pray. (Now would be the right time to get this book out of there.)

Even the Thing knows the *Shemantra:*

Note: When a *Yid* of a certain generation exclaims, *"Sh'ma Yisrael,"* this may not, in fact, be a dying moment. It may just mean they're *plotzing.*

# Four Play the Kabba Way

*Kabba Lah Lah* teaches that there are four worlds: Emanation, Creation, Formation, and Action. As mere mortals, the latter two are our address. Angels, however, live in the 'hood of Emanation. Just like in an ol' skool Jimmy Stewart movie, whenever you do a good deed, you create a new angel.

Certain angels aka *cherubim* and *seraphim* have existed since the beginning of time. Even in English, they roll with their Hebrew names. Naturally, they come from us. What else is new?

Calling on angels is a Jewish bedtime custom.

**Step one:** Say the *Sh'mantra.*

**Step two:** Rap a request for Divine protection of the *Yiddishe kopf* from the Original Fantastic Four aka the Angels of Presence.

**Step three:** *Geh shluffen. Lila tov.* Nighty night.

**Sound off!**
Michael is G-d's main messenger.
Gabriel is the angel of fire.
Raphael is the healing angel.
Uriel is the angel of perfect light.

---

**The traditional Heebster bedtime ritual rap:**
May Michael be at my right.
Gabriel at my left.
Uriel before me.
Raphael behind me.
And Shechinat El [G-d's Presence] above my head.

# Supernal Posse

Whenever a "who ya gonna call" Act of G-d Moment arises, turn to the Angel Yellow Pages. As Enoch knew all too well in his namesake *Book 3,* the forces of nature boast their own special forces.

Baradiel is the angel of hail.

Baraquiel is the angel of lightning.

Galgalliel covers the orb of the sun.

Opanniel covers the disk of the moon.

Kokabriel is on stars, Lailiel on night, and Shimshiel on day.

Matariel knows from rain and Ra'amiel from thunder.

Ra'asiel delivers earthquakes.

Rahatiel, constellations.

Ruhiel brings wind.

And Shalgiel brings snow angel.

Za'amiel stirs up whirlwinds and Za'apiel, hurricanes.

Zi'iel sets tremors in motion and Ziquiel, comets.

# Match the Rabbi Round *Alef:* Heebsters

1.  **The Surfing Rabbi**
2.  **The Comic Book Rabbi**
3.  **The *Simple Wisdom* Rabbi**
4.  **The First Woman Orthodox Rabbi***
5.  **The Second****
6.  **The Third*****
7.  **The Gonzo Rabbi**
8.  **The Gefilte Phish Rabbi**
9.  **The Jewlicious Rabbi**
10. **Transvestite Rebbetzin**
11. **Jerry's Third Cousin**
12. **The Rainbow Rabbi**
13. **The Grateful *Yid***
14. **Comforts the Spiritually Bankrupt**

a.  Rabbi Yonah
b.  Alexander Seinfeld
c.  Hadassah Gross
d.  Simcha Weinstein
e.  Haviva Ner-David
f.  Reb Mimi Feigelson
g.  Irwin Kula
h.  Niles Goldstein
i.  Rav Shmuel
j.  Regina Jones
k.  Nachum Shifrin
l.  Menachem Creditor
m.  Yosef Langer
n.  Chaim Friedman-Mahgel

*Answers:* 1. k, 2. d, 3. g, 4. j, 5. f, 6. e, 7. h, 8. i, 9. a, 10. c, 11. b, 12. n, 13. m, 14. l.

*Some say no such thing as an Orthodox woman rabbi can exist.

**Others disagree.

***And yet, they still debate who placed first, second, and third!

**THE KLUGGEREBBIE SAYS**

The Eskimo practice of naming every type of snow and the Hawaiian practice of naming every type of rain parallel the Jewish practice of naming every aspect of G-d. Where do you think they got it from anyway?

# Name That G-d

*Hashem,* Hebrew for "The Name," serves as a mere approximation of G-d's true essence. That's because The Ultimate Heebster defies all human comprehension. According to Jewish tradition, the Original Masked Crusader actually has seventy-two different names, creating an excellent candidate for multiple personality disorder.

One of Da Boss's names gets more play than any other, the Tetragrammaton aka the four-letter *Yud-Hay-Vav-Hay.* Even this name is a paradox. No one except the ancient High Priest, the *Kohen Gadol,* who pronounced this name on *Yom Kippur* when the Temple stood in Jerusalem, actually uttered the Holiest of Heebster Honorifics. And now, so many years have passed without any living Heeb saying it that every one has forgotten how.

Check it out: G-d has seventy-two names. G-d has a whole bunch of the Coolest Aliases. G-d even has abbreviations like the single Hebrew letter that represents this chapter. And yet, the True Name of G-d may never be said. And that makes the Ineffable Name truly, well, you know, ineffable.

Ready for the beat of more conundrums? The true nature of the Great Heebster in Heaven can never fully be understood. But that's a good thing! Who ever wanted a G-d you fully understood? If you already understood G-d, you would simply be G-d. And then there would be no need to question authority, your existence, or anything else for that matter. And if that were true, you could hardly call yourself Jewish. And what would be the fun of that?

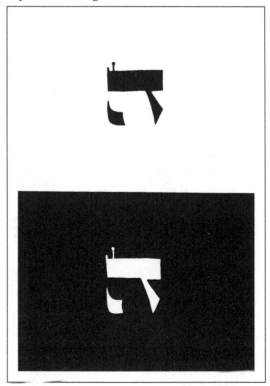

# Jew-It-Yourself G-d Knowledge

In just one quick at-home experiment, you can get a better idea of G-d. Go take a look in the mirror. Take a good, hard look. Done?

Alrighty, then. This is what G-d isn't.

Despite all flattering notions of our physical selves, we are only *spiritually* created in the image of G-d.

G-d has no eyes. But G-d can still see. G-d has no ears. But G-d can still hear. G-d has no hands. But G-d can still touch. If you're completely confused, you're on the right track!

G-d is beyond physical form, beyond everything you've ever understood. Yes, you. Even you.

Question: So if G-d doesn't have eyes, then how can G-d see?
   The only way to answer is, of course, the Jewish way: with another question.
Answer: The One Who gives eyes shouldn't see?

Question: But how can G-d hear?
Answer: The One Who gives ears shouldn't hear?

Question: But how can G-d touch?
Answer: The One Who gives hands shouldn't touch?

**Note:** There are three kinds of Jews when it comes to math. Those who understand and those who don't.

# Missionaries, Shmissionaries!

| THEY SAY | WE SAY |
|---|---|
| Come to church. | Cousin Lurch! |
| Climb the spire. | Uncle Meir! |
| On the altar | Hi, I'm Walter. |
| Try Christ. | No dice! |
| Seek truth! | Dr. Ruth! |
| G-d's son | Not the only one! |
| Died for sins | Love them Twins! |
| It's true. | Not for a Hebrew! |
| Hail Mary | Mail, Harry! |
| Church decree | Makes us flee! |
| Sign of the cross | Get lost! |
| Jew for J? | No way! |
| Must repent! | What's that, lint? |
| Celibate | Doesn't fit! |
| St. James? | *Dreidl* games! |
| Burn in hell! | Ya mean Mel?* |
| Gospel binds | Duncan Hines |
| Accept our faith.? | It's *trayfe!* |
| Shrimp cocktail? | A dirty pail. |
| Calamari squid? | Not for a *Yid*! |
| Quiche Lorraine? | What a pain … |
| Whaddya say, sir? | I keep kosher. |
| Proselytes? | *Shabbos* lights. |
| I give up! | Tofu Pup? |
| Why, thank you. | It's best with Jew Glue! |
| You actually are kinda nice. | I do descend from Mauschwitz Mice. |
| *Oy, gevalt!* Vaht can I do? | Cheer up, brotha. Come home, Jew. |

\* Gibson?

# Kabba Lah Lah For Non-Dummies

The People of the Book have a lesser known but equally fabulous stature as the People of the Numbers. This of course dates back millennia, to the Holiest of Heebsters' pastime of assigning our letters numerical value, as spelled out in our beloved tome of ancient wisdom, the Talmud.

According to our sage Sages, Da Rabbis, G-d created the world with Ten Utterances. And G-d keeps the world existing by speaking it into existence every split second. In contrast to the Original Motivational Speaker Upstairs and Everywhere, each individual Jew is allotted a certain number of spoken words in life. And when they're up, so to speak, so is your number.

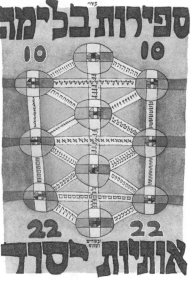

The *Kabba* Creation Story of the Ten Utterances explains the Tribe's widely acknowledged practice of supplying the world with great scientists, economists, mathematical minds, and bargain shoppers. This knack for numbers is one of the many gifts G-d sealed into every Heebster's spiritual DNA. What will you do with it?

When it comes to numbers, Jews play favorites. No. 1, of course, is Numero Uno. The Original One and Only One is G-d. Continuing in the It-All-Comes-from-Us

category . . . G-d, however, loves another: the seven days of the week, the ancient Seven Prophetesses, Lucky Number Seven. Yep, seven is G-d's personal fav.

Count up every one of your fingers and, of course, you get 10: the Ten Commandments, the Ten Utterances, ten Jews make a minyan. Add two for the *bat mitzvah,* 12, and one more for the *bar.* As it "happens," 13 equals the numeric equivalent of the Hebrew word for love, *ahava.* When two human beings come together in love, they reflect Divinity. That's because 13 + 13 = 26. And it just so "happens" that 26 also equals the numerical value for the Tetragrammaton, G-d's name.

Between 13 and 26 is the all-important 18. Elvis, taxi drivers, and *Kabba Lah Lah*-ists everywhere *schlep* a *chai* around their necks because the Hebrew word for life represents the numerical value of 18. That's why Heebsters give charity in multiples of 18.

Not to be outdone is the number 40. It took forty days and nights for the earth to renew itself during the flood. Forty years of wandering in the wilderness for the Children of Israel to transform from slaves into a free nation. Forty days of Moshe on

Mount Sinai for Hashem to transform the *Torah* from a blueprint for the creation of the world into a *Torah* humans could at least try to understand. Like you. Right now. Totally. Well, kinda. Maybe. Just a little bit.

In *Gematria* aka Jewish numerology, forty represents birth, rebirth, and transformation. Remember that when you score a double score! Kinda makes going gray a touch better now, doesn't it? Go on, nod your head now. Uh huh, just like that. Don't worry, nobody is noticing.

Fasten your seat belts and zoom forward now to 613, the total number of commandments in the *Torah*. Now add each digit together, 6 + 1 + 3, and you get 10, a minyan. Then add the 1 and the 0 together and, of course, you get 1. And you're right back exactly where we started. Now that's *Kabba Lah Lah* traction in action. Just as it all begins, so, too, does it end: with One.

### THE KLUGGEREBBIE SAYS

Traditionally, a person must turn forty in order to study *Kabbalah*. To study *Kabba Lah Lah*, a person need only be fourteen. Cancel that. Make it four and a half.

# Mystical Meal

Ten out of ten *minyan*s agree, the more you cultivate your *Kabba,* the more conscious you become. To test this theory, select a fabulous number. Then flip through a Jewish cookbook on pages that are multiples of this number. Miraculously, *Kabba* automatically calculates the perfect menu, just as if the Ultimate Chef planned it all ahead of time!

---

*Kabba*-Listic Digit: 13

**Mystical Theme:** Love

**Cookbook:** *Spice and Spirit* from Chabad Lubavitch Women

**Results:** A lovely dairy meal, perfect for a *Tu B'Av* romantic dinner for two.

13 x 4 = page 52: Traditional Challah

13 x 6 = page 78: Vegetable Frittata

13 x 8 = page 104: Eggplant Soufflé and Cheese Soufflé

13 x 10 = page 130: Summer Fruit Soup

13 x 12 = page 156: Sweet-and-Sour Whitefish

13 x 32 = page 416: Cream Puffs

13 x 36 = page 468: Praline Ice Cream

---

# The Good, the Bad, and the Average

Each month, as every *Kabba Lah Lah*-ist knows, there are good days and days a little less than good. (This is a very Jewish way of saying bad.) These days come to us, naturally, from, where else? The Talmud! Get ready, get set, get your calendars. Each month, the very best day is aka *Rosh Chodesh* with a /ch/ as in Bach. After *Rosh Chodesh,* the New Moon, the twenty-seventh of the month is the next best day. So is the eleventh. This is the time to jDate, premier your new disk on jTunes, get preggers, incorporate, assume the presidency ...

Consider yourself warned. The less than good days each month are the 3rd, 5th, 7th, 13th, 15th, 17th, 21st, 24th, and 25th. All other days are average—not a very Heebster thing to be.

Note: This is deep *Kabba Lah Lah.* It does not work on a *goyish* schedule. The proof is in the (noodle) pudding. To test this theory, snag a free Heebster calendar from the local Jewish Home for the Aged, Chabad, kosher butcher, or, if you're desperate, the mortuary. Then mark your calendar and watch the *Kabba Lah Lah* reveal itself in full glory.

# Lamed Vavniks

Since the beginning of creation, G-d has relied on thirty-six Heebsters to keep the place running. These righteous folk are compassionate spiritual giants, *Torah* scholars, dedicated mommys, and other selfless wonders. The Hebrew letters that represent the number thirty-six are *lamed* and *vav.* So naturally, these Holy Heebs are called the *Lamed-Vavniks.* The thing is, only the Ultimate *Lamed-Vavnik* in Heaven knows who they are. They don't even know who they are. For all you know, it could be you!

# The Real Secret

As the Baal Shem Tov taught, "Think good and it will be good." The power of positive thinking ... Is it no surprise? It *aaaaall* comes from us!

# Birthmarks

According to Jewish tradition, every Heebster already knows *Kabba Lah Lah,* all of it, every single word. Even if you've felt like the biggest ignoramus reading this chapter, deep down inside, you're actually a *Torah* genius! That's because the *Torah* is already in you. The Talmudic *Tractate Niddah 30b* explains that angelic educational emissaries make house visits to every junior cool Jew inside his or her mother's womb.

Just like Baby You, these angels make themselves at home. And while you leisurely suck your thumb and play footsie amongst yourself, these generous souls teach you the entire *Torah.* It's like nine months of In-Utero Yeshiva—all expenses paid!

Right before graduation, one angel comes close, turns to Baby You and says, "Don't be an evil person, a *rasha.* Be a *tzaddik,* a righteous person!" Then the angel touches your face in the little space between the lips and the nose, leaving a little groove above your mouth called the philtrum—among Heebsters this is aka the *gephiltrum.* And with that one touch, you forget all the *Torah* you just spent nine months learning.

It sounds like one giant rip-off but the truth is the spiritual awareness you cultivated remains imprinted deep inside your *Yiddishe neshama.* To retrieve it again from your Jewish soul, all you have to do is read this book 613 times.

---

### FYI: FOR THE YIDDISH IMPAIRED

Moshe Rabbenu, the greatest Yid who ever lived, actually lived to 120. Naturally, the happiest *Kabba Lah Lah* birthday wish is "May you live to 120!" To which an informed Heebster responds, "To 100, like 20!"

---

# The Holy Tongue

Despite its mystical appearance, you don't have to be a Jewru to read Hebrew. Besides you already learned it in the womb!

Do yuo nurdetsnad tihs? Fi yuo do, tehn yuo hvae a bairn. And taht maens yuo cna eailsy laern Hberew! In fact, operators are standing by right now at 1-800-44-HEBRE(W).

Researchers say the hmuan mnid deos not raed ervey lteter by istlef. It raeds ecah wrod as a wlohe. So who ceras how yuo pslel it, in English or Hebrew?

Even fi you cna not raed this so well, yuo can still learn to master the Holy Tongue. Good Lcuk! Or as they say in the Holy Land, *Hatzlacha raba!*

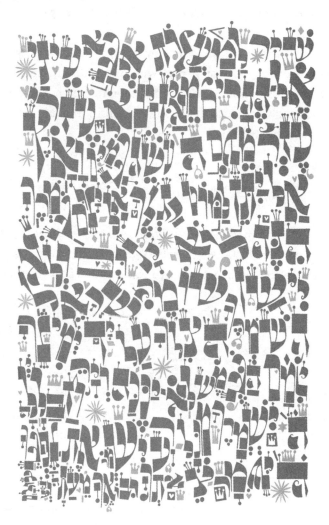

# A Minyan of Heebster Hobbies

1. **Feeding:** your spouse, your kids, your neighbors, your fellow *shul* members, your chocolate cravings, the homeless, Africa
2. **Collecting:** stamps, coins, baseball cards, comics, university degrees, real estate, family history, yarmulkes from weddings, *bar mitzvahs,* and synagogues you'll never visit again
3. **Getting:** a deal, published, on the best-sellers list, on NPR, on *Oprah,* the word out, great seats
4. **Shopping:** especially on Orchard Street, at factory outlets, and going-out-of-business sales
5. **Creating:** new professions, theories, cures, wealth, social change, entertainment, films, art, music, Web sites, JewTube videos
6. **Mocking:** dweeby dating services, certain celebrities, the *goyim,* our frenemies, anti-semites, ourselves
7. **Protesting:** unfair wages, discrimination, injustice, awkward satin yarmulkes
8. **Practicing:** law, medicine, psychiatry, your swing, your pitch, making the ideal *matzah* ball
9. **Praying:** in *shul,* at bedsides, on Israeli buses, in ashrams and meditation centers worldwide, that this diet will finally work, that there's still one left in your size
10. **Growing:** corn, spiritually, beards

# Match the Rabbi Round Bet: Star Search

In the Talmudic book of wisdom, *Ethics of the Fathers,* the ancient sages suggest every person on the planet find his or her own rabbi. That's right. Your very own *Kabba*-ist. Every single one of these celebrities has been spotted hanging with a Rav-a-rooni. Can you make the right match?

1. **Kirk Douglas**
2. **Madonna**
3. **Martin Luther King Jr.**
4. **David Mamet**
5. **Perry Peretz Farrell**
6. **Reverend Al Sharpton**
7. **Bart Simpson**

a. Rabbi Yosef Langer
b. Rabbi Abraham Joshua Heschel
c. Rabbi Shaul Youdkevitch
d. Rabbi Shmuely Boteach
e. Rabbi Mordechai Finley
f. Rabbi David Aaron
g. Rabbi Hyman Krustofski

*Answers:* 1. f, 2. c, 3. b—They marched together for civil rights!, 4. e, 5. a, 6. d, 7. g

# The Beardy Bunch

Everybody loves a good beard. Experiment with these beardoos to reveal the hidden expression of your face.

1. **WEST BANK STYLE AKA ZZ TOP**
   Let my people grow!

2. **TORAH SCROLLED**
   A Hasidic favorite, mystical secrets hidden within.

3. **DEARLY DEPARTED**
   Like Abraham and Lot, you go left. I go right.

4. **SURVIVOR**
   *Baruch Hashem,* the oven didn't get the whole thing.

5. **THE WEAVE**
   A physical manifestation of spiritual integration.

6. **THE BABA SKINNY**
   Sparse is *Kabba Lah Lah*-istic. (Not really, but it's all I can grow.)

7. **THE GOATEE**
   I'm cool. I make films. Oh yeah, and I'm bald.

8. **YESHIVISH**
   Anal retentive, who me?

9. **ORTHO SHAVE**
   Razors are, in fact, permissible, but only the lousy electric ones.

# The Red String

The popular Hollywood red string bracelet is aka a *bendl* in Yiddish. Despite the practices in Tinsel Town, the red string is actually a modest traditional thank you from beggars in exchange for a few coins of charity. It's "sold" widely near the Western Wall in Jerusalem or at the grave of Rachel the Matriarch. It may cost as little as a quarter. The thing is the red string is generally considered a way to ward off the evil eye, the *ayin hara*. Among *Kabba*-ists, it also has other secret meanings. Even more so for airhead celebs . . .

### WHAT THE RED STRING REALLY MEANS

**Note to self:** Buy horseradish. With beets!

**Note from mom:** Remember, red zones mean parking tickets!

**Note to stylist:** Red is my natural hair color. I'm just having a
    blonde moment.

**Note from dentist:** Floss or else!

**Note to jDate:** Bright red temper.

**Note to public:** Stop. This one is dangerous.

# When Do You Swing a Chicken Over Your Head?

Yidden know how to turn everything into a party, transforming even a solemn holiday into a squawking carnival for the birds. Literally. Believe it or not, slinging a feathered friend overhead is a traditional *Yom Kippur* practice aka *shlogen kapores*.

Once a year, before the onset of the holiday, pious Jews recite a prayer asking the Great Cashier on High to accept the chicken as payment for sins. A kosher butcher slaughters the chicken and donates it to feed the poor. Now, don't get all PETA ballistic. The squeamish amongst us reenact the same procedure with clean hard cash. Whip out a twenty, swirl it around your head, and you're good to go!

# Blessing-O-Meter

There are hundreds upon hundreds of blessings to recite "in Jewish." Do you know which *brachot* actually exist? True or False:

A *bracha* when the Yankees win the Subway Series.

A *bracha* when your favorite quarterback fumbles.

A *bracha* when a loved one passes away.

A *bracha* when you wear new Manolos scored from a thrift store.

A *bracha* when you meet a Noble Prize winner.

A *bracha* when thunder rattles *Bubbie's* dentures.

A *bracha* when you stand in a place where your people experienced a miracle.

A *bracha* when lightning sets a tree aflame.

A *bracha* after you pish.

A *bracha* when you reunite with your long lost partner-in-crime from Yeshiva of Flatbush.

A *bracha* when you see a double rainbow.

A *bracha* when Israeli captives are finally freed.

A *bracha* when you meet a blow-your-mind rebbe.

A *bracha* when you see the first blossoms of spring.

A *bracha* when you eat a new fruit each *Rosh HaShanah*.

A *bracha* when you witness a total lunar eclipse (and land a first kiss).

A *bracha* when you get a whiff of sea air up close and personal for the first time in thirty days.

A *bracha* when you see a whale breach.

A *bracha* when you survive a plane crash.

A *bracha* when you first step foot in Israel.

A *bracha* after forty hours of childbirth.

A *bracha* before *and* after a glass of wine.

A *bracha* for suddenly cashing in what you thought was a worthless comic book collection.

A *bracha* when Seinfeld snagged the last marble rye from that old lady at Schnitzer's.

*Answers:* "In Jewish," there truly is a blessing for almost everything, except the Yankees winning, a quarterback fumbling, making a mint on comics, and a Seinfeld (or any other) shortage on rye.

# Hierarchy of Holiness

According to the ancient Jewish sages, there is a spark of holiness in everything.
In the Hierarchy of Holiness,
> the holy of holies is holier than just the holy.

*Shabbat* is holy. But *Yom Kippur* is
> holier. It has to be.
> It's like taking your soul to the
> spiritual dry cleaners, wash-
> ing away the *shmutz* from the
> whole year.

Everyday things also contain holi-
> ness, some more than others.

*In Jewish,* a bee,
> which produces honey,
> is holier than a mosquito,
> which produces inflammation.

A goat is holier than a bee
> because it provides milk, even
> if it's kinda stinky.

A cow is holier than a goat
> because it provides a lot more
> cuts of kosher meat
> (besides, who ever wanted to eat a goat?!).

There is nothing but G-d!
**DEVARIM 4:35**

An excellent brisket is holier than an entire cow,
> parts of which are not kosher, including its rump (roast).

A Heebster is holier than even the most expensive cut of brisket
> because every Heebster can *shteig* to spiritual greatness.

*In Jewish,* that's actually the whole purpose of the brisket.

Even the most evil person on the planet is holier than the finest brisket ever
> because deep inside even the most evil person, a speck of his or her soul remains pure
> no matter how much spiritual $#*! they pile on top of it.

And that pristine pure soul—available in pint, quart, and other quantities—
> is known as the beloved *Pintele Yid.*

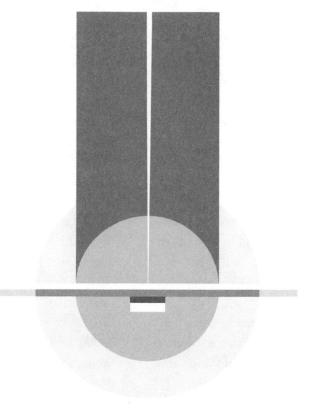

# Divine Providence

Spiritual types call it synchronicity. Shrinkies call it meaningful coincidence. Hippies call it G-d Energy. And Heebsters call it *Hashgacha Pratit*. How do you know when you're experiencing Divine Providence? You decide!

**ALEF**  You cruise into Loehmann's. The skirt you've been longing for all winter is finally on sale. Correction: it's on clearance. Plus you've got a discount coupon. Oh and look, there's only one left. And it's in your size! Is this Divine Providence or just luck?

**BET**  You're riding the bus in downtown Jerusalem on that free trip you won online, when you suddenly spot that crabby bunkmate who short-sheeted you at summer camp. Wow, he's still shorter than the top bunk. Is this Divine Providence or just a typical Israel experience where you eventually run into everyone from your past?

**GIMEL**  You're struggling to come up with a plotline for your new TV sitcom pilot when you watch "The Itche Kadoozy Show" at chabad.org. The swimming gefilte fish who keeps losing his carrot triggers the perfect idea. Is this Divine Providence or just another one of those joyously freaky things that keep happening to you since you've been studying *Kabba Lah Lah*?!

# Jewish Pipe Dreams

*Kabba Lah Lah*-ists believe in miracles. One day, in the not-too-distant future . . .

- Jew, Jewer, Jewisht will enter common parlance.
- gefilte fish will make your breath fragrant.
- chopped liver, *gribenes,* and *shmaltz* will lower cholesterol.
- *tsexy tsnius*\* will enter common parlance.
- dweeby *shtetl* names will deliver high swoonability. Ephraim will be hot. (But Osnat and Dudu may be forever doomed.)
- rhinoplasty will enlarge miniature noses.
- Da Fringe, or another professional athlete with a potentially Jewish-sounding name, will refuse to play on *Shabbos.*
- IBS will once again stand for Isaac Bashevis Singer instead of Irritable Bowel Syndrome.
- Jewish day school tuitions will drop below the per capita income of Wyoming.
- Bonnie Bell Lip Smackers will become available in Manischewitz Blackberry flavor.
- organic kosher foods will cost less because of their inherent spiritual integrity.
- Mallomars will convert to kosher.
- bumper stickers will read KOSHER KISSES TASTE BETTER.
- anti-Jewish graffiti and desecrations of cemeteries will be no more.
- Jewnited Airlines will take flight.
- terrorism insurance will become available.
- the need for terrorism insurance will disappear.
- NYC will host the Rabbi Trading Cards Convention.
- the female equivalent of Matisyahu will hit the airwaves.
- Super Fresh Kike and Jew Boy will be popular terms of endearment.
- the universal spelling of G-DASH-D will change to G-HEART-D.
- *achdut* and *ahava chinam*—unity and wanton love of Jewish breadren—will become a reality.
- the *Moshiach* (Yiddish for "messiah") will usher in a revolutionary peace that knows no boundaries.
- Jewish physicists will solve the mystery of the hole in the bagel.

---

\* *Tsnius* is "modest" in Yiddish. "*Tsnius* is tsexy" appears as a fantasy T-shirt slogan in *Yom Kippur a Go-Go,* a memoir by Heebster Matthue Roth.

# Light and Truth

Where did Jew haters ever come up with that story about Jews having horns? It all goes back to Michelangelo. An artistic genius for sure, but that *goy* didn't know a beam of mystical light from an antler. When Michelangelo was prepping for his sculpture of Moses, he relied on the Vulgate, the Latin translation of the Bible. In Exodus 34:29–35, the Torah explains that as Moses descended from Mt. Sinai, a remarkable brilliance emanated from his face. His encounter with the Divine had so uplifted him that he was sending forth "beams of light" aka *keren*. A great name for a Heebsterette, Keren translates to "ray, beam, or horn," depending on the context. Poor Michelangelo had only the Vulgate to go on, which rendered the phrase "horns of light." Michelangelo actually carved Moshe physical horns of marble protruding from his forehead, fueling the fires for future antisemites, who took the concept one giant devil-step further and gave us tails, too. Proof they're actually jealous? The Pope's formal wardrobe includes the "Mitre," a cloth crown with two horns!

## Recycle, Reuse, Reshmooze

*Sure, your* Yahrzeit *candles served their purpose with dignity. But why throw out a perfectly good glass?*

Fill with sand and a stick of sandalwood for a unique incense burner.
Serve giant shots of whiskey to remember the departed.
Fill to the brim with *Zaydie's* daily pill doses to keep him alive
    and well.
Do a *mitzvah:* soak his dentures overnight.
Substitute for cupcake and muffin tins.
Collect as a *Shavuos* set for mini sundae cups.
Display ingredients on your countertop and provide a running narrative as you host
    your very own (pretend) Jewish cooking show!
Line up nine glasses. Fill each with two inches of water and 1/4" extra virgin
    olive oil. Drop in a floating wick to create a *Chanukiah*—a *Chanukah* menorah.
    Add food coloring for a rainbow of flames!
Use a pair as neck bolts for a snowy Rabbi Frankenshtein.

# Hebrew Coat of Arms

Yale University adopted the Hebrew words for light and truth for its coat of arms back in 1722. *Urim* and *Thummim* (*oo-REEM* and *too-MEEM*) appear in Exodus 28:30 in the description of the breastplate of the high priest, the *Kohen Gadol*. He consulted the breastplate like an oracle on questions of national import. Commentators debate whether the *Urim* and *Thummim* were a) mystical divine names of G-d written on paper and placed inside the breastplate; b) actual or engraved stones set in the breastplate, names used in the *Kohen Gadol's* meditation; c) borders of the tribal territories; d) astrological signs or e) ancient Aramaic for "Call your mother."

# Vatican or Vati' Won't?

Way back when, that no-goodnik Roman Emperor Titus captured ancient treasures from the Temple in Jerusalem and *schlepped* them back to Rome. Sleuthing Heebster conspiracy theorists suspect they still remain in the Vatican!

How did this legend take root? During his lifetime, a rabbi known as Reb Raphel (1804–1894) reportedly befriended a pope. Together, the *kippa'd* pair explored the Vatican's archives where the rabbi identified sacred vessels stolen from the ancient Temple.

Is this tale fact or fiction? Does it even matter? Since when did the Vatican give anything back to Jews?! Vatican or Vati' won't?

# Every Last Bissel

If you haven't realized it yet, it *all* comes from us, even this:

The *shmo* says, "What's mine is mine and what's yours is yours."
The *schlepper* says, "Mine is yours and yours is mine."
The *rasha* says, "Mine is mine and yours is mine."
But the *shteiger* says, "Mine is yours and yours is yours."*

*Pirke Avot*, Chapter 5:13.

# Favorite Causes

Jews for Cheeses
Neil Tzedaka Fund
Shiksa Support Hotline
Kike-aholics Anonymous
Kosher Ham Radio Nation
Herring Preservation Society
Milk & Meat Friendship Circle
Mothers Against Unmarried Daughters
Animal Lovers for the Protection of *Shtreimls*

# Show G-d the Money!

Those silly socialites. What's all this *meshugass* about social climbing? Naturally, Heebsters know better. Should you chose to accept it, your Mission Is Possible is to gather the broken sparks of mystical energy to repair our world.

How do you do that? You strive for spiritual greatness! In Yiddish, you're either *shteiging,* climbing, or you're falling. There is no standing still.

There are lots of ways to start *shteiging.* The Ten Commandments are just ten. But we've got a whole slew of others!

Let's start with your pockets. "In Jewish," money is not evil. It is a vehicle for spiritual transformation. That's why, whether you have a little or a lot, you should give it away at a rate of 10 percent.

Counterintuitive but true. Giving away your moola to charity is a *mitzvah,* a commandment, that creates a spiritual vessel for you to receive more good. Not visible to the naked eye, but definitely there all right.

Test the theory yourself. In the it All-Comes-From-Us Category, the more you give, the more you get. Where else do you think they got it from?

# Fork It Over

When you've got a friend taking a long trip, a modest gesture is all it takes to evoke a little *Kabba.* With minute largesse, you can instantly transform your ordinary friends into righteous *shteiging* emissaries!

**Step one:** Get out your wallet.

**Step two:** Fork over a dollar. This is not a piddly contribution to their expenses. No, this is how you purchase spiritual traveler's insurance *and* make a vessel for yourself to receive more good *all-in-one!*

**Step three:** Give the dollar to your friend on the condition that he or she give it to charity after arriving at the destination. This intention activates the policy. If only health insurance were this easy!

**FINE PRINT:** With this special *Kabba* un-contract, your pal will be traveling with the best bodyguard of all: The Great Underwriter Upstairs. That's because anyone involved in a *mitzvah* automatically receives Divine protection—no matter where, no matter when!

When you're really down with the *mitzvah,* hand over a second greenback for the trip home. Now that's *shteiging!*

## THE KLUGGEREBBIE SAYS

You're carrying a Jewish star, a Magen David, around all the time. There's one on every dollar bill. Can you find it?*

# Jewish Origami

When the Heebsters purchase spiritual travelers' insurance for friends, they fold each buck just the right way to reveal a hidden *Kabba* message in every otherwise ordinary dollar bill.

Looking at the front of a dollar, imagine three lines running equidistant across the bill horizontally. Fold down the top third to cover up Da Prez. Now take the bottom third and fold it up.

Next, imagine three vertical lines dividing the bill into three equal parts. Remember right over left, love over discipline? Take the right third and fold it toward the center. Then take the left third and fold it toward the center, too. Tuck the left flap into the right flap and press it flat. Now turn the bill over to reveal the secret message that was there all along.**

---

\* Did you know? Thirteen stars form one big Star of David above the eagle on the back of every buck!

\*\* "In G-d We Trust: ONE."

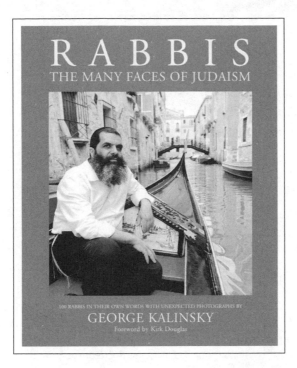

# Match the Rabbi Round *Gimel:* Alias

1. **Leprechaun Look-Alike Rabbi**
2. **Meaningful Life Rabbi**
3. **The Hineni Rebbetzin**
4. *Moshiach?*
5. **The First Renewal Rabbi**
6. **The Singing Rabbi**
7. **Civil Rights Rabbi**
8. **Rabbi of Reference**
9. **First Conservative Woman Rabbi**
10. **First Reconstructionist Rabbi**
11. **First Reform Woman Rabbi**
12. **Rabbi of 84th Street**
13. **Rabbi Yitz**

a. Esther Jungreis
b. Amy Eilberg
c. Joseph Telushkin
d. Simon Jacobson
e. Haskel Besser
f. Menachem Mendel Schneerson
g. Blu Greenberg
h. David Aaron
i. Mordechai Kaplan
j. Zalman Shalomi-Schachter
k. Abraham Joshua Heschel
l. Sally J. Priesand
m. Shlomo Carlebach

*Answers:* 1. h, 2. d, 3. a, 4. f, 5. j, 6. m, 7. k, 8. c, 9. b, 10. i, 11. l, 12. e, 13. g

# RABBI CHALLAH FAME

Elevation to the *Ranks of Righteousness* is an honor open only to the real *shteigers,* mountaineers of the highest spiritual altitude. As we say in Yiddish, *shep nachas.* Take pride in their accomplishments because where you look is where you go. It's *shteiging* time, baby. Be great. *Shteigate!*

**BEN BAG BAG** and **BEN HEH HEH** (around the time B.C.E. changed to C.E.). The first rabbinic rap duo, originators of "No pain, no gain." For real. *Pirke Avot,* Chapter 5:26.

**The RAMBAM** (1135–1204) **aka Rabbi Moshe ben Maimon aka Dr. Maimonides.** Used a leech like nobody's business. Rumor has it, he studied for his doctorate on the can.

**RASHI** (1040–1105) **aka Rabbi Shlomo Yitzhaki.** Unparalleled biblical commentator and vintner. His portrait is around here somewhere but his namesake wine bottle has much less facial hair.

**The BESHT** (1698–1760) **aka Baal Shem Tov aka Yisrael ben Eliezer aka Srulik.** The founder of Hasidism was repeatedly kicked out of *shul*s for excessive somersaulting. Seriously.

Yeshivas Etz Chaim *Shul* in Volozhin, 175 years ago

**REB CHAIM** (1749–1821) **aka Chaim of Volozhin aka the Volozhiner.** Established the Mother of All Yeshivas with thriving progeny from Amsterdam to Zimbabwe.

# aka THE OF BLESSED MEMORY GALLERY

**HOLY FIRE** (1889–1943) **aka Harav Kalonymus Kalman Shapira, the Grand Rabbi of Piazeczna aka the Children's Rebbe.** The only rebbe of congregants too young to constitute a minyan, he ran a secret *shul* inside the Warsaw Ghetto and preserved his Torah teachings by burying them in the ground.

**THE LUBAVITCHER REBBE** (1902–1994) **aka Rabbi Menachem Mendel Schneerson.** So in love with the Jewish people, he sent ambassadors to Kinshasa, Kishinev, and Kowloon. Never met him? Ask his posse to deposit your note at his grave: ohel@therebbe.org.

**THE BABA SALI** (1890–1984) **aka Rav Yisroel Abuchatzeira aka the Praying Father.** A miracle worker, his *hillula/yahrzeit* triggers waves of ecstatic parties across Israel.

**RABBI SHLOMO CARLEBACH** (1925–1994) pictured with his singing protégé, daughter Neshama. The "Highest of the High, the Deepest of the Deep" coined a new vocab for his Holy Hippilach at Haight-Ashbury's House of Love & Prayer. *Mamash a gevalt!* The most famous singing *Hasid* in the Pre-Matisyahu Era.

**Honorable Mention THE FACE** (1906–1995) **aka Emmanuel Levinas.** Born in Lithuania and drafted by the French, he began writing philosophy as a German POW during WWII. Indecipherable even in translation but quickly becoming *the* philosopher of Z Generation.

# Real Life Talmudic Riddles

**Rabbi Hillel says,** "If I am only for myself, who am I? If I am not for myself, who will be for me? And if not now, when?"

**Rabbi Elazar ben Azariah says,** "If there is no flour, there is no *Torah*. If there is no *Torah*, there is no flour."

**Rabbi Elazar HaKappar says,** "Against your will you were born. Against your will you live. Against your will you die."

**Reb Simcha Bunim says,** "A Jew walks through the world with a piece of paper in each pocket. One says, 'The whole world was created for me.' The other says, 'I am nothing but dust.'"

# UNITED COLORS OF BUBBELEH

Heebsters are so cool, everyone wants a piece of us. And, actually, everyone may *be* a piece of us. From east to west and north to south, we're everywhere—everywhere you want to be and every place your ancestors dreaded and fled. We're so diverse, we've got a handful of obscure languages to prove it. Who would have thunk the Tribe would have so much in common with other exotic peoples? And if that weren't surprising enough, growing numbers of our own confirmed breadren are returning to stake out their claims among the *beshtreimled*. Will you be among them?

---

### FYI: FOR THE YIDDISH IMPAIRED

*Beshtreimled* is a unique condition used to describe those individuals who adopt the lifestyle of Hasidic members of the Tribe. Started by the Besht three hundred years ago in the Ukraine, the term is based on the Hasidic headdress called a *shtreiml,* a black hat with a large, fur-covered brim. It's all the rage in Boro' Park.

---

**THE KLUGGEREBBIE SAYS**

Assimiliation is antithetical to the Heebster credo. Why disappear when you can have your herring and eat it, too?

# Jewish Diversity
# aka Where We've Been, Where We're At, Where We're Going

Just as there is herring in cream sauce and herring in wine sauce, the essence of each remains herring. So, too, are there Sephardic Jews, Ashkenazic Jews, Ethiopian Jews, and many, many other types of Jews. Each has its own distinct cuisine. But, as Dr. Paul Root Wolpe writes in *The Great Latke-Hamantaschen Debate,* in their deepest essence, each is also exactly the same in that they are all hungry. The rest is just sour cream and onions.

"GIVE ME YOUR TIRED, YOUR POOR   I LIFT MY LAMP

# Planet Jewish

Heebsters really do rule the world. At least with our tongues. Do you know which forms of *Yid*-speak actually exist? True or false:

1. Judezmo
2. Jewish Arabic
3. Jewish Yemenite
4. Jewish Italian
5. Jewish Persian
6. Jewish Neo-Aramaic
7. Jewish Malayalam
8. Jewish Crimean Tatar
9. Jewish Provençal
10. Jewish Portuguese
11. Jewish Slavic
12. Jewish Alsatian
13. Jewish Berber
14. Judeo-Georgian
15. Jewish Slavic/Canaan
16. Jewish Tajik/Bukharan
17. Jewish Tat
18. Karaite
19. Jewish Franyol

*Answers:* It's aaaaaall true! In fact, No. 1 is another name for Ladino aka Judeo-Spanish, No 5. is aka Dzhidi, No. 7 hails from Southern India, and No. 17 from the Caucasus. Accept it. We're everywhere!

"Give me your tired, your poor,
Your huddled masses yearning to breathe free,
The wretched refuse of your teeming shore.
Send these, the homeless, tempest-tost to me,
I lift my lamp beside the golden door!"

Sheebster Emma Lazarus penned the poem, "The New Colossus," that appears on the Statue of Liberty.

## Talkers Jew-nite!

Even Esperanto, the most widely spoken *planned* language, has Jewish roots. At the end of the nineteenth century, conflicts among Poles, Byelorussians, and Yiddish-speaking Jews in Bialystok saddened a nice Jewish boy named L. L. Zamenhof aka Ludovic Lazarus aka Ludwik Lejzer. When he was still a teenager, L. L. envisioned a universal language to unite people of diverse backgrounds.

How Heebster can you be? Next time you're doing your do, try asking in Esperanto, "Kie estas mia afro pick?"

## Lost Tribes: Who's Who

Back in the biblical day, Jacob and his two wives, Rachel and Leah, and his two concubines, Zilpah and Bilhah, had a total of ten sons. One of those boys, Joseph, also had two sons, Efraim and Menashe. All together, they formed a very important posse: the seeds of the Jewish people for eternity. The lineup reads like this: Gad, Reuven, Shimon, Asher, Levi, Dan, Zevulon, Issachar, Menashe, Efraim, Naftali, Judah, and Benjamin.

These days, most *Yiddelach* are presumed descendants of the tribes of Judah and Benjamin. The other ten dispersed throughout the world after the destruction of the First Temple, more than two thousand years ago. Inquiring minds want to know, how could they all just disappear? Doesn't this sound like some strange antisemitie *shmear* campaign? Really, now, could we be that bad with directions?

# Brotha From Anotha Motha

Since Jews don't proselytize, that makes us even cooler. Everybody is looking for a way in. Rastas say they're a lost tribe of Israel. Hawaiians do, too. Native Americans may descend from Judah. With amazing grace, the Black Hebrews, a group of African-Americans, claim they once were lost, but now are found. Ethnic peoples in India and Africa want in. Contemporary hippies known as the Rainbow Family believe they are the thirteenth Tribe. And the imperial family of Ethiopia claims it descends directly from King Solomon. There are so many theories about the lost tribes. Hey, maybe they're all true! Are we breadren?

| CATEGORY | HASIDIC JEW | RASTA | NATIVE AMERICANS | HIPPIE |
|---|---|---|---|---|
| Source of Life | Hashem | Jah Rastafari | Great Spirit | G-ddess, Mother Earth |
| Philosophy | Tikkun Olam, Repairing the World | "Livity" and Conscious Living | Knowledge, Love, Respect (Mandan) | Harmony |
| Prophet | Moses | Marcus Garvey | Four Bears (Mandan), Sitting Bull, Black Elk, and Crazy Horse (Lakota) | Amma-chi aka Hugging Mother |
| Recent Oppression | Holocaust | Slavery | Genocide | 1970 Controlled Substances Act |
| Promised Land | Israel | Africa | Turtle Island (aka North America among South Eastern tribes) | U.S. National Forest |
| Headcover | yarmulke/hat | "crown" | feather headdress (Northern Plains) | bandanna, headwrap |
| Hairstyle | Payis (sidelocks) | Dreadlocks | Braid (Lakota) | Dreads, lice |
| Gathering | Farbrengen | Nyabinghi | PowWow | Drum Circle |
| Greeting | "Shalom aleichem" | "One love!" | "Hau!" (Mandan) | "Hey!" |
| Refreshments | food a must at all events | pot a must at all events | food a must at all events | food, pot, zoozoos (sweets), "Whatever . . ." |

# Rasta

You've seen the Jewish stars. You've heard the longing for Zion. *Whaddaya gwan wit dat?\** 

Jamaican Rastafarians trace the lineage of their Black *Moshiach,* Haile Selassie, the former Emperor of Ethiopia, all the way back to the wisest *Yid* who ever lived: King Shlomo. Truth be told, tabloid fodder it ain't. In the Book of Kings II, Da Queen of Sheba visits Jerusalem and leaves with "everything she wanted." And what she wanted was to get it on with Da King, husband to one thousand women. Jewish tradition confirms Da Queen was "with child" when she returned to Ethiopia.

Rasta say, "I and I give thanks and praise to The Most High. Yes—I!"

# Marley or Matisyahu?

Jews and Rastas even sing alike. Bob Marley and Matisyahu are two men with one (largely mutual) message. Take a look at these lyrics. Can you tell the difference?!

**Marley or Matis?**

1. *Fire descends from on high in the shape of a lion; burn the sacrifice up right and right under Mount Zion.*  ☐  ☐

2. *Jah sitteth in Mount Zion/And rules all creation.*  ☐  ☐

3. *Give thanks and praise to the Lord and I will feel all right.*  ☐  ☐

4. *And I sing to my G-d songs of love and healing, I want Moshiach now!*  ☐  ☐

5. *Huh, it remind I of the days in Jericho/When we troddin' down Jericho walls.*  ☐  ☐

6. *Hear nobody but His majesty; My spirit, you'll be free.*  ☐  ☐

7. *Jerusalem if I forget you, let my right hand forget what it's supposed to do.*  ☐  ☐

*Answers: Marley, 2, 3, and 5. Matis, 1, 4, 6, and 7.*

\*Translation: What's going on with that?

# Top Seven Reasons
# Jews and Japanese Are Related

1. They got Buddha. We come from Judah.

2. The number ten in Japanese is "Jew." And to read the Torah scroll, ten Jews must gather together.

3. Japanese religious leaders blow a seashell horn. Jewish blow a ram's horn.

4. The ancient crest of the Imperial House of Japan resembled a sunflower similar to the mark on King Herod's Gate, aka the Flower or Sheep's Gate, in the Old City of Jerusalem.

5. In Japanese Shinto shrines, just as in Jewish *shuls*, no idols allowed.

6. Japanese priests strap a black box on their foreheads just as Jews strap *tefillin* boxes on theirs.

7. The Japanese are very homeogeneous. Jews are just plain genius.

Kohenic measure of
the grain offering.

# Top Seven Reasons
# Jews and Hawaiians Are Related

Hang loose, howlie!

1. Jews reserve a particular term for G-d: the Ineffable Name, known in Hebrew as the *Shem Havaya*. This term closely resembles the authentic pronunciation of Pacific islanders. Hawaii is pronounced Ha-VAI-ee. Get it? *Havaiee, Havaya*.

2. Israel and Hawaii split the globe; they are located about halfway around the world from each other.

3. Jews *hora* and blow *shofar*. Hawaiians hula and blow conch shells.

4. Jews light ritual candles and pray at sunset on holidays and Sabbaths. Hawaiians light torches, sing songs, and dance at sunset on special occasions. At these times, Jews dine on roast brisket. Hawaiians dine on roast piggy.

5. Jews long for the Land of Israel. Hawaiians long for their lost singer, Israel "Iz" Kamakawiwo'ole, who sang the most awesome Hawaiian rendition of "Somewhere Over

the Rainbow" before his untimely death in 1997 at age thirty-eight.

6. Jews respect the ancient priesthood of *Kohanim*. This is called *Kahuna* in Hebrew. Likewise, Hawaiians revere their *Kahuna,* a healer/spiritual leader.

7. The Hawaiian symbol for "Hang loose, howlie!" and the *Kohenic* method for measuring out the grain offering in the ancient Temple in Jerusalem are exactly the same.

# Top Seven Reasons
# Jews and Mayans Are Related

1. Both believe in angels.
2. Both like puns.
3. Both have an incomprehensible mystical tradition.
4. Both honor a Higher Power.
5. Both wear special robes on unique occasions.
6. Both built pyramids.

7. Both still exist, defying all logic.

# Top Seven Reasons
# Jews and Rappers Are Related

Many Jews helped start the rap industry. What else do we have in common?

1. Elder Jews—*alter kackers*—and rappers both wear Grampy Gear: tracksuits, sunglasses, and ol' skool tennis shoes.
2. Both love bling.
3. Both love riding in long sedans.
4. Both have deep tribal identification.
5. Both have good Jewish lawyers.
6. Both sag their pants.
7. Both say "Oy!" but rappers say it backwards.

# Jewish Gangsta Tags

Just like tough bloods, Heebsters have hand signs, too. Non-Jewish gang tags, like "Blood," "Chicago," and "Crip" simply sound threatening. Naturally, Jewish tags are somewhat more cerebral, like a spelling bee.

O-J-G                    J-E-W                    Jewish star in formation
Original Jewish Gangstas

# Contemporary Rabbinic Luminaries

Rabbis David Aaron, Simon Jacobson, Joseph Telushkin, Irwin Kula, Rabbi Zalman Schachter-Shalomi, Rebbetzin Esther Jungreis, Rabbi Tirza Firestone, Avivah Gottlieb Zornberg, and Mimi Feigelson.

# Fictional Rabbinic Luminaries

*SNL*'s Hanukkah Harry and Linda Richman of "Coffee Talk," Mordechai Baruch Netanyahu aka the Hebrew Hammer, and Hershel Pinkus Yerucham Krustofski aka Krusty (Schmoikel) the Clown from *The Simpsons*.

# Heebster Rap-inic Luminaries

Antithesis, Blood of Abraham, Brimstone127, Emunah, Etan G, Hadag Nahash, Hip Hop Hoodios, Original Jewish Gangsters, Mariposah, MC Hy with Pep-Love, Matisyahu, Mook E, Joshua Nelson, Remedy, RZA and Cilvaringz, Sagol 59, Socalled, Solomon, Subliminal, Y-Love.

# The Rabbi and the Rapper

The rabbi says, "Let's read Talmud."
The rapper says, "You know it's all good."
The rabbi says, "It's almost *Shabbos.*"
The rapper says, "I'm practically jobless."
The rabbi says, *"Gevalt! Oy vey!"*
The rapper says, "Yo, I'm from the Bay!"
The rabbi says, "Are you sure it's kosher?"
The rapper says, "Ask my boy, Moshe!"
The rabbi says, "Don't *hock* me in *chainik!*"
The rapper says, "Get offa my ----!"
The rabbi says, "Embrace the *Torah!*"
The rapper says, "Break dance the *hora!*"
The rabbi says, "It's almost *shkiyah*" (sunset, i.e., time to pray).
The rapper says, "Oh yeeeeeah!"

# Vulcans

The Vulcan greeting on the original *Star Trek* comes from, where else? The *Torah*. The so-called Vulcan Hand Salute is how Jewish priests, the *Kohanim,* held their hands when they blessed the Israelites in the ancient Temple in Jerusalem. Today, Jews presumed to descend from these priests recite the blessing in synagogues everywhere with the same hand sign. Leonard Nimoy, the actor who portrayed Spock, is, of course, Jewish. And the Vulcan blessing is a version of the traditional *Kohenic* one. "Live long and prosper," where do you think Spock got it from anyway? Compare it to the original:

### THREE-PART *KOHENIC* BLESSING
### *BIRKAT KOHANIM*

May *Hashem* bless you and keep you.

May *Hashem* make His countenance to shine upon you and
be gracious unto you.

May *Hashem* lift up His countenance to you and grant you peace.

**Note:** *Kohanim* form their fingers into three prongs to resemble the Hebrew letter *shin,* which represents G-d.

---

**FYI: FOR THE YIDDISH IMPAIRED**

Anyone with the name Aronov, Aronson, Azulay, Tzudikoff, Kagan, Katz, Cahn, Kahn, Kohn, or Cohen, as in Sacha Baron, may very well be a descendant of Moshe's brother, Aaron, the very first Kohen.

# Jewish Blood

Recent advances in DNA testing suggest there is really something to the claim of Jewish blood. Jewish men who identify as descendants of the priestly class called *Kohanim* actually carry a genetic mutation passed down from father to son—just like the tradition of being a Jewish priest! What's more, a black South African tribe called the Lemba claims to be Jewish. And more than half of the males in the Lemba priestly clan called the Buba carry the same genetic mutation prevalent among *Kohanim*.

The amazing stories don't stop there. One Hispanic man living in the American Southwest decided to test his family lore, which suggests he is a descendant of the Catholic Saint Teresa d'Avila. He wrote repeatedly to the Vatican, wanting to confirm a widely *shmeared* belief that Teresa was born Jewish but forced to convert to Catholicism during the Spanish Inquisition. The Vatican could care less. So he sent his own DNA samples to laboratories in England and the United States to test for genetic indicators of ethnicity. Just as he suspected, both labs confirmed he has Jewish ancestry. He even showed the genetic mutation of the *Kohanim,* the Jewish priestly descendants of Aaron.

But he was already a priest—a Catholic one! Padre Bill, as he is known, has embraced his ancestry by preaching a message of brotherhood and tolerance from his pulpit. "We are all," Padre Bill says, "children of Abraham."

## SHABOT 6000 by Ben Baruch

© Ben Baruch

# Latinos

In 1492, the Spanish Inquisition forced Jews in Spain, Portugal, and Spanish territories to convert to Catholicism under threat of expulsion. Many of these "conversos" practiced their "Jewish" in hiding, passing on traditions to their descendants. Some were put on trial for "Judaizing" and burned at the stake. Centuries later, Latinos around the world are still reclaiming their Jewish identity. How do you know you're really Jewish? Check it out:

- ☐ You've been longing for a reggaeton song with Klezmer samples.
- ☐ You like *hummus* more than salsa.
- ☐ Your father, your father's father, and your father's father before him, as far back as you can recall, have always been named Moises.
- ☐ During the long winter nights, you played with a spinning top for Chiclet.
- ☐ You always thought Zorro was Jewish.
- ☐ Your great-grandmother lit candles every Friday night in the linen closet.
- ☐ Instead of dyeing Easter eggs pink and yellow, your mother scorched them with a match—just like the egg on the Seder plate!

Did you score? Straight up, you're kickin'!

# European Reunion

Yes, Poles, Germans, and Spaniards persecuted us horribly in the not-so-distant past. But now they're trying to make nice. If your ancestors were forced out of these countries, you may be able to restore lost citizenship. Of course, plenty of fine print applies, including residency requirements. And it may cost some serious moola. But the added bonus? The much-coveted E.U. passport.

# Where the Yids Are

All across the North America, clusters of Jews have taken root, primarily on both coasts, in capital cities and other metro areas, but also in various locales midway. In no particular order, here are a few highlights. Naturally, the biggest concerns in every community are where to meet and what to eat!

1. **New York City:** Upper West Side, Upper East Side, Village, Lower East Side, Yeshiva University, Stern College, Brighton Beach, Boro' Park, Da 'Burg, Flatbush, Crown Heights, Washington Heights, Young Israel of Willowbrook, Einstein and Mt. Sinai Hospitals, Riverdale, Kew Garden Hills, Wall Street

2. **Greater New York:** Catskills, Monsey, Great Neck, Five Towns (Cedarhurst, Lawrence, Woodmere, Hewlett, and Inwood), New Square, Kiryas Yoel

3. **Jersey:** Cherry Hill, Teaneck, West Orange, Lakewood, Morristown, Passaic, Deal

4. **LA:** Pico-Robertson, Fairfax, the Valley, Venice

5. **Illinois:** Skokie, Chicago, Highland Park, Rogers Park

6. **Florida:** Miami, Boca Raton, Bal Harbor, Ft. Lauderdale

7. **San Francisco:** the Mission, Sunset, and Richmond Districts, Silicon Valley, Berkeley

8. **Maryland:** Baltimore, Pikesville, College Park, Silver Spring

9. **Massachusetts:** Brookline, Cambridge, Sharon, Brandeis

10. **Ohio:** Cincinnati, Cleveland, Columbus

11. **Pennsylvania:** Philadelphia, especially West Mt. Airy, Elkins Park, and Main Line; Pittsburgh/Squirrel Hill.

12. **Colorado:** Boulder, Denver

13. **Missouri:** St. Louis

14. **Georgia:** Atlanta, Savannah

15. **Iowa:** Postville Rubashkin butchers

16. **Nevada:** Las Vegas

17. **Connecticut:** Hartford

18. **Arizona:** Scottsdale, Phoenix

19. **North Carolina:** Charlotte

20. **Michigan:** Ann Arbor, Detroit

21. **Texas:** Austin, Dallas, Houston

22. **Tennessee:** Nashville, Knoxville

23. **Canada:** Toronto, Montreal, Vancouver

# Jew by Choice

Think you might be Jewish or wanna be? If you're not born a Heebster, don't worry. You've still got options. If you're hunkering to be an MOT, the slowest step is the wisest step. Becoming Jewish is rough, so rough that most Jews don't understand why anyone in their right mind would join us. In fact, becoming a Jew by conversion is highly discouraged. But if you're still interested in joining the tribe, consider these facts:

Membership requires circumcision for all males. And though it is rare, some *moyels* make mistakes. Membership also requires loving other Jews. And about 612 other laws.

Still want to join? There are no Jewish missionaries. It takes a lot more than a few sprinkles of holy water, a dunk, and some "Hail Moshes" to become a Yid.

## THE KLUGGEREBBIE SAYS

As a rite of consideration, road test honorary membership. The cost? *Gornisht!*

1. Attend an annual Passover seder and learn a few blessings. No commitment required.
2. Get yourself an "Honorary Heeb" shirt. How do you feel wearing it in public? Converting is not a T-shirt you can just throw in the laundry when it starts to stink!
3. Offer to turn on the lights on the Sabbath for Orthodox friends as a reliable *Shabbos goy*. If any of your friends ask what the heck you're doing, just explain how cool it was that Elvis did the same for his upstairs neighbors.
4. Consider becoming Noahide rather than Jewish. Only seven laws involved!

**SHABOT 6000** by Ben Baruch

© Ben Baruch

# Kosher Converts

Once upon a time, these guys weren't kosher either!

Oreo

Funyuns

Slurpee*

Cheez-It

Frangelico**

Jelly Belly candy

See's Candies

Marshmallow Fluff

Godiva Chocolatier

Burger King—Israel

Coffee Bean & Tea Leaf

Bac-Os Bacon Flavor Bits

Krispy Kreme Doughnuts*

Elite Bazooka Joe Bubble Gum

Campbell's Vegetarian Vegetable Soup

Binyamin & Yirmiyahu's aka Ben & Jerry's

McDonald's—Buenos Aires and Jerusalem

Subway—Brooklyn, the Upper West Side, Cleveland, LA, and more!

*Select locations. Be wary in antisemitie territory.
**The definition of crypto-kosher: The bottle is shaped like a monk and belted with a rope!

# The Covenant of Noah

Noahide is English for spiritual descendants of the biblical Noah. If you think about it, this refers to the entire human race! In Heebster parlance, the Noahide Laws are also known as the Naugahyde Laws, which take their name from vintage faux leather. You see, Naugahyde is to leather as Noahide is to Jew. Noahide looks a lot like the real thing, but requires much less furniture polish.

Attention *shiksah, shaygetz,* and *goyim* of all stripes: Unlike kosher kikesters, as a Noahide, you may still eat bacon cheeseburgers, Chicken Parm, and Eggs Benedict. They are not taboo-boo. But anarchy is. Incest is. And so is that Chinese delicacy, live monkey brains.

Otherwise, to be Noahide, just be good. Very very good. And if you can't be good, be careful. Very, very careful.

## Recycle, Reuse, Reshmooze

*Yes, the intestinal festival is (finally) over. But when the whole world loves it, why throw out perfectly good matzah?*

Build a *matzah* high-rise with gefilte landscaping and *charoset* caulking.

Conduct surveys of the blind to reveal hidden *Kabba Lah Lah*-istic messages.

Chalk a sidewalk bull's-eye and play flying *matzah* toss.

Feed the remains to the birds.

Crush, fry in an egg batter, and eat with jam, maple syrup, or cinnamon sugar for *matzah brei*—the Jewish answer to French toast!

Soak in Manischewitz, layer with chocolate icing, and chill for a "Go in Peace" *Pesach* cake.

Decorate for protest signs and oversized business cards.

Use colored frostings to design an edible Monopoly board. Winner eat all!

Trade beautiful specimens with friends.

# Frumology

Rebelling against parents is a common Jewish experience. It happens in nearly every generation. But in many contemporary Jewish families, marrying "out" is no longer a form of rebellion. The best new way to freak out your family is to become a Super Jew, that is, a Super Religious Jew. This is also called getting *frum,* which is Yiddish for "pious." Heebsters call this "*frummin'* out." You've got to admit, it sounds a whole lot better than "Born Again Jew."

In most instances, "returning" in this grand fashion will make your family—well, there is no kind way to say this—*plotz.* If you come from a comfortable home, this will likely represent a shocking rejection of your parents' secular lifestyle. And this may upset them. But it will, after all, be toward a much higher purpose—making crab cakes a thing of your past!

In the rare event you already come from a religious home, becoming irreverent is the obvious rebellious option. An even more shocking alternative is to become Hasidic. That way, you'll develop a fondness for Slivovitz, get to dress like an original Blues Brother, increase your tolerance for vodka shots, *and* go to heaven!

# Top Seven Reasons to *Frum* Out

1. You always knew you were different. Now you're truly an anomaly among your friends and family.

2. Until you figure out what it really means to be kosher, you're bound to lose weight. Everything feels off limits! (This *will* change once you begin the practice of eating three large meals every *Shabbat!*)

3. If you are the unfortunate recipient of a bald spot or receding hairline, covering it makes you belong. Under all those hats and *yarmulkes,* nearly everyone else is bald, too!

4. You now have an automatic excuse for turning down invitations to overpriced restaurants—except kosher ones. (You're on your own for that!)

5. Unless you live in Boro' Park or Da 'Burg, you'll get lots of attention! Your new headcoverings and *tzitzit* will attract really colorful street people, antisemities, psycho strangers, and other crazies who will ask if you have cancer or have discovered eternal truth.

6. You can now be super philosophical and answer in the most Jewish way: Never answer. Instead, ask more questions!

7. Now you can finally say you don't roll on *Shabbos* and mean it! To quote the Big Lebowski: "Three thousand years of beautiful tradition from Moses to Sandy Koufax. You're damn right, I'm living in the f—n' past!"

# Shock Value

What's the EKG—Estimated *Kvetch* Grade—of your return to religion? The answer is simple. The higher your assimilation factor, the greater the shock!

## BACKGROUND

If your parents attend some sort of synagogue at least once a year, score 1 point.

If your Jewish parents raised you in a spiritual commune or a cult, score 10 points.

If your parents don't know what the word *shul* means, score 50 points.

## ORIENTATION

If you're Modern Orthodox and decide to become *Chabad Lubavitcher Hasid,* score 50 points.

If you're a hippie and decide to become *Yeshivish,* score 300 points.

If you're a Red Diaper Baby—the child of communists—and you decide to keep kosher and keep the Sabbath, score 3,000 points.

## FAMILIAL TIES

If your grandparents were religious, score 50 points.

If your great-grandparents were religious, score 100 points.

If you can't remember who was the last religious person in your family, score 1,000 points.

## DIET

If the last time you ate bacon was never, score 0 points.

If your parents cook bacon at home, score 100 points.

If your parents insist on bacon on *Yom Kippur,* score 5,000 points.

## RESULTS

If your score is between 101 and 500, you may walk around in a stupor for four to six months, but eventually, your *neshume-le* will understand that you have come home. You will not only adjust accordingly. You will become quite content with your new lifestyle, thrive, and prosper. Go forth and conquer. G-d is on your side!

If your score is between 501 and 9,000, you are advised to take baby steps and find yourself a fun-loving rebbe with a rock 'n' roll band. Becoming religious will add meaning and contentment to your life, once your parents relent and stop serving bacon and eggs whenever you're home for *Shabbat*. Don't take no for an answer and don't give 'em a chance to think!

And if your score is above 9,000, becoming religious will demand a lot from your psyche. Find yourself a good Jewish shrink. Long-term therapy, if not daily dunking in a ritual bath, the *mikvah,* may be required. This will calm your nerves. In the meantime, you may need prescription drugs.

# Need a Label?

*Mazal tov,* you're a *Yid!* It really all boils down to that. But if you insist, adopt a label as-is or mix and match to express your kind of Jew.

| | |
|---|---|
| Ultra | Reform |
| Gonzo | Conservative |
| Iconoclastic | Orthodox |
| Confused | Conservadox |
| Strict | Slackadox |
| Traditional | Renewal |
| Lite | Reconstructionist |
| Committed | Zionist |
| Sunday morning | Lox and bagelist |
| Heavy | *Shtetl* guitarist |
| Spiritual | Cultural humanist |
| Indie | Mind-set |
| *Hasidishe* | Soul |
| Bitter | Outlook |
| *Machmir** | Individualist |
| *Makel** | *Kabba Lah Lah*-ist |
| Spiritual | Israeli |
| Federation | Pocket |
| Post modern | Chabad Lubavitcher |
| Raised | B'nai Akiva |
| Neocon | Carlebachian |
| Left-wing | Rav Kookian |
| Right-wing | Progressive |
| Neurotic | Rainbow hippie |
| Fusion | Ashkenazic |
| Mizrachi | Sephardic |
| Bipolar | Ashkephardic |
| Apathetic | "I had my bar/bat mitzvah. Now I'm done." |
| Fanatical | Post-lableficationist |

* *Machmir* and *makel* are Talmudic terms for *stringent* and *lenient.*

# Got Frum?

So you're a "BT," a *baal tshuva,* a recent returnee to observing Jewish law. That changes everything: how you speak, how you dress, what you eat. Don't freak. Here's your shortcut to fitting in fast.

1. **Insist** everyone call you by the Old Country alias used by your great, great: Blooma Shendel Moskowitz or Menachem Mendel Felsenfeld.

2. **Cover up.** If you're a *Yid,* put on a lid. If you're a *maidele,* don't throw out your miniskirts and spaghetti strap tops. Just layer them over pants and long sleeves!

3. **Clean up your speech.** Stop cursing to make conversation colorful. Instead, pepper your tongue with energetic expressions of praise in Hebrew. These include *Baruch Hashem,* "Blessed be the Name," *Im yehrtzei Hashem,* "If G-d Wills it," and *Has v'chalilah,* "Heaven Forbid!"

4. **Keep the Sabbath.** From Friday afternoon, eighteen minutes before sunset, to one hour after sunset Saturday night, start keeping "Pumpkin Time." Turn off your cell, your TV, your oyPod. Instead, hang with the homies at *shul* and go home with the rabbi for dinner. If your friends don't understand, remind them of the Cinderella story or tell them you're experimenting with being Amish.

5. **Eat kosher.** Always. Pickled piggie feet, puffed pork skins, and squid in its own ink are gross anyway!

6. **Study Torah.** Tribal tradition is filled with timeless wisdom. Haven't you heard that enough already? As Rabbi Hillel said, "Go and learn it." Soon you'll be quoting *Bava Metziah* as if it were the Bhagavad Gita or whatever your hippie parents read you at bedtime!

7. **Visit Israel.** Experience the beauty of Bamba, Israel's peanut-ty answer to the Cheeto. Imagine noshing a bag while you float in the Dead Sea, reading a newspaper upside down and backwards. Now that's paradise!

Repeat until this feels natural. This *is* actually possible!

# Frumster™ Heebonics

When you're a frummie, you are automatically given a new universal vocabulary that works in *all* countries, *all* foreign languages, and *all* situations. From now on, the key is to avoid specifically answering questions. That's because the objective of every conversation is not actually to exchange information or reveal your state of mind. No, your sole objective is to express your resolute faith in the Source of All Life. Your personal welfare remains a mystery.

Question: Did you pass a kidney stone?
Response: *Baruch Hashem.*
Translation: Blessed be the (Holy) Name.

Question: How did it feel?
Response: *Mamash, a gevalt.*
Translation: The highest of the high.

Question: Will you survive if you have to pass another?
Response: *B'siata d'shemaya.*
Translation: With the help of Heaven.

Question: Will you be well enough to come for *Shabbos* dinner?
Response: *Im yehrtzei Hashem.*
Translation: *If G-DASH-d wills it.*

Question: You promise?
Response: *Bli neder.*
Translation:Without a vow, because for all I know, I might be carrying around a dozen in there.

## BONUS ROUND

If you know anyone whose name ends in "el," you now have a great way to show off your new-found piety. In Hebrew, another name for G-d is "El." So in everyday conversation, religious Jews avoid pronouncing this word to prevent taking the L-rd's name in vain. Instead, they say "kel." For added religious oomph, pronounce Eliana as "Kelly-ana" and Daniel as "Danny-kel." This method also works for many desinations, such as Kel Segundo and Kel Cerrito, and the beverage known as Ginger K'Ale.

# Superstition

Keep the evil eye away by peppering conversations with these doozies.

1. *Has V'Shalom*—Literally peace forbid. Used similarly to "Heaven forbid."
2. *K'ayin Ahora*—Alternatively spelled *Kaynahara* or other variations thereof. Against the evil eye. Add a P.S.: "phfoot, phfoot, phfoot," "too, too, too" or the Americanized "poo, poo, poo" for a kick. Even better, at the end of a sentence, hock up a wet one and spit for final emphasis, as in, "I just got a great new job. *K'ayin Ahora*, too too too, fwuwhoot!" Just make sure you're not hanging out among the Daughters of the American Revolution when you let this one rip.
3. *Neged Ayin HaRa*—The Hebrew equivalent of *K'ayin Ahora*.

There are approximately 361 additional superstitious expressions, but this should keep you for a while.

# Beg Your Pardon

Forget hookups. In ultra-religious circles, men and women don't touch. *At all.* They don't even shake hands. Now *you* have to figure out how to be modest. In Yiddish, the word is *tznius*. Try that out loud. If it sounds like you've suppressed a sneeze, you're saying it just right!

**The Spiritual Handshake**—Place palms together in prayer position and bow like you're Jewpanese.

**The *Tznius* High Five**—Reach your arms up high as if you're going to slap palms with your buddy. Instead, let your hands intentionally miss each other but yelp as if you actually connected! Also known as the **High Fly Me**.

**The *Tznius* Hug**—Invoke these words and it's as if you've really embraced! Doubles as an excellent e-mail sign-off.

**The *Tznius* Kiss**—Ditto. Make like a starlet and blow air kisses with wild abandon!

**A Handshake in Thought**—The ultra-modest expression of affection, for whom even a thought-hug or -kiss feels grossly inappropriate!

# Finding a Mate

Courtship in religious circles is often conducted at warp speed. Among the ultra-religious, deciding to get married within three or four dates is standard. The process is usually simplified through introductions made by a matchmaker, a *shadchen* in Yiddish. Like a Jewish PI, a good *shadchen* does character checks in advance of an introduction. This stands in stark contrast to the other insta-weddings on the globe, where there are no *shadchens,* only shotguns.

# The Perfect Date

### YOU KNOW YOU'VE FOUND
### A REAL SHEEBSTER WHEN,

*She* says, "Guys look hot in *kippas.*"

*She* digs it when you imitate Matisyahu, Borat, or Yuri Baranovsky.

*She* loves her own Babs-like *shnoz.*

### YOU KNOW YOU'VE FOUND
### A REAL HEEBRO WHEN,

*He* makes a mean *matzah brei.*

*He* does a horrible Matisyahu, Borat, or Yuri Baranovsky, but you never let on.

*He* calls you a "radiant Jewish beauty," even with your Babs-like *shnoz.*

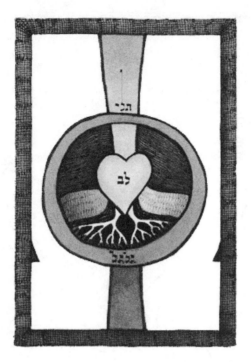

# Hasidic Pickup Lines

- You know what they say about men with long beards …
- You even make the *cholent* look beautiful!
- Anyone here know how to carve a ham?

# MR. AND MRS.

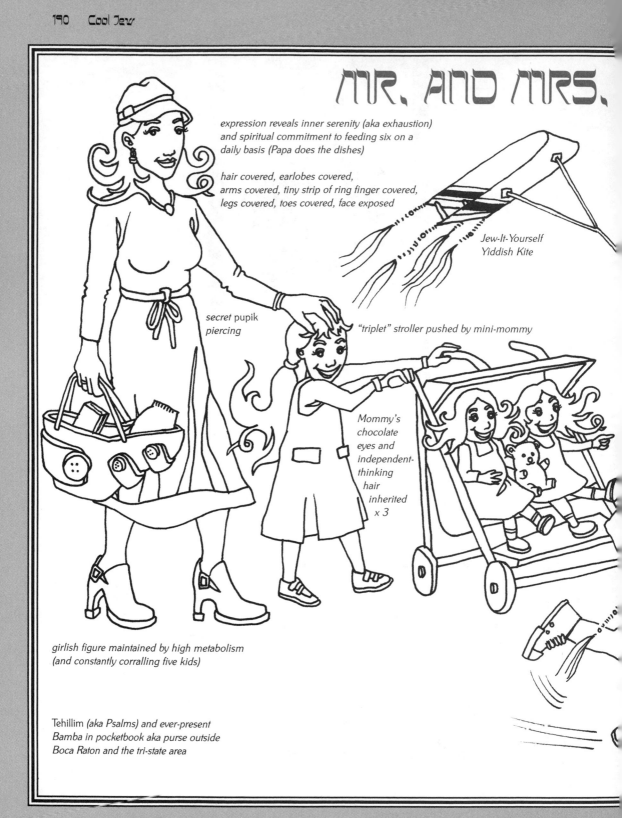

expression reveals inner serenity (aka exhaustion) and spiritual commitment to feeding six on a daily basis (Papa does the dishes)

hair covered, earlobes covered, arms covered, tiny strip of ring finger covered, legs covered, toes covered, face exposed

Jew-It-Yourself Yiddish Kite

secret pupik piercing

"triplet" stroller pushed by mini-mommy

Mommy's chocolate eyes and independent-thinking hair inherited x 3

girlish figure maintained by high metabolism (and constantly corralling five kids)

Tehillim (aka Psalms) and ever-present Bamba in pocketbook aka purse outside Boca Raton and the tri-state area

# FRUMMED OUT

hat conceals tie-dyed yarmulke and receding hairline

genetically programmed beard, sidelocks tucked behind ears

characteristic contagious congeniality

Papa's beloved guitar, Leslie West autographed pick

Netivot Shalom, Hasidic teachings for absorbing wisdom every spare moment

proud fringe bearers

oyPhone loaded with Daf yomi, (daily Talmud study) G-dcasts, and stock quotes tucked into pants pocket

Heebster t-shirts, including "My Rabbi is Fly," marketed online by Mama

mini-me x 2, future beards, thick eyebrows and male pattern baldness inevitable

All-Jewish-Stars in all Jewish sizes

Moshav band stickers peeling from underside of family heirloom

# IF YOU CAN'T SAY ANYTHING NICE, SAY IT IN YIDDISH.

## Word!

Hanging with Heebsters means navigating unspoken social checks and balances. Mastering the massive monstrosity of Mosaic murmurations requires patience, discipline, and a keen intelligence. That's because Jews are not only the People of the Book. We are also the People of the Verb, Imperative, Pronoun, and Pluperfect!!! For generations, we have cherished, polished, and refined a multitiered tradition of expressing ourselves with great emotion, conviction, and gesticulation . . . like the man who fell overboard, began to drown, cried for help, waved his arms wildly, miraculously climbed back on ship, and explained, "If I veren't yelling so loud, I never vould have made it."

This annotated guide to the linguistic Heebster vibe will get you hip-hopping your Hebraic, putting the rap in Rappaport, and Shebrewing your shizzy in no time. Before you know it, you, too, will be *Da Bim Bom!* *

---

### FYI: FOR THE YIDDISH IMPAIRED

To hock is to remove phlegm from the throat with a deep guttural rumble. It is pronounced with a similar sound, a kkhh from within. Hock is also Yiddish for "pestering." Traditionally paired with *chainik,* a teakettle, or *koperein,* "in the head." As in "stop hocking me in *koperein!*"

---

* A holy compliment combining "You da bomb" with the traditional *Shabbos* hymnal, "Bim Bom, Bim, Bim, Bim Bom, Bim, Bim, Bim, Bim, Bim, Bom, Cheery Beery Beery!"**
** repeat

# The Other *Alef Bet*

**K** is a Jewish letter.

Think *kvetch, knaidlach, knish, klutz* . . .

**M** is more Jewish than **N**.

*Maven, mensch, macher, minyan vs nudnik, nebich, nincompoop.*

**S** might be Jewish.

**SH** is definitely Jewish. In fact, SH is the Jewish version of a dipthong.

*Shmaltz, shmendrick, shmegegi, shlemiel,* and on and on without end!

The English pronunciation of **CH** (as in "church") ruins you for Hebrew (but not for Yiddish).

*Chaim* and *Tanach* (both Hebrew) but *cholent* (Yiddish).

**Q** is *goyish.* Reclaim *goyish* letters by combining them with Jewish letters. In "*goyish* school,"
   **Q** must always be followed by **U**, which hamstrings you (pun intended) in Scrabble,
   among other places. In Jewish, **Q** is followed by **V**.

Her Highness, the Qveen of England. That sounds better already.

**W, Y,** and **Z** are totally Jewish. It doesn't get more Jewish than that.

The surname Yoskowitz is a perfect example.

**X**, however, is a Catholic letter.

Xmas. Need we say anymore, Xavier?

The further you progress in the other *alef bet*, the more Jewish it gets.

Vowels validate this theory.

**A** is not Jewish.

Archbishop.

**E** is not Jewish.

Evangelical.

**I** is often Jewish.

Ich!

**O** is definitely Jewish.

*Oy!*

**U**, as we know, is Jewish.

You again? Uch!

And **Y** . . . not sometimes, but always.

Yankel. *Yidden.* Yiddish. Yello?!

It should be noted, providing a clear explanation is *goyish.*

It's Jewish not to have to explain.

# The Yiddish Invasion

Even if you don't speak a shpeck of *Die Mama Loshen,* you can fake it well with a critical sound, the all-purpose /sh/. Get shmart. Test your Yiddish know-how with these All-Shtar Minyan Makers, plus one for good luck!

1. **shpiel**
2. **a shidduch fon a shadchen**
3. **sheitl**
4. **shehecheyanu**
5. **shaygetz**
6. **shiksah**
7. **shtark**
8. **shpilkes in tuchis**
9. **shtick**
10. **shanda**
11. **shtipn araiyn**

a. strong as a horse

b. a blessing stated on holidays, new threads, eating a fruit for the first time each year, a bris and other eventful occasions. Also refers to the occasion itself and, sarcastically, for a big deal that is really no big deal at all

c. a male gentile

d. literally "to stuff into," used for "shove it in"

e. a funny bit, a *Purim* play, a put-on, also used for sex

f. needles in the arse; as in "sitting on pins and needles," raring to go!

g. *kitsch,* clowning, or emotional baggage

h. a matchmaker-made match

i. wig worn by ultra-Orthodox women

j. female *shaygetz*

k. a shame, an embarrassment

*Answers:* 1. e, 2. h, 3. i, 4. b, 5. c, 6. j, 7. a, 8. f, 9. g, 10. k, 11. d

די קאַץ דער פּאַיאַץ

Dɪ KATS
DER
PAYATS

*The Cat in the Hat by Dr. Seuss
in Yiddish*

פֿון ד"ר סוס
יודיש: שלום בערגער

**Fun Dokter Seuss**
**Yidish: Sholem Berger**

# Proofiness: It All Comes From Us

Many common English expressions are translations of Hebrew phrases from the Good Book. Despite what Harry Potter may have you believe, even the concept of the phoenix, a bird that lives for one thousand years, dies, and is then resurrected from its ashes, is a Jewish teaching. It's all there in Job 29:18.

You know that. And I know that. But do *they*? Whenever someone unknowingly uses a Jewish expression, quietly cite its source, then mumble, "It all comes from us."
Note: This works especially well when speaking with self-haters and antisemities ill-advisedly ill-disposed to the Tribe.

| EXPRESSION | SOURCE |
|---|---|
| *My brother's keeper* | Genesis 4:9 |
| *Dust of the earth* | Genesis 13:16 |
| *Sweat of your brow* | Genesis 3:19 |
| *Man shall not live by bread alone* | Deuteronomy 8:3, |
| *Apple of my eye* | Deuteronomy 2:10, Zechariah 2:8 |
| *Eye for an eye, tooth for a tooth* | Exodus 21:24, Leviticus 24:20, Deuteronomy 19:21 |
| *Golden calf* | Exodus 32 |
| *How the mighty have fallen* | Samuel 1:19–27 |
| *Drop in the bucket* | Isaiah 40:15 |
| *No peace for the wicked* | Isaiah 48:22 and 57:21 |
| *Can a leopard change his spots?* | Jeremiah 13:23 |
| *Not by might, nor by power, but by my spirit, said the Lord of Hosts* | Zechariah 4:6 |
| *From the mouths of babes* | Psalms 8:2 |
| *At my wit's end* | Psalms 107:27 |
| *A rose among thorns* | Song of Songs 2:2 |
| *There is nothing new under the sun* | Ecclesiastes 1:9–14 |
| *There is a season, turn, turn, turn* | Ecclesiastes 3:1–8 |
| *Eat, drink, and be merry* | Ecclesiastes 8:15 |
| *Weighed in the balances and found wanting* | Daniel 5:5 |
| *Writing on the wall* | Daniel 5:5 |

# The Proof Continues: Expressions from Yiddish

Seek and ye shall find.

Go jump in the lake!

This is for the birds!

Drop dead!

A chip off the old block!

The wheel turns round.

A penny saved is a penny earned.

The one who can't dance says the band
    can't play.

Money doesn't grow on trees.

Silence speaks louder than words.

Flattery will get you nowhere.

Honesty is the best policy.

After nine months, the truth comes out.

A jest is a half truth.

A half truth is a whole lie.

The bottom line.

## LESS FAMILIAR BUT, NATURALLY, STILL FABULOUS

Sleep faster—we need the pillows!

You can't dance at four weddings with
    two feet!

Better a Jew without a beard than a beard
    without a Jew.

Your health comes first; you can always
    hang yourself later!

Five minutes of happiness, a hundred years
    of grief!

# Loving Me, Loving Jew: The Heebster Sexicon

**Akerensyado** Ladino for object of affection

**Chibookim** Hebrew for hugs, /ch/ as in Bach

**Mishmish** Hebrew for apricot, a gentle nibbling of the earlobe

**Namorikos** Ladino for flirtation

**Nishikot** Hebrew for kisses

**Pook** A Yiddish non-kiss, a goodnight kiss fake-out. Pucker up, make contact with skin, and imitate the sound of natural gas emissions. Safe for putting a child to bed. Aka in English as a raspberry.

**Potch in tuchis** a love pat on the tush, or a more severe spanking

**Shmuck** Yiddish for the male member, doubles for idiot. Eg. With a *sheiner tuchis* like yours, that *shmuck* let you go?

**Shtup** literally, Yiddish for push or stuff, the foulest word for the most intimate of acts. Known in Hebrew as *ten zayin;* the latter word is also the Hebrew letter for this chapter.

**Tashmish HaMita** the preferred Talmudic term for knowing in the biblical sense

Not necessarily in this order ...

## G-d Bless!

First things first, you should be well. That said, the practice of blessing a sneezer dates back to ancient Israel. Back in the day, there was no sickness before death. A little soul, a little snot, and, boom, it was all over. People sneezed, then died ... end of story. That's why, says the Ba'al Shem Tov, we kindly bless each other when we let one rip!

### SNEEZE PRONUNCIATION GUIDE

In contemporary times, the sneeze serves a new dual purpose. Besides ridding the *shnoz* of foreign bodies, it also provides a way to identify the native tongue of fellow MOTs. Naturally, a well-educated Heebster always responds in kind.

| Sneeze | Mother Tongue | Heebster Response |
|---|---|---|
| **Recha!** | Yiddish | **Zei Gesund!** Be healthy! |
| **Apchee!** | Hebrew | **La briute!** To your health! |
| **Achoo!** | English | Look, as long as you're healthy, that's what's important! |

# Sounds Like Hebrew

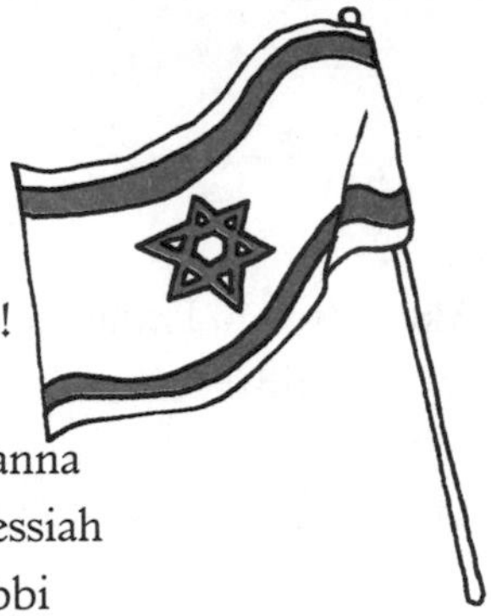

These words sound like Hebrew for a good reason. Because they are!

abracadabra

alphabet

amen

behemoth

cabal

camel

cherub

cider

cinnamon

copasetic (from the
Hebrew for *kol b'tzedek*,
"everything is just")

groan

hallelujah

Jew

Joe Shmo (the Jewish John
Doe; literally, "Yosef is
his name")

jubilation

jubilee

kosher

leviathan

manna

messiah

rabbi

Sabbath

sabbatical

sapphire

selah

seraph

Shibboleth

sodomy

Uzi

Zion

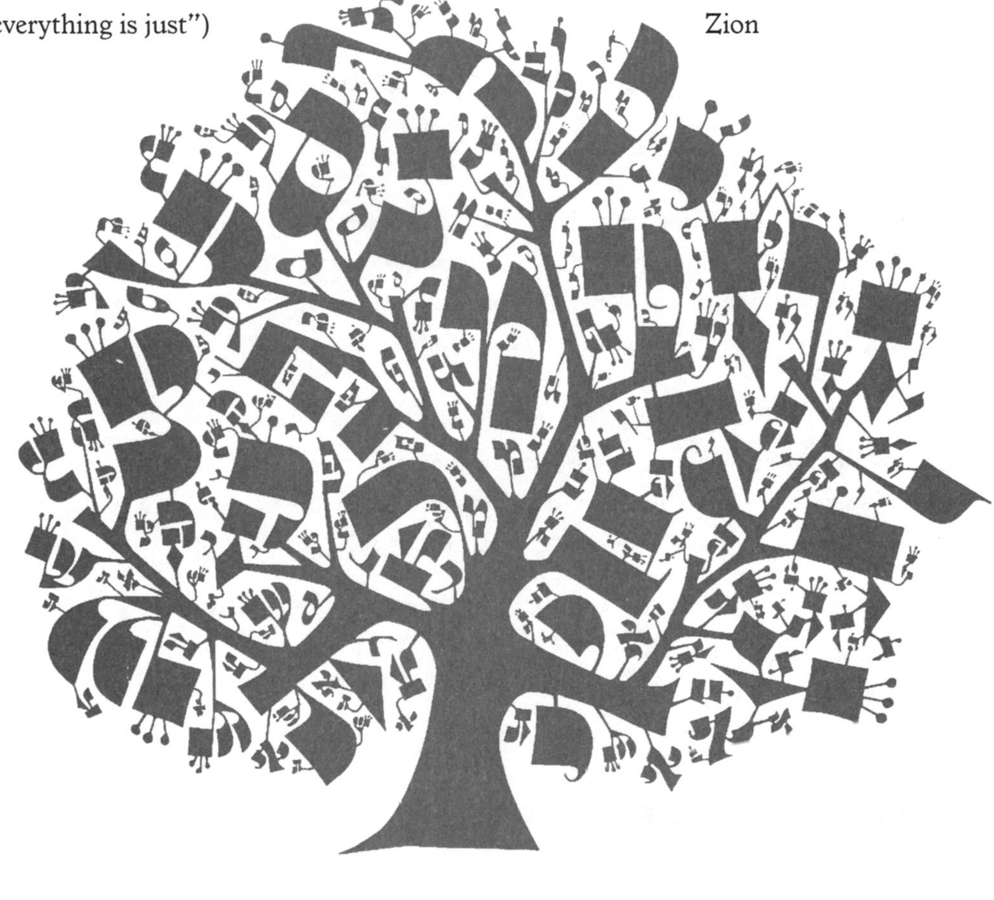

# Biblical Destinations

**Bethesda:** Maryland

**Burning Bush:** Georgia, Pennsylvania, Texas; Ontario, Canada

**Canaan:** Alabama, Arkansas, Connecticut, Indiana, Maine, North Carolina, New Hampshire, New York, Vermont, New Brunswick

**Eden:** California, Idaho, Maryland, New York, North Carolina, South Dakota, Texas, Utah, Vermont, Wisconsin; Manitoba, Ontario, Canada

**Ephrata(h):** New York, Pennsylvania, Washington

**Galilee:** Arkansas, Missouri, New Jersey, New York, Pennsylvania, Rhode Island, Texas; Queensland, Australia

**Garden of Eden:** Illnois, Texas; Ontario, Canada

**Hebron:** Connecticut, Indiana, Illinois, Kentucky, Maryland, Mississippi, Nebraska, North Dakota, New Hampshire, Ohio; Newfoundland, New Brunswick, Nova Scotia, Canada

**Jericho:** Indiana, Mississippi, New York, Ohio, Kentucky, Texas, Vermont

**Jerusalem:** Alabama, Arkansas, Georgia, Maryland, Michigan, Rhode Island, Ohio, Vermont, New York

**Moab:** Utah, Washington

**Mt. Hermon:** California, Louisiana, Kentucky, New Jersey, Maryland, Massachusetts, Virginia

**Mt. Sinai:** Alabama, Indiana, New York, North Carolina, Ohio, Texas, Tennessee

**Mt. Zion:** Arkansas, Ohio, Tennessee, Missouri, Kentucky

**Nineveh:** Indiana, New York, Ohio, Pennsylvania, Texas, Vermont, Virginia, Solomon Islands

**Rehoboth:** Massachusetts, New Mexico

**Rehoboth Beach:** Delaware

**Safed:** United Kingdom

**Salem:** Arizona, Idaho, Illinois, Indiana, Massachusetts, Missouri, New Hampshire, New Mexico, New Jersey, Ohio, Oregon, South Dakota, South Carolina, Virginia; New Brunswick, Canada

**Salome:** Arizona

**Sharon:** California, Connecticut, Kansas, Massachusetts, North Dakota, Oklahoma, Pennsylvania, South Carolina, Tennessee, Vermont, Wisconsin; Ontario, Canada

**Shiloh:** Alabama, Arkansas, Georgia, Idaho, Illinois, Maine, Michigan, Missouri, Mississippi, New Jersey, North Carolina, Ohio, Tennessee, Virginia

**Shushan:** New York

**Sinai:** Florida, South Dakota, Kentucky, Mississippi, Virginia; Colombia

**Zion:** Illinois, National Park, Utah

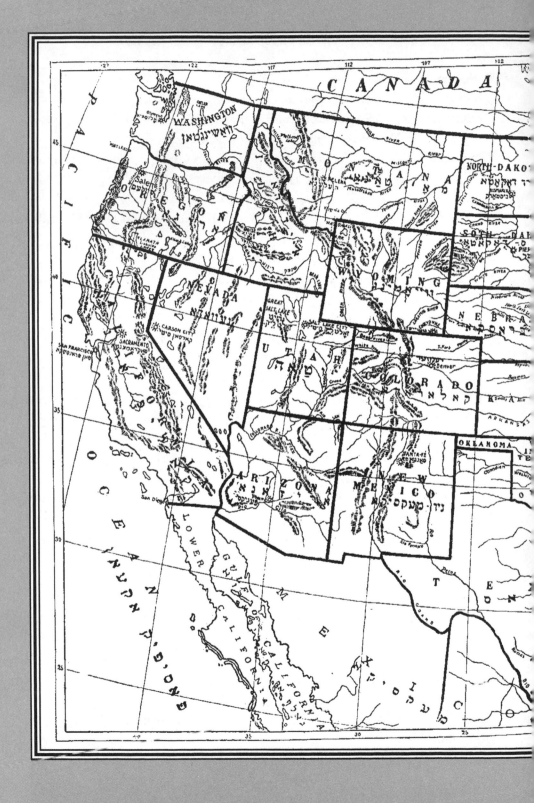

# Hebrew Slanguage

Put the emphasis on the second syllable to sound like a local (or as if you've slept with one).

*Achi* Bro

*Achla* Awesome

*Bassa* Bummer

*Ben Zona* Literally "son of a whore." Put emphasis on "Ben," to connote bad ass, and awesome.

*Challas* Enough

*Hatich* Piece. A hot Jewish guy.

*Haticha* The female equivalent.

*Haval al haZ'man* Literally, "a waste of time;" used for "totally awesome."

*P'tzatza* Literally "explosion." Hot Jewish chick.

*Pitzootz* Also means "explosion." Synonymous with "that's da bomb."

*Sababa* Once cool but no longer. Use at risk of ridicule.

*Sof haDerech* Literally, end of the world, used for amazing!

*Yalla* Move it on, people!

# Sounds Like Yiddish

| | | | |
|---|---|---|---|
| Bludgeon* | Herring | Nincompoop* | Spatula |
| Canasta | High falutin | Numbskull | Tumult |
| Clunker | Hoi polloi | Ow | Umbrage |
| Cockamamy | Hoity-toity | Pickle | Watusi |
| Dregs | Hotsy totsy | Pooch | Woe |
| Doozy | Hullabaloo | Shebang* | Woozy* |
| Far-fetched | Kaniption | Shindig | Yack |
| Far-flung | Kaput | Slug | Yada yada yada |
| Farkleberry* | Kumbaya | Smooch | Yahtzee! |
| Finagle | Mishmash** | Smug | Yank* |
| Floozy* | Mooch | Snooze* | Yokel |
| Glitch** | Muckety muck | Snug | Yucky |

# E-mail Sign-offs

Another opportunity to exhibit your inherent Heebster know-how!

| **Sign-off** | **Translation** |
|---|---|
| *Blessed art thou!* | You're the biggest sinner! |
| *Farshteist?* | Undaztood? |
| *Power to the payis!* | May you always be blessed with two phallic symbols hanging from your head! |
| | |
| Happy *Chanukah* | *Shmearing* cheer throughout the year. |
| Love you a latke! | Props to you and Da Tribe! |
| Got *shpilkes?* | Feelin' jittery, Heebster? |
| Signed, Your little *oy*-ster! | From one anxious MOT to another. |
| May the Schwartz be with you! | Props to Mel Brooks's *Space Balls* |
| Big *tznius* hug! Air kisses! | The perfect non-contact, modest send-off for religious friends of the opposite sex. |
| | |
| *Ahava Echad* | Hebrew for "one love" |
| *Shabbat Shalom*-y, Homie! | *Shalom* out! |

\* According to Webster's, these terms are of "unknown origin." Where do *you* think they come from?
\*\* These actually are *mama loshen!*

# Sentence Restructuring

To speak like a MOT, simply employ these traditional methods.

1. Answer any question with a question.

   **Question:** *How are you?*
   **Answer:** *How should I be?*

2. The infamous /ch/ sound not only clears the throat of all phlegm. It also instantly puts the speaker *in the know,* making her sound Jewish even if she is not. It is also especially effective to convey emphasis.

   **Example:** *This* **ch**allah *is delicious with* **ch**uch*!*

3. Repeating a word and adding *"shm"* at the beginning provides sarcasm, rejection, judgment, or skepticism.

   **Example:** *Hungry, shmungry.*
   **Example:** *Tired, shmired.*
   **Example:** *Dying, shmying.*

4. Withholding a well-deserved *"mazal tov"* is an accepted way to respond to life-altering good news. Easily conveys skepticism, or sarcasm and/or criticism.

   **Example:** *I just got accepted to Harvard!*
   **Response:** *You? Harvard, shmarvard.* Nebich. *Go clean your room!*

---

### FYI: FOR THE YIDDISH IMPAIRED

In the hard-to-believe-but-sounds-likely category, some say, *"Oy vey!"* is actually an alternate pronunciation of the ineffable name of G-d, spelled in Hebrew *Yud-Hay-Vav-Hay.*

# An Alef Bet of Insults

Not that you would ever use any of them …

| | | | |
|---|---|---|---|
| 1. | **Ay chileria!** | a. | pig |
| 2. | **Chaim Yankel** | b. | loser |
| 3. | **chucham*** | c. | first cousin to *shlemiel*** |
| 4. | **fresser** | d. | drunk |
| 5. | **gonif** | e. | thief |
| 6. | **khazzer** | f. | devourer |
| 7. | **klutz** | g. | *putz* |
| 8. | **kvetch** | h. | moocher |
| 9. | **macher*** | i. | unlucky misfortune |
| 10. | **nebich** | j. | wise one* |
| 11. | **nudge** | k. | pipsqueak |
| 12. | **putz** | l. | jerk |
| 13. | **schlepper** | m. | A cholera upon you! |
| 14. | **shiker** | n. | rag |
| 15. | **shlemazal** | o. | complainer |
| 16. | **shlemiel** | p. | braggart (literally, "one who sweats") |
| 17. | **shlub** | q. | no name |
| 18. | **shlump** | r. | clumsy |
| 19. | **shmegegi** | s. | mover and shaker* |
| 20. | **shmendrick*** | t. | drag |
| 21. | **shmatte** | u. | what's his name |
| 22. | **shmo** | v. | pesterer |
| 23. | **shnook** | w. | a gossip, a busybody … her line of business? Yours! |
| 24. | **shnorrer** | x. | one who drags himself along (bad dresser) |
| 25. | **shvitzer** | y. | oaf |
| 26. | **yente** | z. | pitied patsy |

*Answers:* 1. m, 2. u, 3. j, 4. f, 5. e, 6. a, 7. r, 8. o, 9. s, 10. c, 11. v, 12. l, 13. t, 14. d, 15. b, 16. i, 17. y, 18. x, 19. g, 20. k, 21. n, 22. q, 23. z, 24. h, 25. p, 26. w.

**Note:** Allowing for regional variations in nuance, many terms are actually interchangeable!

* Requires a bitter intonation, otherwise, it may be misconstrued as a compliment!
** As heard on *Laverne and Shirley.*

# What 1 Like About Jew, Two

When you're in love with the Tribe, the whole world is Jewish. *Shmear* affection for your fellow MOTs with this *alef bet* of TLC: Tribal Loving Care.

*Bubbeleh* Jews call their loved ones granny as a blessing!

*Chamud* Hebrew for "adorable," feminine version is *Chamuda,* Yiddishized form is **Chamudeleh. Chamudalah** is also acceptable, /ch/ as in Bach.

*Chatikh* (m), *chatikhah* (f) Hebrew for "hunk," like those hot Israelis playing *matkot* at the beach.

*Habibi* Hebrew slang borrowed from Arabic, used by men for their women and between platonic pals

*Hamantaschen* Synonymous for "darling," as in "You're so yummy, my little *hamantaschen*." Who knew it represents an ancient fertility symbol of female anatomy?! (Now you wish you didn't.)

*Kreplach* Close to ditto, but not quite. Yiddish substitute for "My little dumpling."

*Maidele* Yiddish diminutive for "girl." Doubles for "cute young thing."

*Mameleh* Why you'd call your girlfriend your mother remains a mystery!

*Motek* Hebrew for "sweetie;" for a guy. Morphs to *Metuka* for a girl. Shortens nicely to Mo and Mo-ie.

*Neshama* Literally, Hebrew for "soul," doubles for "precious one;" also heard, *Neshume-le* in Yiddish

*Shayna* Yiddish for "pretty" or "beautiful," especially inside

*Shayna punim* Yiddish for "pretty face," a real looker, Ms. Congeniality

*Sheiner tuchis* beautiful arse

*Soysuza* Ladino for "vixen"

*Tzatzkellah* cute little one

*Zeesie* Yiddish dimunitive for "sweetie"

*Zeeskeit* Yiddish for "sweetness." Not to be confused with *meeskeit* (ugliness, internal, too), as in "Feh! Did he turn into a *meeskeit*!"

# Jewsticulations

The People of Da Book talk with da hands.

1. **The Tug** The excruciating yanking of your cheek by your Aunt Chaya Rivka. With all that arthritis she *kvetches* about, it's surprising she can pull so hard!

2. **The Clamp** The smushing of your face between two elderly palms; may be topped off with a cracked lipstick kiss that has haunted you since the first grade.

3. **The *Potch in Tuchis*** S&M-lite, the affectionate tush tap among lovers; used in the Old Country non-affectionately as a spankin' for naughty little ones, sometimes used as a mere threat of punishment.

4. **The Hand** A wave or thrust that varies in form, position, and speed to reflect highly individualized forms of emphasis, as in "*Nu?*" or "And then, to top it all off ..."

5. **The *Rak Rega*** The gathering of all five fingers into a teepee pointing upward; Israeli for "Would you hold your frickin' horses already?"

6. **The Bird** Giving the finger to obnoxious drivers; pairs well with the curse *Geh kackin af'm yam!* (Yiddish for "Go crap in the sea!")

7. **What's with You?** Exploding your entire hand into five screaming exclamation points when obnoxious drivers threaten your sanity. Also known as "Meet the whole *mishpocha!*"

8. **The Dismissive** Waving away bothersome friends, family, and salespeople.

# Words Rarely Spoken

**Almemmar** *bima,* pulpit

**Beadle** *shul* caretaker

**Benediction** blessing

**Conventicle** *Shtiebl,* little *shul*

**Judaize** to make Jewish

**Judaizer** Heebster

**Phylacteries** *tefillin*

**Rabbinism** rabbinic teachings and wisdom

**Ritualarium** *Mikveh,* ritual bath

**Sabbath pudding** *kugel*

# The Meaning of Jew

Western culture has tragically often made the Jew its scapegoat. To defuse the potential anxiety of this discussion, pour yourself a Mani.

Now then, look no further than the Christian Book of Hebrews. Like a pain in the Lower Mongolian Nether Regions, the text explicitly condemns Jewish religious practices. Uh huh, right there in the drawer of every *goyish* hotel room. Forget that $#*%!

Shocking but true, further proof of historic Christian intolerance exists in almost any dictionary. We can live with Webster's definition for hebdomad, a period of seven days. But the rest of it? Jew hatred waaaay past its prime, if it ever had one. Remember, may his name be erased, Hitler? He's dead. Get with the program, not the pogrom. This stuff has got to go.

| WEBSTER'S | HEEBSTER'S |
|---|---|
| **Hebe** is a derogatory term coined in the early twentieth century. | **Heebster** is a complimentary term coined in the twenty-first century! |
| **Hebetude** means to make dull. | **Heebitude** means to make it your own. |
| **Hebephrenia** is a form of schizophrenia. | **Heebephilia** is a love for all things Jewish, which is itself a cure. |
| **Jewfish** is a large, dark grouper with a thick head and rough scales. | Everybody knows jewfish is code for that delicacy with the carrot on top! |

# The Right Kind of Revisionism

We all know the Holocaust really happened. There's no denying it. But what about you? Who says you always have to keep it real? Edit your reality to improve your life instantly!

**Your Personal Jewish History**
Antisemities blew up our mailbox.
Oh, this big bandage on my *shnoz*?

Judge, we need more time for
   the continuance.

**Your New Reality**
We won a free demolition!
My doctor insisted on excavating my breathing
   passage. Now it's a wide-open highway, just a
   half-inch shorter!
Your honor, next Tuesday is the Jewish Holiday
   of *Ta'iti Od Pa'am.* *

---

### FYI: FOR THE YIDDISH IMPAIRED

How does a *maven* say, "I was mildly disappointed?" He *krekhtzes* mit a loud "uch!," throws his arms in the air, and exhales as he barely manages to utter the words, "I was ready to kill myself!"

---

# Goyish Gone Jewish

In a non-Jewish world, polite *goyim* sometimes just don't make sense.

| WHAT THEY SAY *Goyish* | WHAT THEY MEAN Jewish |
|---|---|
| This situation does present a few challenges. | What a crock of $#*! |
| Are we clear? | Did you understand even ONE THING I've said? |
| I'm busy. | You're so aggravating. |
| Okay. | I feel you. |
| That's really quite remarkable. | Go away! |
| I'd like to underscore that point. | I'm telling you! |
| P.S. | And another thing! |

* Heeb for "I screwed up again."

# Heebonics

| DON'T SAY | SAY |
|---|---|
| Exegesis | *Midrash* |
| I saw Jesus! | Eisegesis* |
| Jaw harp** | Jew's harp |
| Bluegrass heebie jeebies | Jewgrass the creeps |
| Jew him down | Jew him up! |
| *jeu d'esprit*** | *Jew d'esprit**** |

# How to Behave in the South, Siberia, and Other Hostile Territories

Sure, the Nazis are gone. The czar is dead. And the Inquisition is long over. But Jihad rages on. And the KKK is out there somewhere. Whether the threat is real, perceived, or merely a terrifying television rerun, Heebsters are always prepared. Because frenemies, *friendly enemies,* come in all shapes and sizes.

At all costs, do not let this book fall into antisemitie hands. Consider it a tribute to all those who came before you, those who managed to survive when the ones-whose-names-should-be-erased-from-history actually roamed the planet.

# Skills For the Neurotic Among Us: Antisemitism Translator

**WHAT THEY SAY**

You have a rather exotic look.

You're a creative shopper.

I believe your share is $300.

My, what an interesting ritual.

You have a sensitive management style.

**WHAT THEY MEAN**

That's some *shnoz*!

What a *shnorrer*!

No way are you gonna Jew me!

You're living in ancient history!

You're a Jewish mafioso! Are you, uh, going to kill me now to bake my blood into *matzah?!*

* Reading your own ideas into a biblical text.
** A lyre-shaped instrument for the mouth.
*** A witty comment or disposition.
**** A Heebster.

## THE KLUGGEREBBIE'S
# Rap For the Fearful

When you suspect bad guys about, trust your suspicions. Listen up to
    your doubt.

Don't you dare get caught feeling feeble. Or this may be your last day
    as a Heeble.

Deli mustard up your strength. Take control of the situation. Tune in your
    hearing aids right now. And listen up for elongation!

When Jewish holidays are pronounced wrong, wizened Heebsters don't
    stick around long!

Just for once, forget having fun. When you hear "Happy *Tcha-tcha Noo-
    kah,*" grab your gear and run!

And like brotha Lot leaving Sodom and Gomorrah, bring along your loved
    ones, get away from the horror.

Pretend you're All Jewish-Stars tanked on crack and never ever, don't Jew
    ever look back!

I said, never ever, don't Jew ever look back!

Historic Heebster hero.

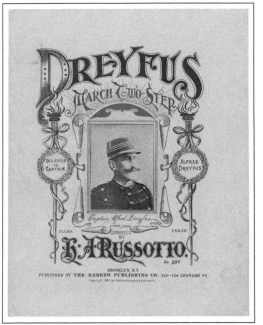

Modern Jewish martyr.

# Heebster Undercover

When traveling in Siberia, surrounded by farm animals or strange white-hooded beings engaged in pyrotechnics, Heebsters wisely avoid all outward forms of Jewish expression. If you are so blessed as to speak the Holy Mother Tongue, do not attempt spoken Hebrew in public or even amongst those you may suspect are fellow MOTs. Instead of Jewish, speak *goyish*. Do whatever you can to preserve your *matzah* balls.

| DON'T SAY | INSTEAD SAY |
|---|---|
| *Shabbat* | abbat-shay |
| *Shalom* | alom-shay |
| *Shabbat Shalom* | Shatiga-batigat Shatiga-lotigom. |
| How far is it to the border? | Howtigow fartigar iti-is to-ito bortigor-dertiger? |

# Emergency Terminology

Administer in cases of severe hunger while traveling in frenemy territory.

| ENGLISH | PIG LATIN | DOUBLE G |
|---|---|---|
| *matzah* ball soup | atzah-may all-bay oup-say | matiga-zahtigah batigall soutigoop |
| gefilte fish | efilte-gay ishfay | gehtigeh-fitigil-tehtigeh fitigish |
| I eat only raw foods. | Iay eetay onay awray oodsfay. | Itigai eatigee otigon-litige ratigaw footigoods. |
| Oy gevalt! | Oyay evaltgay! | Oytigoy getigeh-vatigalt! |

# CV: The Circumcised Version

To cut conversational calories, cultivate community, and *kvell* over their own ingenuity, Heebsters prefer communicating in code. But when Hebrew, Yiddish, Ladino, and other forms of Heebonics aren't options (when you-know-whos are around), the Circumcised Version is. With minimal effort and maximal fun, Heebsters can say as much or as little as they want. The added bonus: insulation against antisemites. The ominous they won't have any idea what's being said or why. Perfect for Generation Text!

> I was DF for L&B when I ran into my old classmate. She rolls with Christina SSN, but she's the ultimate JBA and joined me RTNT for FH... as if! Naturally, H&H is COS, so on Sunday, EAP. So M&M, MOTs GW. NJ&Gs visiting from YULA for a YU conference with AKs from BGU. TTBA. Then, this HH Chris hangs with at the JCC walks up to her and says, "Let's BTJ for some POR!" I was so "WAICL?" "You?" he says. "THH, KAH PPP. Not like me, TGFW. I'm only JBI."

AK = *Alter Kacker*

BGU = Ben Gurion University of the Negev

BTJ = Blow this Joint

COS = Closed on *Shabbos*

DF = Down For

EAP = Everything's a Party

FFB = Frum from Birth, Berkeley, Botswana

FH = Free Ham (the Jewish dilemma)

GW = Gone Wild

H&H = Purveyor of New York bagels

HH = Honorary Heeb, Heebster Hustle, or Hot Heebster, depending on context

JCC/J = Jewish Community Center.

JBA = Jew by Association

JBI = Jewish by Insertion, i.e., *shtupping*

JST = Jewish Standard Time

KAH = *K'ayina Ahora,* followed by PPP

L&B = Lox and Bagels

MOT = Member of the Tribe

M&M = Making a Mani Cocktail, also describes a rockin' good time

NJB = Nice Jewish Boy

NJG = Nice Jewish Girl

NJBGB/NJGGB = NJB or G Gone Bad

NMOT = Non MOT

POR = Pastrami on Rye

PPP = Poo Poo Poo! Preceded by KAH

RT&T = Right Then and There

SSN = Such a *Shiksah/Shaygetz* Name

TBA = Temple Beth Anywhere, applied to loud gatherings of Jews

T = Totally, used before other codes

TGFW = Too Goyish for Words

WAICL = What Am I, Chopped Liver?

YU = Yeshiva University

YULA = YU (high school) of Los Angeles

# The Art of Nu

No word in any language compares with *Nu*. This single-syllable nudge pesters and prods others to action. *Nu* also means "So?," but conveys considerable feeling, impatience, and anticipation. The longer it is draw out, as in *mooooo*, the more emphasis the cow, correction, the speaker applies.

One friend to another after a date: *Nu?*

Husband to wife in labor: *Nuu?*

Wife to husband after giving birth: *Nuuu?*

Rabbi to spouse after the sermon: *Nuuuu?*

Kluggerebbie to you after reading this book: *Nuuuuu?*

---

## Recycle, Reuse, Reshmooze

*Book, shmook. Of course you've absorbed every precious morsel of these pages. But who lets a masterpiece sit and collect dust?*

Prop in your east-facing window to identify Jerusalem, the direction for prayer. You've instantly turned this book into a *mizrach.* So Jew!

On *Purim,* dress up like a religious fanatic and clutch as your faux Bible.

Fake out religious friends and relatives by putting it in the bookshelf where they keep their many volumes of Talmud. Dude, it'll fit right in.

Tear out three pages you've already memorized and twist into an impromptu candle for the *havdalah* ritual to say good-bye to *Shabbat.* (Wrap base in foil to prevent boo-boos.)

Wave the remaining book like a fan to clear smoke from your new *havdalah* candle.

Commit the rest to memory during your trans-Atlantic flight to Israel.

When you land, present as an impromptu gift for the nephew of your fourth cousin twice removed for picking you up at the airport.

---

### FYI: FOR THE YIDDISH IMPAIRED

The ultimate Jewish expression of "way to go" is *yasher koach*/"May your strength increase." It's a verbal pat on the back that dates back centuries. The correct pronunciation is merely two syllables, slurred together into one Ashkenazi whopper: *shkoiyach!*

# נו?

You've read it. You've said it. You've practically bled it. We're just about done here. *Nu*, are you a Heebster yet or vaht? Check it out. Literally!

☐ You've danced the *hora* to "Havana Nagila," Hula Hooped and thrown away your inhibitions at a big phat Jewish wedding!

☐ You've served herring to the homeless with humility.

☐ You've polished, purchased, or prospered from marketing treasured Jewish ritual items.

☐ You've eaten a full *kiddush,* gone home for *Shabbat* lunch, and still hunkered for thirds of Saturday night pizza and ice cream.

☐ You've drunk Manis, served Manischewitz Manna, adopted a pet manatee, and named your first child Manny—short for Emmanu-kel.

☐ You've founded, attended, or broken away from an indie *minyan.* (You know who you are.)

☐ You've stayed up all night studying *Torah* on *Shavuos,* gorged on cheesecake, and pulled it off without No Doze, Red Bull, Meth, or speed. That's right, some how, you got high on *Torah.*

☐ You've expanded your vocabulary to include, "I've got *shpilkes.* Wanna see my *pupik?*"

☐ You've interviewed your *faintly ghetto* grandparents and discovered your real Jewie name is Shprintza Dina Basha Fayga Gittel or Saadia (Shraga) Nissim Menachem Irachmiel— with two /ch/s as in Bach Bach.

☐ You realize driving a German car doesn't help you get back at those Nazi bastards. But making a mint eBaying one you've customized into a Heebster-mobile does!

☐ You changed your cell phone ring to that *Shabbat* classic, *L'cha Dodi,* for your pope costume on *Purim* and never changed it back.

☐ You've never felt more at home calling yourself a Member of the Tribe. *Shkoiyach!*

# Mazal Tov!

You've read *Cool Jew.* You've said the *Shemantra.* Now start *shmearing* the Jew Glue, starring in your own Heebster Hustle, and shining your Hebraic out loud and proud. Get your *tuchis* grooving and give the world not seconds but thirds of what it's been waiting for: you, informed, downtown, and vibe-in' Da Jew pride!

But first, on this momentous occasion, perform the ritual circumcision of the opposite page. It will hurt a lot less than the original. Post it between your *mezuzah* and your (future) *ketubah.**

One day, your grandchildren will thank you. Until then, may G-♥-D bless us with the peace that knows no boundaries. And protect us from heartburn, gastroenteritis, and colonic polyps forever more! And let us say, "Ahhhhhh-mayn!"

Love,

קלוגרבי

The Kluggerebbie

*Jewish marriage contract.

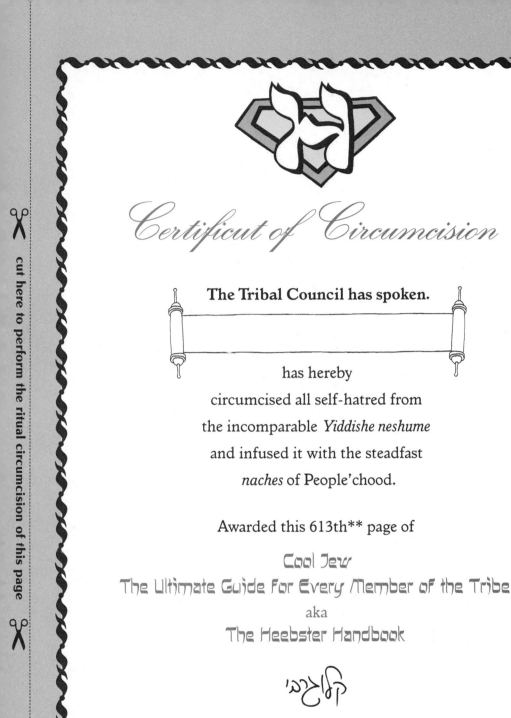

# *Certificut of Circumcision*

**The Tribal Council has spoken.**

has hereby
circumcised all self-hatred from
the incomparable *Yiddishe neshume*
and infused it with the steadfast
*naches* of People'chood.

Awarded this 613th** page of

## Cool Jew
## The Ultimate Guide For Every Member of the Tribe
aka
## The Heebster Handbook

לוג רבי

The Kluggerebbie
*Shayna Brachos* Dahlink

**Give or take a few hundred pages.

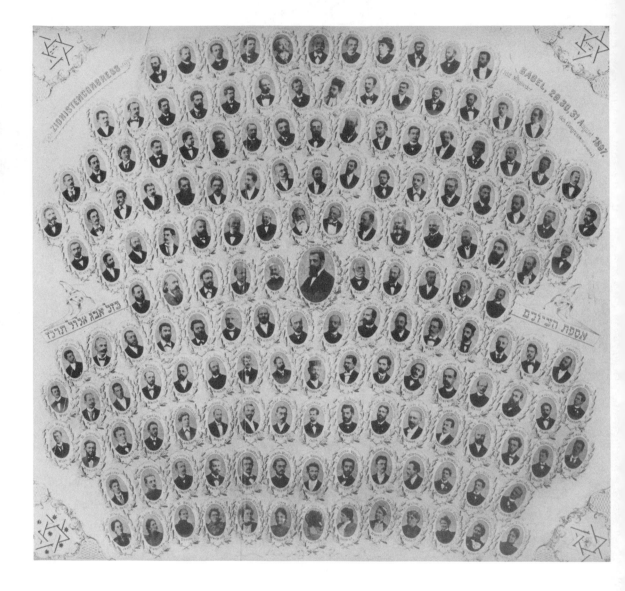

APPENDIX

# People of Da Book: Heebster Essentials

The Torah is a considered a Tree of Life. All the rest is commentary. Haven't you heard it enough already? As Rabbi Hillel said, "Go and learn it."

## THE FUNDAMENTALS

1. The Bible, known in Hebrew as *Tanach* (which rhymes with Bach)
2. The *Mishnah*
3. The *Talmud*
4. The *Zohar*
5. The *Tanya*
6. The *Siddur* aka Prayerbook
7. The *Shulchan Aruch*, Code of Jewish Law

## JUDAISM 101

1. *Back to the Sources*, Barry Holtz
2. *Book of Our Heritage, Vol. I, II, and III*, Eliyahu Kitov
3. *The Jewish Holidays*, Michael Strassfeld
4. *Jewish Literacy: The Most Important Things to Know About the Jewish Religion, Its People and Its History*, and other books, Joseph Telushkin
5. *Jewish Meditation, Outpouring of the Soul*, and other books, Rabbi Aryeh Kaplan

## LIVING LARGE

1. *On Being a Jewish Feminist*, Susannah Heschel
2. *On Women and Judaism, How to Run a Jewish Household*, Blu Greenberg
3. *Between G-d and Man*, Rabbi Abraham Joshua Heschel
4. *Toward a Meaningful Life*, Rabbi Simon Jacobson
5. *To Be a Jew: Guide to Jewish Observance in Contemporary Life*, Hayim Halevy Donin

## THE SHOAH (AKA THE HOLOCAUST)

1. *Maus I: A Survivor's Tale: My Father Bleeds History*; and *Maus II: A Survivor's Tale: And Here My Troubles Began*, Art Spiegelman
2. *Diary of a Young Girl*, Anne Frank
3. *Night*, Elie Wiesel
4. *Man's Search for Meaning*, Viktor Frankl
5. *If This Is a Man*, Primo Levi

## FICTIONAL HISTORY

1. *As a Driven Leaf*, Milton Steinberg
2. *The Chosen, The Promise, My Name is Asher Lev, Davita's Harp*, and all titles by Chaim Potok
3. *Exodus*, Leon Uris
4. *Inside, Outside* and *Marjorie Morningstar*, Hermon Wouk
5. *The Source*, James A. Michener
6. Works by Philip Roth, Michael Chabon, Saul Bellow, Anita Diamant, Allegra Goodman, Dara Horn, Cynthia Ozick, Naomi Ragen, and many others.

# Da Tribe Online

By the looks of things, Jews really do run the world.

*2Jewish.org* Jewish Cultural Arts

*92y.org* Jewish programs abound

*AIPAC.org* Israel political support

*Aish.com* Online Torah galorah

*AE.COMYU.edu* Albert Einstein Med School

*AJC.org* Safeguarding *Yiddelach* worldwide

*AJPA.org* Jewish Press Association

*AJSS.org* Teenage summer social justice

*AJWS.org* Jewish World Service

*Akhlah.com* Kid stuff

*AlefsInWonderland.com* Art by Josh Baum

*ALEPH.org* The Jewish Renewal Movement

*AmchaCJC.org* Jewish activism and advocacy

*AmericanJewishArchives.org* In Cincinnati

*AmericanSephardicFederation.org* Homie headquarters

*ArchieMcPhee.com* Judaikitsch gifts

*AskMoses.com* Live rabbis, 24/6

*AvodaArts.org* Art, creativity, and ideas

*Avodah.net* Jewish Service Corps

*Ayecha.org* Jews of Color

*BaalShemTov.com* Hasidic meditations

*Babaganewz.com* More great kid stuff

*BangItOut.com* New York events and more

*Bariff.org* Gear emporium

*BecholLashon.org* Jewish diversity

*BegedIvri.com* Ancient customs, jThreads

*BGU.edu.ac.il* Ben Gurion University

*BiblioMaven.com* jLibrary links

*Bikkurim.org* jIdeas incubator

*birthrightisrael.org* Are you between eighteen and twenty-six? Visit Israel for free. It's your birthright!

*Brandeis.edu* Jew U since '48

*CanfeiNesharim.org* Envirodox *Yidden*

*CardozoYU.edu* The law 'n' Jews

*CarlebachShul.org* Rock Friday night!

*Chabad.org/kids* The Itche Kadoozy Show

*Chochmat.org* Jewish meditation

*ChutzpahtheGroup.com* True *chutzpah*

**Chutzpah**

*Circle.org* Community, culture, activism

*CJH.org* Center for Jewish History

*CJP.org* Combined Jewish Philanthropies

*CLAL.org* Center for Learning n' Leadership

*COEJL.org* Environment and Jewish Life

*Columbia.edu/cu/lweb/projects/digital/lcaaj/* Spoken Yiddish archive

*CoolJewBook.com* You know!

*CreativeZionism.com* Summer leadership

*CryptoJews.com* Research and networking

*CSMC.edu* Cedar Sinai Medical Center

*DeliciousPeace.com* Shalom in a cuppa joe
*Dinur.org* jHistory at Hebrew U
*Drisha.org* Deep Torah for S/Hebrews
*DryBonesblog.com* Comics from Israel
*EdAlliance.org* Helping Heebs since 1889
*EncyclopaediaJudaica.com* Word!
*FamousRabbis.com* The Beardy Bunch
*Farbrengen.com* A party in print
*Folksbeine.org* National Yiddish Theatre
*Frumster.com* Operation soul mate
*G-dcast.com* Animated Torah
*GenerationJ.com* Gen X zine
*GesherCity.org* Bridges for *Yidden*
*GetThreaded.com* Threaded Heritage gear
*Ghetto Plotz.com* Yup.
*GoIsrael.com* Da Land of Milk and Honey
*GuiltandPleasure.com* Quarterly mag
*Hadassah.org* Support for Israel, jYouth

*HadassahGross.com* An unorthodox
　*rebbetzin*
*Havurah.org* National Havurah HQ
*Hazon.org* Enviro-activism on wheels
*HebrewHammer.com* Cult film favorite
*HebrewNational.com/store* Gear galore
*HeebMagazine.com* Radical jExpression
*Hillel.org* Jewish campus life
*Hineni.org* Rebbetzin Esther Jungreis

*HODS.org* When
　you croak, do
　some good
*HUJI.ac.il/huji/
　eng/* Hebrew
　U for Y-O-U
*IJS-online.org*
　Spiritual
　nourishment

*IKAR-LA.org* Torah and social justice
*IMJ.orgil* The Israel Museum in J-town
*ImmigrantHeritageTrail.org* DIY jTours
*IsabellaFreedman.org* Re-Jewva-Nation
*Israel21c.org* Israel beyond the conflict
*IsraelOnCampusCoalition.org* Go blue!
*IsraelServiceCorp.org* Exactly
*Isralight.org* Rabbi Aaron and friends
*JBooks.com* Hebraic books-plus
*JCCA.org* Home to the Js of the U.S. of A.
*JCCMaccabi.org* Athletes and artists
*JewishChildren.museum* jKids 'zeum
*JDate.com* Need we say more?
*JDC.org* Da Joint, help for *Yiddelach*
*JDubRecords.org*
　jTunes reign supreme

*JerusalemCamp.org*
　Hippie summer
　camping
*JESNA.org* Jewish
　education for all

*Jewcy.com* Eclectic culture, clothes, fun

*JewishCartoon.com* All in the jFamily

*JewishCulture.org* The Foundation for ...

*JewishFamily.com* Parenting with meaning

*JewishGen.org* Tribal family tree

*JewishHospital.com* For real

*JewishImpactFilms.com* In Hollywood!

*JewishJustice.org* Inequality beware

*JewishLeaders.net* Coachin' and mentorin'

*JewishLife.org* Philanthropy central

*JewishMilestones.org* Make 'em count

*JewishMuseum.org* On Museum Mile, NYC

*JewishNetwork.com* Yid-friendly events

*JewishOrganizing.org* Ol' skool activism

*Jewish-Place.com* Model temples

*JewishResearch.org* Diversity spoken here

*JewishRNB.com* jTunes

*JewishRobot.com* Getting diggy wid it

*JewishService.org* Heebster Peace Corps

*JewishSports.com* Track the Tribe

*JewishStudentWeekly.com* Word!

*JewishSupers.com* Home for heroes

*Jewish TVNetwork.com* Exactly.

*JewishVirtualLibrary.org* Info emporium

*Jewlarious.com* Funny stuff 'bout us

*Jewlicious.com* Tribal unity in a blog

*JewliciousFestival.com* Heebster a-go-go

*JewSchool.com* Blogarama

*JewsforJudaism.org* Nu, vhat else?

*JewsRock.org* Heavy *shtetl*

*Jewz.com* All day, all things J

*JFREJ.org* Jews for Justice in Jew York

*JiddischKurs.org* Online Yiddish learning

*JNF.org/goneutral* Carbon footprinting

*JOI.org* Outreach to the intermarried

*JPhilanthropy.com* No explanation needed

*JRetroMatch.com* Matchmakers unite!

*JRF.org* Home of Reconstructionist Jewz

*JSinglesCruise.com* Vay-kays n' swee-tays

*JudaicVilnius.com/en* Study Yiddish abroad

*Juedisches-museum-berlin.de* jMuseum

*Jvibe.com* Teen site

*JVibe.com/homer* Count Da *Omer* with Homer

*JWA.org* Jewish Women's Archive

*KabbalahArt.com* Artwork by Avraham Lowenthal

*KlezKamp.org* Camp for grown-ups!

*KolEchad.org* Jews Without Borders

*Kolot.org* Women and Gender's Studies

*Kosherfest.com* It's all in the name

*Kosherica.com* Lux family cruises

*Koshertreks.com* Ditto

*Kosmic-kabbalah.com* Art by David Friedman

*Kulanu.org* Helping lost tribespeople

*LaitsUTexas.edu/gottesman* Yiddish history

*LeadingUp.org* Jewish leaders magnet

*LeagueforYiddish.org* Yiddish support team

*LegacyHeritage.org* jVision
*LimmudNY.org* Jewish learning bonanza
*LivingTraditions.org* Go Yiddish!
*LowerEastSideNY.com* Free tours
*MaccabiUSA.com* Da *Yiddishe* Olympics
*Magnes.org* Judah L. Magnes Museum
*Makor.org* Cool programs in Jew York City
*MasaIsrael.org* Moola for Israel programs
*MatanKids.org* Jewish learning for all
*MatisMusic.com* Rockin' Hasidic reggae
*Matzoball.org* Xmas jFun
*Mazon.org* Fight against hunger
*MeaningfulLifeCenter.org* Get one!
*Metivta.org* Jewish meditation
*Mfa.gov.il* Israel Foreign Ministry
*Mimaamakim.org* Hip lit mag
*MinuteMatrimony.com* Cross-cultural short
*MJHNYC.org* Museum of Jewish Heritage
*ModernTribe.com* Gifts amundo
*Mosaica.ca* Jewish arts-plus
*MosaicOutdoor.org* MOTs in the Woods
*MOTL.org* March of the Living
*MountSinai.org* Kosher medical care
*MuseumOfTolerance.com* Word!
*MyJewishLearning.com* More to explore
*NACOEJ.org* Support for Ethiopian Jews
*Natan.org* Philanthropic *shteigers*
*NationalMahJonggLeague.org* Mahj HQ
*NBN.org.il* The Zionist dream lives on
*NJCD.org* Including the Jewish disabled
*NeoHasid.org* *Hasidus* without borders
*NewVoices.org* Student jMag
*Nextbook.org* jBooks, writers, events
*NiceJewishGirlsGoneBad.com* Live, on stage
*NIF.org* The New Israel Fund

*NJOP.org* Read Hebrew America/Canada
*nypl.org/research/chss/jws/jewish.html*
NYC Pubic Library Dorot Jewish Division
*OnlySimchas.com* Good news for Jews
*OrientalTrading.com* Shtick-a-rama
*ORTAmerica.org* Global breadren support
*OU.org* Orthodox Union headquarters
*OyBayW.orgdPress.com* Blogging by the Bay

*Oyhoo.com* Downtown Arts Development,
    NYC, music and more
*Panim.org* Leadership, values, good stuff
*Peje.org* Support for jDay schools
*Peoplehood.org* Uncensored rants
*PJAlliance.org* Progressive Jews
*PopJudaica.com* Gear heaven
*PresentenseMagazine.org* Idea marketplace
*ProjectOtzma.org* Service in Da Holy Land
*RabbisDaughters.com* Hip, *heimishe* gear
*Rebooters.net* Music, journal, and more
*RitualWell.org* Old meets new
*RJ.org* Home to Reform Judaism
*ROI120.com* Expanding Jewish
    involvement and leadership
*Romemu.org* jRaves in Jew York
*RotemGear.org* Jewie shirts and gifts
*SafedCandles.com* *Havdalah* gear and more
*Sar-El.org* Volunteering in Israel
*SawYouAtSinai.com* Matchmaking a go-go
*ScatteredAmongtheNations.org* ¡Help
    abroad

*Serverccoakton.edu/~friend/chinajews.html*
Promotes Judaic studies in China
*Shabot6000.com* Robot comix
*Shalem.org.il* Ideas to sustain the Tribe
*Shamash.org* Info-a-plenty
*Shemspeed.com* Happening jTunes, gear
*Shma.com* Journal of Responsibility
*Shmaltz.com* He'Brew shtick
*Sholom-aleichem.org* A writer's world
*Sino-judaic.org* Egg rolls and *kreplach*
*Skirball.org* LA Cultural Center
*SocialAction.com* Repairing the world
*STARSynagogue.org Shul* renewal
*Storahtelling.com Torah* teaching theatre
*SuburbanHomeboy.com* Smooth E comedy
*Sulha.com* Grassroots peace project
*TAU.ac.il* Tel Aviv Jew U.
*Technion.ac.il* Israel's M.I.T.
*Temple.edu/isrst/Affiliates* Jewfro meets
Afro, exploring our diasporas
*Tenement.org* Revive the Lower East Side
*TevaAdventure.org* Nature and *Yidden*
*TheBBI.org* Brandeis-Bardin Institute
*TheForestFoundation.net Tikkun Olam*
*TheLandofIsrael.com* All the dirt!
*TJSSC.com* Educational toys
*Toldot.org* Online kids museum
*TotallyJewishTravel.com* Exactly

*TravelJewish.com* ditto
*TribeTheFilm.com* Heebster history
*Tzadik.com* Radical Jewish music label
*UJA.org* Federations across the nation
*UniversalFace.org Kabba* for everyone
*USCJ.org* Home of Conservative Judaism
*USHMM.org* U.S. Holocaust Memorial
Museum
*Ushpizin.com* Ultra-ortho *Sukkot* dramedy
*VirtualJewishLibrary.com* Clicks away
*WhyDateJewish.com* It's all in a URL
*Wiesenthal.com* Simon Wiesenthal Center
*WorldManna.org* Stop world hunger
*YadVashem.org* Holocaust Memorial
Museum
*YiddishBookCenter.org* The *gantza megillah*
*YiddishCulture.org Mama Loshen* lovers
*YiddishKaytLA.org* Ditto
*YiddishRadioProject.org* Audio treasure box
*YiddishWeb.com* Yiddish in French
*YIVOInstitute.org* Classes, archives …
*YoungIsrael.org* Nearly 150 Ortho *shuls*
*YU.org* Yeshiva University
*Yungntruf.org* Keep Yiddish alive
*WexnerFoundation.org* Leadership
programs
*Zeek.net* Progressive pontification
*Zemerl.com* Belt it out in song

## Da Heebster Jewke Box

*2000-Year-Old Man,* Carl Reiner and Mel Brooks

*Abayudaya, Music from the Jewish People of Uganda,* Various artists

*Agua Pa'la Gente* and *Raza Hoodia,* Hip Hop Hoodios

*Avadim Hayinu: Once We Were Slaves, Let Us Break Bread Together,* The Afro-Semitic Experience

*Babylon & Beyond,* Hieroglyphics

*Bagels & Bongos,* Irving Fields Trio

*Balkan Beat Box,* Eponymous

*BTRock I and II,* Various artists

*Bubbemeises: Lies My Grandma Told Me, Krakauer Live in Krakow* and more, David Krakauer

*Celebrate Hip Hop,* Jewish Artists From Around the Globe

*Celebration 25,* Various artists from the Chabad Telethon

*Celestial Wedding, Day & Night, Garden,* Sheva

*Chutzpah,* Eponymous

*Code: Red,* Remedy

*Come Listen,* Ta-Shma

*The Compendium of All Things Close to Home,* Benjamin Hesse

*Connie Francis Sings Jewish Favorites,* Connie Francis

*Count It (7 Sefira),* Y-Love and Yuri Lane

*Davka Live* and more, Davka

*The Days of Awe,* David Chevan with Frank London and the Afro-Semitic Experience

*DJ Handler Presents Y-Love, The Mixtape,* Y-Love

*Emunah,* Eponymous

*EyeDollarTree,* Blood of Abraham

*Four Songs for You,* Michelle Citrin

*Freilach Time,* Golden State Klezmers

GOLEM!

*Fresh Off the Boat,* Golem

*From Avenue A to the Great White Way:
Yiddish & American Popular Songs From
1914-1950,* Various artists

*Funny Accent,* DJ Balagan

*Ghettoblaster, Let's Get Wet, The SoCalled
Seder,* SoCalled aka Josh Dolgin

*Greetings from the Isle of Klezbos,* Isle of
Klezbos

*A Groyse Metsi'e,* Eponymous

*The Hanukkah Lounge: Instrumental Jew Age
Music,* Various artists

*Hanukkah Rocks,* The Levees

*Hanukkah Swings!,* Kenny Ellis

*Haran* and more, Pharoah's Daughter

*Hazanos* and more, Frank London

*Hebrew National Kosher Classics,* Various
artists

*The Hidden Gate: Jewish Music Around the
World,* Various artists

*Hip Hop Shabbat,* Original Jewish Gangstas

*HipHopKhasene,* Solomon & SoCalled

*The Hip-Hop Violinist,* Miri Ben-Ari

*Holy Brothers and Sisters,* Rabbi Shlomo
Carlebach

*Human Beat Box,* Yuri Lane

*Hyperlink,* iSQUAD

*The Idan Raichel Project,* Idan Raichel

*The Israel Question,* Antithesis

*Jewface,* Reboot Stereophonic

*Jewish Funkey Monkeys,* Joshua Sitron

*Journey,* Neshama Carlebach

*Kedem,* Diaspora Yeshiva Band

*The Last One,* Adi Ran

*Laughter Through Tears,* Oi Va Voi

*Live at Stubs, No Place to Be, Shake Off the
Dust . . . Arise, Youth,* Matisyahu

*The Long Night,* Nadav Samin & Co

*Meditations,* and other albums from
C. Lanzbaum and Soul Farm

*Meditations of the Heart: Hasidic Aspirations
For Voice & Piano I and II, The Breslav
Tradition,* Israel Edelson and Alon
Michael

*Mein Albumf,* Good for the Jews

*Merkavah,* Amen

*Metamorphosis,* Brimstone127

*Mish, Mash, Mosh,* Aaron Alexander

*Moshiach, Moshiach, Moshiach,* Mordechai
Ben David

*My Awakening, 70 Faces,* Blue Fringe

*Noble Station* and *Uproot the Weeds,*
    Benjamin Hesse

*Now That Sounds Kosher,* Various artists

*Nu Med,* Balkan Beat Box

*On the Seventh Year,* Adam Weinberg

*Pallelujah,* MC Paul Barman

*The Passover Lounge: Instrumental Jew Age
    Music,* Various artists

*Path,* Mosh Ben Ari

*Plea for Peace,* The Afro-Semitic Experience

*Presence,* Sam Glaser

*Protest in Disguise,* Myself

*Protocols,* Rav Shmuel

*Push the Button,* Teapacks

*Reggae Chanukah, Reggae Passover,* Alan
    Eder and Friends

*Return Again* and more, Moshav Band

*Road Marks,* Yosef Karduner

*Rock Refuge Sublime,* Mare Winningham

*Rooftop Roots, Jdub Mixtapes I, II and III,*
    Various artists

*Sandwiches & Cats,* Michael Schowalter

*Shabbat Alive! The Hope Live,* and other
    albums by Rick Recht

*Shalosh,* Rashanim

*Shema Yisrael,* Mook E

*Shemspeed Alt Shule,* Juez

*Shir Zion,* Aaron Razel

*Smadar,* Eponymous

*South Side of the Synagogue,* Etan G

*Sugar Shack,* Alicia Jo Rabins

*The Two Sides of Purple 59,* Hip Hop
    Einstein, Sagol 59

*The Upwelling,* Eponymous

*Trilectic,* Jewlia Eisenberg

*Twenty Songs of the Chosen Surfers,*
    Meshugga Beach Party

*Voices for Israel,* Various artists

*V'sham Nashir,* Reva L'Sheva

*We Can Rise,* Chana Rothman

*Wonder Wheel,* The Klezmatics, Lyrics by
    Woody Guthrie

*Woody Guthrie's Happy Joyous Hanuka,*
    Woody Guthrie

*Yiddish Radio Project: Stories from the
    Golden Age of Yiddish Radio,* as heard
    on NPR's *All Things Considered*

# Let's Bless! Bendigamos

These traditional Sephardic words of praise are the swan song for celebratory meals. Everyone loves the tune to *Bendigamos,* but few know the Ladino words or what they mean. Not any more!

| | |
|---|---|
| Bendigamos al Altísimo, | *Let us bless the Most High,* |
| Al Senor que nos crió, | *The L-rd who nurtured us,* |
| Démosle agradecimiento | *Let us give G-d thanks* |
| Por los bienes que nos dió. | *For the good things given us.* |
| | |
| Alabado sea su Santo Nombre, | *Praised be His Holy Name,* |
| Porque siempre nos apiadó. | *Because He always took pity on us.* |
| Load al Senor que es bueno, | *Praise the Lord, for He is good,* |
| Que para siempre su merced. | *For His mercy is everlasting.* |
| | |
| Bendigamos al Altísimo, | *Let us bless the Most High,* |
| Por su Ley primeramente, | *First for His Law,* |
| Que liga a nuestro pueblo | *Which binds our people* |
| Con el cielo continuamente. | *With heaven continually.* |
| | |
| Alabado sea su Santo Nombre, | *Praised be His Holy Name,* |
| Porque siempre nos apiadó. | *Because He always showed us mercy.* |
| Load al Senor que es bueno, | *Praise the L-rd, for He is good,* |
| Que para siempre su merced. | *For His mercy is everlasting.* |
| | |
| Bendigamos al Altísimo, | *Let us bless the Most High,* |
| Por el pan segundamente, | *Secondly for the bread,* |
| Y también por los manjares | *And also for the foods* |
| Que comimos juntamente. | *Which we have eaten together.* |
| | |
| Pues comimos y bebimos | *For we have eaten and drunk* |
| alegremente, | *happily,* |
| Su merced nunca nos faltó. | *His mercy has never failed us.* |
| Load al Senor que es bueno, | *Praise the Lord, for He is good,* |
| Que para siempre su merced. | *For His mercy is everlasting.* |

Bendita sea la casa esta,
El hogar de su presencia,
Donde guardamos su fiesta,
Con alegría y permanencia.

Alabado sea su Santo Nombre,
Porque siempre nos apiadó.
Load al Senor que es bueno,
Que para siempre su merced.

Hodu LaShem ki tov,
Ki le'olam khasdo.
Hodu LaShem ki tov,
Ki le'olam khasdo!

*Blessed be this house,*
*The home of His presence,*
*Where we keep His holy day,*
*With happiness and permanence.*

*Praised be G-d's Holy Name,*
*For His mercy is everlasting.*
*Praise the Lord, for He is good,*
*For His mercy is everlasting*

*Praise the Lord, for He is good,*
*For His mercy is everlasting.*
*Praise the Lord, for He is good,*
*For His mercy is everlasting!*

## About the Author

The daughter of immigrants from Poland and Panama, Lisa Alcalay Klug's school lunches were filled with unusual combinations like gefilte fish and coconut. Her ever-convertible last name has earned her a host of aliases including Klugsta, Klugeriffic, and Inspector Klugeau. Oh yeah, and she writes, coaches, and shoots—with a camera. She has reported from Hong Kong, Ketchikan, and other far flung venues for a whopping list of publications including the *New York Times,* the *Los Angeles Times,* and the internationally acclaimed *Shtetl Town Crier!* She holds the position of Senior Professor of *Kabba Lah Lah* Yoga at the Jewlicious Festival, teaches classes on Jewish women *supersheroes* at retreats in Maui, and serves on the advisory board for Schmooze, the Sidney Krum Jewish Culture Conference. She has performed stand-up comedy in New York, San Francisco, and Jerusalem and is addicted to Manischewitz Manna (see page 116). You can find her online at—where else?—CoolJewBook.com.

## About the Illustrator

Artist, shmartist. It was Amos Goldbaum's uber-Jewish moniker that landed him in the pages of the tome also known as *The Heebster Handbook.* Before embarking on this odyssey, the only Hebrew Amos was packin' under his Jewboy belt were the letters on a *dreidl.* He did, however, possess more than a *bissel* of the *mama loshen* as well as advanced levels of *kvetch*-ability culled from his Bronx-based mentors, Yetta, of blessed memory, and Boomie, may he live long and prosper. A freelance illustrator who lives and draws in his native San Francisco, Amos roots for the Golden State Warriors. Visit his gallery at amosgoldbaum.com.

# Credits

Original drawings by Amos Goldbaum as conceived by Lisa Alcalay Klug © Lisa Alcalay Klug, all rights reserved.

### TABLE OF CONTENTS
Border design © Downtown Arts Development, image courtesy of Downtown Seder/Oyhoo.com, original design by David Bias, ThisDesignStudio.com.

### ALEF: CHAPTER 1
*Tallit* © Rabbi Samuel Skaist aka Rav Shmuel. Reprinted with permission.

*George der Naygeriker* provided courtesy of Yiddish House. Reprinted with permission. *Curious George* © 1941 and © renewed 1969 by Margret E. Rey, copyright assigned to Houghton Mifflin Company in 1993, Yiddish translation © 2005 Zackary Berger.

Curious George dreidl photo © Lisa Alcalay Klug.

Hammer in the 'chood movie still from *The Hebrew Hammer* © Tool Time LLC. Images courtesy of ContentFilm, Inc., TheHebrewHammer.com.

Irving Berlin sheet music courtesy of Brown University Library.

Man Ray (1890–1976) © ARS, NY, Man Ray, 1931. Gelatin silver print, 6 3/4 x 5". Gift of James Thrall Soby. (104.1941), Location: The Museum of Modern Art, New York, NY; Photo credit: Digital Image; Photo credit: The Museum of Modern Art/Licensed by SCALA/Art Resource, NY, ART307999.

Harry Houdini courtesy of Photofest, PhotofestNYC.com.

Maccabiah Games courtesy of Swann Auction Galleries, SwannGalleries.com.

Menorah Man T-shirt image © Alan Oirich, jewishsupers.com, CafePress.com/jewishsuperhero. Image provided by CafePress.com, Inc. Reprinted with permission.

Jacket cover © Leviathan Press, an imprint of Salisbury Press, LLC from *Up, Up, and Oy Vey!* by Simcha Weinstein. Reprinted with permission.

### BET: CHAPTER 2
Blackberry Manischewitz photo © Lisa Alcalay Klug.

*Shabot 6000* "Shabot Crimper" comic strip © William Levin aka Ben Baruch. Reprinted with permission of William Levin and Shabot6000.com.

Jacket cover copyright © 2005 by Random House, Inc., from *Bar Mitzvah Disco* by Roger Bennett, Jules Shell, and Nick Kroll. Used by permission of Crown Publishers, a division of Random House, Inc.

Bar Mitzvah poster, product image provided by CafePress.com, Inc. Reprinted with permission.

*Marry a Yiddisher Boy, Living Corpse,* and *Mismor L'David* courtesy of Brown University Library.

Doggie Shayna Punim shirt © RabbisDaughters.com, courtesy of Daniella Zax.

*The Hebrew Hammer* poster © Tool Time LLC. Images courtesy of ContentFilm, Inc.

*Hamsa* by Josh Baum, all rights reserved © Josh Baum, AlefsinWonderland.com.

He'Brew perfect for weddings needlepoint, Lenny Bruce RIPA bottle photo, and He'Brew Beer logo © Shmaltz Brewing Company, Shmaltz.com. Reprinted with permission.

*Kosmic* © David Friedman, Kosmic-kabbalah.com. Reprinted with permission.

Nissim and Yehudit Alcalay z'l wedding photo, author's collection.

Farklempt Mrs. Carver movie still from *The Hebrew Hammer* © Tool Time LLC. Images courtesy of ContentFilm, Inc., TheHebrewHammer.com.

*Yiddisher Cowboy* courtesy of Brown University Library.

## GIMEL: CHAPTER 3

Mashuga Nuts © Torn Ranch, TornRanch.com. Reprinted with permission.

Jewish Fortune Cookies © Creative Cookie, courtesy of PopJudaica.com.

Katz's Deli Since 1888 postcard © Katz's Deli, KatzsDeli.com. Reprinted with permission.

Hebrew Bazooka Bubble Gum photo © David Abitbol. Reprinted with permission of Topps, Topps USA, and Elite-Strauss, Israel.

Kosher symbols courtesy of the Kosher Information Bureau and organizations listed on pp. 66–67.

Latke Crisps and Babka Bites © Thou Shall Snack, ThouShallSnack.com. Reprinted with permission.

Maccabeans Legendary Jelly Beans © Maccabeans, Maccabeans.com. Reprinted with permission.

*Protocols* Rav Shmuel album cover © Jewish Music Group, JewishMusicGroup.com, art by Rav Shmuel, RavShmuel.com.

King and Queen yarmulke photo © Lisa Alcalay Klug.

*Yiddisha Rag* courtesy of Brown University Library.

Manischewitz, Jewcy, and Hasidic Double Dutch T-shirt photos © 2007 Jewcy Partners, LLC, Jewcy.com. Reprinted with permission.

Tel Aviv and Love T-shirts © Threaded Heritage LLC, GetThreaded.com. Reprinted with permission.

He'Brew Beer T-shirt © Shmaltz Brewing Company, courtesy of PopJudaica.com.

Sammy Davis Jr. Mensch T-shirt, © The Original Lefty's, courtesy of PopJudaica.com.

WWBD, Heeb, Honorary Heeb, and Moses Is My Homeboy T-shirt photos by Seth Olenick for *Heeb Magazine,* © Heeb Media, LLC, HeebMagazine.com. Reprinted with permission.

Jew Boy belt © Peter Svarzbein/Mongovision.com for HeebMagazine.com. Reprinted with permission.

Tallit T-shirt photo by Brenda Staudenmaier for *Heeb Magazine,* © Heeb Media, LLC, HeebMagazine.com. Reprinted with permission.

Bubeleh tank, Tush sweat pants, and Yiddish travel bag © RabbisDaughters.com, courtesy of Daniella Zax.

Tenement T-shirt courtesy of Tenement Museum, Tenement.org.

Sephardilicious T-shirt © Rotem Gear, RotemGear.com. Product image provided by CafePress.com, Inc. Reprinted with permission.

Hebrew School Drop Out logo and hoodie © hebrewschooldropout.com. Reprinted with permission.

I (heart) Hashem messenger bag (aka *tallit* bag) © David Abitbol, Jewlicious.com. Reprinted with permission. CafePress.com/Jewlicious.

*Mamaleh* necklace © RabbisDaughters.com, courtesy of Daniella Zax.

*Pakn Treger* magazine cover, © The Noble Rooster (Berlin, 1922), courtesy of *Pakn Treger* magazine and the National Yiddish Book Center.

Honda Element © American Honda Motor Co., Inc. Reprinted with permission.

Scion, a marque of Toyota Motor Sales, USA, Inc., © Toyota. Reprinted with permission.

Xebra car photo © ZAP, ZapWorld.com. Reprinted with permission.

Gefilte fish sticker, art/concept by Jay Sheckley, © Dark Carnival Books, Berkeley, Calif.

## DALET: CHAPTER 4

Seder star © Downtown Arts Development, image courtesy of Downtown Seder/Oyhoo.com, original design by David Bias, ThisDesignStudio.com.

*Return Again* album cover © Moshav Band, art by Michael Blumenthal, MoshavBand.com. Reprinted with permission.

*Rosh HaShana* postcard, courtesy of American Jewish Historical Society, Newton Centre, Massachusetts and New York, NY.

*Shofar* blowers, public domain image, courtesy of Downtown Seder/Oyhoo.com.

## HEY: CHAPTER 5

Yale University Shield © Yale University, courtesy of Yale University Office of Public Affairs, Yale.edu/opa.

*Tzedaka* box photo © Lisa Alcalay Klug.

Share: Jewish Relief Campaign poster, Library of Congress, Prints & Photographs Division [LC-DIG-ppmsca-05663], 1917.

*Rabbis: The Many Faces of Judaism* book cover, © Georger Kalinsky, *RABBIS*, Rizzoli/Universe New York, 2002. Reprinted with permission.

Maimonides image, public domain.

Rashi Moscato D'Asti © Royal Wine Corp., Bayonne, NJ. Produced and distributed by Royal Wine Corp., RoyalWines.com.

Baal Shem Tov image, Volozhin *shul* photo, and Aish Kodesh photo, public domain.

Rabbi Menachem Mendel Schneerson © Chabad.org. Reprinted with permission.

Baba Sali © J. Reznik Studios, JReznikStudios.com. Reprinted with permission.

Shlomo and Neshama Carlebach photo by Joan Roth, © Joan Roth. Reprinted with permission.

Emmanuel Levinas by Bracha L. Ettinger, reprinted under the Creative Commons License (CC-BY-SA 2.5 License).

*Unification* by Avraham Lowenthal © Tzfat Gallery of Mystical Art, KabbalahArt.com. Reprinted with permission.

### VAV: CHAPTER 6

Stieglitz, Alfred (1864–1946) © ARS, NY, The Steerage. 1907. Photogravure, 12 5/8 x 10 3/16". Provenance unknown. (136.1986), Location: The Museum of Modern Art, New York, NY. Photo credit: Digital Image © The Museum of Modern Art/Licensed by SCALA/Art Resource, NY, ART166161.

Mother of Exiles Hanukkah lamp by Mae Rockland Tupa, Brookline, MA, commissioned by the Stiftung Jüdisches Museum, Berlin, 2006; © Mae Rockland Tupa, photo by Myron A. Tupa, courtesy of Mae Rockland Tupa.

"The New Colossus" by Emma Lazarus, American Jewish Historical Society, Newton Centre, MA, and New York, NY. Reprinted with permission.

*Be'chol Lashon* logo © Be'chol Lashon, Institute for Jewish & Community Research, JewishResearch.org.

*Meshugga Beach Party* album cover © Meshugga Beach Party, MeshuggaBeachParty.com. Reprinted with permission.

Oy/Yo © David Chevan, Chevan.addr.com/ase.html. Reprinted with permission.

Gangsta hand tags modeled by Yonatan Gutstadt, photos © Lisa Alcalay Klug.

Heroes of the Torah © Fishs Eddy, Inc., FishsEddy.com. Reprinted with permission.

Leonard Nimoy as Spock in *Star Trek,* courtesy of Paramount/Photofest, PhotofestNYC.com.

*Kohenic* Judaica photo © Lisa Alcalay Klug.

Alcalay family photo, author's collection.

*Shabot 6000* "Spain Sucks" and "Goyish Conversion" comic strips © William Levin aka Ben Baruch. Reprinted with permission of William Levin and Shabot6000.com.

Hebrew Bazooka Bubble Gum © Elite-Strauss, reprinted with permission of Topps, Topps USA and Elite-Strauss, Israel.

Vintage Manischewitz *Matzos* boxes © R.A.B. Food Group/Manischewitz, Manischewitz.com. Reprinted with permission.

*Mitzvah* bike photo courtesy of Rabbi Yosef Langer, ChabadSF.org. Reprinted with permission.

*Axis, Cycle & Heart* © David Friedman, Kosmic-kabbalah.com. Reprinted with permission.

*Shabot 6000* "Hole in Sheet" comic strip © William Levin aka Ben Baruch. Reprinted with permission of William Levin and Shabot6000.com.

*Ellis Island* courtesy of Brown University.

*Long Live the Land of the Free,* Library of Congress, Hebraic Section, New York: Hebrew Publishing Co., 1911, copyright deposit, 1911 (52.5), Heskes no. 386.

*Chantshe in Amerika.* From the operetta Chantshe in Amerika. Music by Joseph M. Rumshisky, lyrics by Isidore Lillian. (New York, NY: Hebrew Publishing Company, 1913; copr. no. E305266, March 4/8, 1913, MUS, Hebr). Music

Division and Hebrew Section, African and Middle Eastern Division.

The New Success of Peoples Theatre of the Operetta *American Beauty,* Library of Congress, African & Middle Eastern Division [amedmisc awh0036], Hebrew Publishing Company; New York, NY, c. 1910.

### ZAYIN: CHAPTER 7

If You Can't Say Anything Nice, Say It in Yiddish bumper sticker product image provided by CafePress.com, Inc. Reprinted with permission.

*Poale Zion* journal by RotemGear.com. Product image provided by CafePress.com, Inc. Reprinted with permission.

*Di Kats der Payats* provided courtesy of Yiddish House. Reprinted with permission. *The Cat in the Hat* TM & © 1957 Dr. Seuss Enterprises, L.P. All Rights Reserved.

"Abolish Slavery" Jewish women protestors, Library of Congress, Prints & Photographs Division, [LC-DIG-ppmsca-06591], May 1, 1909.

*Tree of Life* by Josh Baum, all rights reserved © Josh Baum, AlefsinWonderland.com.

Yiddish map, American Jewish Historical Society, Newton Centre, MA, and New York, NY.

Egged and Israeli Coins posters courtesy of Swann Auction Galleries, SwannGalleries.com.

From *Yiddish with Dick and Jane* by Ellis Weiner and Barbara Davilman by permission of Little, Brown and Company.

1951 Israeli Mother's Day poster courtesy of Swann Auction Galleries, SwannGalleries.com.

*Bar Kochba* and *Dreyfus* courtesy of Brown University Library.

First Zionist Congress, Basel, Switzerland, August, 1897, public domain, author's collection.

### APPENDIX

*Chutzpah* mafiosos © 2007 Danny Rothenberg, courtesy of Chutzpah, ChutzpahtheGroup.com.

Hadassah Gross © Amichai Lau-Lavie, HadassahGross.com.

OJGs, Original Jewish Gangstas logo © Jonathan Gutstadt, HipHopShabbat.com. Reprinted with permission.

JDub Ground Up Tree © JDub Records, JdubRecords.org. Reprinted with permission.

American Jewess courtesy of the Jewish Women's Archive (www.JWA.org/research/americanjewess).

Oyhoo Festival logo © Downtown Arts Development, image courtesy of Downtown Seder/Oyhoo.com, original design by David Bias, ThisDesignStudio.com.

Oyhoo Music Star © copyright Downtown Arts Development, image courtesy of Downtown Seder/Oyhoo.com, original design by David Bias, ThisDesignStudio.com.

*Balkan Beat Box* © JDub Records, JdubRecords. org.

*Golden State Klezmers* album cover © 1998 Zinovy Goro, courtesy of Jewish Music Group LLC, JewishMusicGroup.com, and the Golden State Klezmers, GoldenStateKlezmers.com, art by Stuart Balcomb.

*Golem!* album cover © JDub Records, JdubRecords.org, GolemRocks.com. Reprinted with permission.

*Jewface* album cover © RebootStereophonic.com.

Good for the Jews photo © Seth Kushner Photography, SethKushner.com. Reprinted with permission.

*Rooftop Roots III* phonograph album cover © JDub Records, JdubRecords.org. Reprinted with permission.

*The Klezmatics Wonder Wheel* album cover courtesy of Jewish Music Group LLC, JewishMusicGroup.com, and the Klezmatics, Klezmatics.com.

*Ain Sof* © David Friedman, Kosmic-kabbalah.com. Reprinted with permission.

Stake Out movie still from *The Hebrew Hammer* © Tool Time LLC. Images courtesy of ContentFilm, Inc., TheHebrewHammer.com.